# Plato's *Republic*

**Critical Essays on the Classics**
General Editor: Steven M. Cahn

This new series is designed to introduce college students to major works of philosophical and political theory through the best critical essays on those works. The distinguished editors of each collection have selected essays for their scholarly excellence and their accessibility to students. Each collection is meant to serve as a companion to the work itself, providing a gateway into a deeper understanding of the text.

Forthcoming in the series:

Descartes's *Meditations:* Critical Essays
  *edited by Vere Chappell*

Kant's *Groundwork on the Metaphysics of Morals:* Critical Essays
  *edited by Paul Guyer*

Mill's *On Liberty:* Critical Essays
  *edited by Gerald Dworkin*

Mill's *Utilitarianism:* Critical Essays
  *edited by David Lyons*

Plato's *Republic:* Critical Essays
  *edited by Richard Kraut*

# Plato's *Republic*

## *Critical Essays*

EDITED BY
RICHARD KRAUT

ROWMAN & LITTLEFIELD PUBLISHERS, INC.
*Lanham • Boulder • New York • Oxford*

ROWMAN & LITTLEFIELD PUBLISHERS, INC.

Published in the United States of America
by Rowman & Littlefield Publishers, Inc.
A wholly owned subsidary of The Rowman & Littlefield Publishing Group, Inc.
4501 Forbes Boulevard, Suite 200, Lanham, Maryland 20706
www.rowmanlittlefield.com

PO Box 317
Oxford
OX2 9RU, UK

British Library Cataloguing in Publication Information Available

**Library of Congress Cataloging-in-Publication Data**

Plato's Republic : critical essays / edited by Richard Kraut.
    p. cm. — (Critical essays on the classics)
  Includes bibliographical references and index.
    ISBN 0-8476-8492-X (cloth : alk. paper). —ISBN 0-8476-8493-8 (pbk.: alk. paper)
    1. Plato. Republic. I. Kraut, Richard, 1944– . II. Series.
JC71.P6.P53   1997
321'.07—dc21                                                    97–15773
                                                               CIP

ISBN 0-8476-8492-X (cloth : alk. paper)
ISBN 0-8476-8493-8 (pbk. : alk. paper)

Printed in the United States of America

♾™ The paper used in this publication meets the minimum requirements of American
National Standard for Information Sciences—Permanence of Paper for Printed Library
Materials, ANSI Z39.48–1984.

# Contents

# Introduction

Plato (427–347 B.C.) is the first Western philosopher who wrote systematically about the wide range of questions that make up the subject of philosophy, and it is in the *Republic* that he most fully expresses his conception of what philosophy is and what conclusions it can be expected to reach. Within this dialogue, we find an exploration of such diverse subjects as justice, education, politics, religion, gender, the family, reason, emotion, science, understanding, the role of art, the immortality of the soul, and the nature of reality. And yet these topics are given a unified treatment, because all of them contribute in one way or another to a single argument carried out over the course of the whole work—an argument that shows what justice is and why it is good. And the *Republic* is remarkable not only for the artful way it unifies its many parts but also because everything it says is thoroughly controversial: it proposes that the real world is invisible and that what we see is a mere shadow of it; it argues that a human being is not one object but three, and that we can achieve a kind of unity only if we live in extraordinarily favorable circumstances; it attacks democracy and popular arts because they undermine the health of the soul; and it portrays an ideal city as one in which philosophers have absolute power, women are educated and hold office, and sexual liaisons are arranged for eugenic purposes. It would be a rare reader who is not offended—and intrigued.

What led to the creation of this unique work? When Plato wrote it (probably during the 380s or 370s B.C.), he had already composed quite a few dialogues, all shorter than the *Republic,* and none as ambitious. All of them feature a character called "Socrates," who explores abstract moral questions in conversation with, and often in opposition to, others. This dramatic figure was not a pure creation of Plato's imagination, but was in some way based on his conception of the real Socrates, the

Athenian philosopher who was tried and executed on the charge of impiety in 399 B.C., when Plato was twenty-eight years old. There can be little doubt that the personality, ideas, and death of Socrates had a profound impact on Plato's philosophical development and on his decision to devote himself to a life of inquiry and writing. Socrates had a similar effect on others; Plato is only one of several who wrote Socratic dialogues.

What Plato learned from Socrates was that we can make discoveries of great significance to our lives if we use the method of question and answer that was the hallmark of Socratic conversation. We see this method at work in Book I of the *Republic* and in many other dialogues. Socrates typically asks his interlocutor about something we assume we understand well enough—what is justice? what is piety? what is courage? and so on. These questions presuppose that there is such a thing as the real nature of justice, piety, and courage; that there is not only a multiplicity of virtuous acts and people but also an underlying unity that explains why they are virtuous; that these are not merely arbitrary or conventional matters that change from one person, community, or time to another; and that we can discover what that unified and real nature is by entering into dialogue with each other, proposing and testing answers and looking for hypotheses that survive all objections.

A reader of the dialogues that Plato wrote before he composed the *Republic*—the *Euthyphro,* the *Charmides,* and the *Laches,* for example—may find it surprising that he was so deeply influenced by the Socratic method of question and answer, for in all of these works that method seems to achieve no positive results. Book I of the *Republic* is meant to remind us of this record of failure, because it portrays Socrates as someone whose efforts to understand justice proved unsuccessful. Various accounts of justice are proposed, but all are found wanting.

It would be a mistake, however, to see in these early works or in Book I of the *Republic* nothing but a series of disconnected and fruitless attempts to discover what the virtues are. On the contrary, every search for a definition in these dialogues contains unmistakable signs that significant progress is being made. For example, the first account of justice proposed in the *Republic*—that it is speaking the truth and returning what one has borrowed—is easily revealed to be superficial, and it is replaced by proposals that raise increasingly fundamental questions. As the conversation progresses, we arrive at some significant negative and positive conclusions: that the conventional assumption that we must return harm for harm is indefensible, that attempts to prove that justice is disadvantageous end in failure, that in fact justice is a great good. When Socrates is asked, at the beginning of Book II, to give new and more persuasive arguments, we must not take this to mean that his method of question and answer was flawed, but simply that he did not carry it far enough. And the rest of the *Republic* is meant to show that the Socratic method can answer his questions, provided that we use resources that are richer than the ones deployed in the earlier dialogues and in Book I of the *Republic*. The Socrates of those works did not show much interest in the nature of the soul or in the existence of a nonvisible and changeless realm of permanent entities. What Plato is saying, then, is that the Socratic method can lead to results that transform our lives and our communities if we recognize that justice and the other virtues cannot be understood in isolation, but must be linked to the soul and all the other aspects of reality that a philosopher must strive to understand.

Plato would not have arrived at this theory if Socrates had been the only important influence on his thinking. It is clear from his dialogues that Plato was interested not only in the moral questions that Socrates was raising but also in the science and mathematics of his time. A group of thinkers had emerged in the fifth century B.C. who were greatly interested in mathematical research because it seemed to offer an insight into the nature of reality. These Pythagoreans (so-called because they were followers of the sixth-century B.C. sage Pythagoras) were the first to investigate numerical ratios and the properties of lines and planes. The fact that musical harmonies can be mathematically represented encouraged them to believe that what accounts for the organization of the entire visible world is not its material composition but some hidden structure that can remain the same in different bodies. Some of Plato's closest associates were Pythagoreans, and he evidently saw some connection between their activities and the methodology of Socrates. When Plato asked himself, "Why was Socrates able to make significant progress in his ethical inquiries?" his familiarity with the Pythagorean conception of the world suggested an answer: justice, courage, and piety are, like numbers and figures, unseen realities whose nature can be discovered only through independent rational inquiry. We cannot understand the basic structure of the universe or the nature of goodness and virtue simply by using our senses; these deep realities can be discovered only through an intellectual and critical process.

In fact, Plato's hypothesis that the deepest realities are unseen was an idea that was shared by a diverse group of thinkers, not solely the

Pythagoreans. Heraclitus (born around 540 B.C.) had said that "nature loves to hide" and had argued that some single unifying factor lies beneath the apparent diversity of the world. Parmenides (born around 515 B.C.) argued that reality consists in one perfect being and that the eyes lie to us when they report a world of change and diversity. Zeno of Elea (born around 490 B.C.) proposed several stunning paradoxes to prove how absurd it is to assume that there is such a thing as motion and plurality. Anaxagoras (born around 500 B.C.) argued that the basic seeds of the material universe are invisible and infinitely divisible, whereas Democritus (born around 460 B.C.) held that they must be *in*divisible, and that we must also recognize the existence of not-being—parts of the world that have no being in them. The intellectual climate was favorable to the idea that there is far more to the world than meets the eye, that the deepest realities are hidden. Plato's hypothesis that there is an independent realm of noncorporeal, imperceptible, and unchanging entities was a bold and new idea, but it belonged to a tradition of thought that posited the existence of unobservable but basic realities.

Aside from his association with Socrates and several contemporary philosophers, we know little of Plato's life. According to accounts written many centuries after his death, he traveled several times to Sicily, where he unsuccessfully tried to exert some influence on the political program of its new ruler, Dionysius II. But he spent nearly the whole of his life in his native city, Athens, despite his conviction that its democratic political system was deeply and inherently defective. Here he established a new school, the Academy, as a center for research and learning. It attracted some of the leading thinkers of the day (Aristotle studied there for nineteen years) and continued to exist for many centuries; but one century after Plato's death, its leaders had abandoned the basic tenets of his philosophy and had instead adopted the skeptical policy of suspending judgment about all disputed or disputable questions. Though we may think of Plato and Aristotle as the two giants of ancient philosophy, there were long periods of time when neither was as influential as the schools of thought—Skepticism, Stoicism, and Epicureanism—that arose at the end of the fourth century B.C. Plato's works have occupied a leading position among philosophers only during certain periods of history. In the third century A.D., one of his most profound students, Plotinus, wrote a series of essays (the *Enneads*) that emphasized and developed the otherworldly aspects of Plato's framework. In later centuries, particularly during the Renaissance, Plotinus's mystical and apolitical conception of Platonism was deeply influential.

In our own time, Plato's philosophical richness and literary skill are widely recognized. Hundreds of scholarly articles, monographs, and books appear every year about every aspect of his thought. In universities and colleges, every serious student of philosophy is expected to have at least some acquaintance with his writing. And yet it may seem somewhat puzzling that he is still the object of so much attention. For we live in an age that is in many respects hostile to Platonism. His unworldliness, so appealing to Plotinus, is not in favor; we assume that perception is what gives us knowledge, and there is considerable skepticism about his thesis that eternal realities and permanent truths provide the foundation of understanding happiness. And the worldly aspects of his philosophy also meet with deep suspicion, for there is widespread agreement that democracy, freedom, and equality—all condemned by Plato—are worthy goals. Yet he continues to fascinate us, because even if we reject many of his radical conclusions, we recognize in him a powerful and disturbing critic of some of our most cherished assumptions, and sometimes we are even willing to concede some ground to him. We may agree, for example, that understanding requires going beyond appearances, that democracy is not an entirely unproblematic form of government, that the human soul is often a locus of conflict, and that if justice is entirely conventional or a mask for oppression, then it does not merit our allegiance or respect.

The essays that have been selected for this volume examine questions about the *Republic* that are still a matter of lively debate. Does his argument that justice is a great good hold up under examination? Can we make sense of his comparison between the parts of a city and the human soul? Do the analogies he uses in the central books of the *Republic*—the sun, the divided line, and the cave—fit together coherently? Can we applaud his attitude towards women? Does he raise legitimate concerns about the nature of art? Those who have long studied Plato express considerable disagreement about these and other matters. Plato's *Republic* has both detractors and defenders, for there is no consensus among scholars about the plausibility or worth of his ideas, or about precisely what those ideas involve. Although Plato is that rare thing—a great philosopher who is often a great pleasure to read—the pleasures he brings are mixed, for his writings are deliberately elusive and troubling. If the essays collected in this volume help the reader develop a better sense of the complexity of Plato's thinking in his most wide-ranging dialogue, they will have served their purpose.

# Acknowledgments

David Sachs, "A Fallacy in Plato's *Republic*" originally appeared in *The Philosophical Review* 72 (1963): 141–58.

John M. Cooper, "The Psychology of Justice in Plato" originally appeared in the *American Philosophical Quarterly* 14 (1977): 151–57. Reprinted with the permission of the *American Philosophical Quarterly* and the author.

C. C. W. Taylor, "Plato's Totalitarianism" originally appeared in *Polis* 5 (1986): 4–29. Reprinted with the permission of the author.

Bernard Williams, "The Analogy of City and Soul in Plato's *Republic*" originally appeared in *Exegesis and Argument: Studies in Greek Philosophy Presented to Gregory Vlastos,* ed. E. N. Lee, A. P. D. Mourelatos, and R. M. Rorty (Assen, The Netherlands: B. V. van Gorcum and Co., 1973), 196–206. Reprinted with the permission of the publisher and the author.

Jonathan Lear, "Inside and Outside the *Republic*" originally appeared in *Phronesis* 37 (1992): 184–215. Reprinted with the permission of B. V. van Gorcum and Co. and the author.

Arlene Saxonhouse, "The Philosopher and the Female in the Political Thought of Plato" originally appeared in *Political Theory* 4 (1976): 195–212. Reprinted with the permission of Sage Publications and the author.

Gregory Vlastos, "Was Plato a Feminist?" originally appeared in the *Times Literary Supplement,* No. 4, 485, Mar. 17, 1989, 276, 288–89. Reprinted with the permission of Mari Vlastos and Stephen Vlastos.

Julia Annas, "Understanding and the Good: Sun, Line, and Cave" originally appeared *An Introduction to Plato's Republic* (Oxford, England: Clarendon Press, 1981), chap. 10, pp. 242–71. © 1981 Julia

Annas. Reprinted by permission of Oxford University Press and the author.

Iris Murdoch's essay is taken from *The Sovereignty of Good* (London: Routledge & Kegan Paul, 1970), 90–104. Reprinted with the permission of Routledge.

Gregory Vlastos, "A Metaphysical Paradox" originally appeared in *Proceedings and Addresses of the American Philosophical Association* 39 (1966): 5–19. Reprinted with the permission of the American Philosophical Association, Mari Vlastos, and Stephen Vlastos.

Richard Kraut, "The Defense of Justice in Plato's *Republic*" originally appeared in *The Cambridge Companion to Plato,* ed. R. Kraut (New York: Cambridge University Press, 1992), 311–37. Reprinted with the permission of Cambridge University Press and the author.

James O. Urmson, "Plato and the Poets" originally appeared in *Plato on Beauty, Wisdom and the Arts,* ed. J. Moravcsik and P. Temko (Totowa, N.J.: Rowman & Littlefield, 1982), 125–36. Reprinted with the author's permission.

# 1

# A Fallacy in Plato's Republic

## David Sachs

Recent writers on the *Republic* tend to refrain from detailed discussion of the argument about justice and happiness, the main argument of the work.[1] In the last decades there have been few assessments of Plato's conclusions about the relationship of justice and happiness, namely that just men are happier than any men who are unjust, and that the more unjust a man is, the more wretched he will be. Equally rare have been attempts to examine critically the argument by which Plato reached those conclusions.[2] In this paper I make such an attempt. My aim is to show that Plato's conclusions are irrelevant to what he sets out—and purports—to establish. The fallacy of irrelevance that, in my judgment, wrecks the *Republic's* main argument is due to the lack of connection between two conceptions of justice that Plato employs. I begin with an account of the two conceptions. While discussing them, I try to correct some errors and possible confusions about Plato's argument and his understanding of it. In particular, I try to show that Plato consistently viewed his defense of justice as one made solely in terms of justice's effects. I then examine the fallacy in detail. At the end, I briefly speculate about why Plato proceeded as he did.

### The Two Conceptions of Justice

Like other dialogues that have been called "aporetic" or "dialogues of refutation," *Republic* I ends with an avowal of ignorance by Socrates. Plato has him say that, not knowing what justice is, he can hardly know whether it is a virtue and whether its possessor is happy or not. An

1

impression likely to be made by Socrates' last words in Book I is, as Richard Robinson remarked of the early dialogues as a whole, "that Socrates thinks that there is no truth whatever about *x* that can be known before we know what *x* is."[3] Robinson observes that though Socrates never actually says this, Socrates also never places any limits on the priority of answering questions of the form "What is *x*?" As a result, there is a general problem about the dialogues of refutation; do they include any assertions of doctrine by Plato?[4] Thus, in *Republic* I, Socrates makes various statements about justice; is his avowal of ignorance intended to question all of them? Certainly no doubt is cast upon one repeatedly implied claim, a claim taken for granted in the later books and presupposed by the over-all structure of the *Republic:* namely, that whether one should lead a just or unjust life is to be decided by determining which life is the happier.[5] It is, however, indispensable for evaluating the main argument of the *Republic* to realize that this claim cannot be understood in the same way throughout; it cannot, because of the two conceptions of justice in the *Republic.* I will call the first the vulgar conception of justice, the second the Platonic conception.

### *The Vulgar Conception*

Toward the end of *Republic* IV, immediately after the first exposition of the Platonic conception of justice, there is an important text for what I am terming the vulgar conception of justice. Socrates, speaking to Glaucon, says:

> "We might . . . completely confirm . . . our own conviction . . . by applying . . . vulgar tests to it." "What are these?" "For example, if an answer were demanded to the question concerning that city and the man whose birth and breeding was in harmony with it, whether we believe that such a man, entrusted with a deposit of gold or silver, would withhold it and embezzle it, who do you suppose would think that he would be more likely so to act than men of a different kind?" "No one would." "And would not he be far removed from sacrilege and theft and betrayal of comrades in private life or of the state in public? . . . And, moreover, he would not be in any way faithless either in the keeping of his oaths or in other agreements. . . . Adultery, surely, and neglect of parents and of the due service of the gods would pertain to anyone rather than to such a man. . . . And is not the cause of this to be found in the fact that each of

the principles within him does its own work in the mattter of ruling and being ruled?"[6]

As Plato states them in this passage, the vulgar criteria for justice consist in the nonperformance of acts of certain kinds; and, of course, injustice, according to the vulgar conception, consists in performing such acts. The passage shows that Plato supposes that the just man—as he conceives him—is less likely than anyone else to perform those acts, to embezzle, thieve, betray, behave sacrilegiously, fail to keep oaths or agreements, commit adultery, neglect his parents or the service he owes to the gods. Plato thinks the conduct of his just man, far from being at variance with the vulgar conception of justice, will exemplify it.

The vulgar conception is shared at the start of the *Republic* by all of Socrates' interlocutors: Cephalus, Polemarchus, Thrasymachus, Glaucon, and Adeimantus. (This is not to say that the vulgar conception exhausts the notions of justice they hold, or that they all believe in behaving in accord with it.)

Thrasymachus, at 344a 3–5b 5, describes consummate (τελεωτάτης) injustice and several kinds or "parts" (μέρη) of injustice; his list of kinds of injustice emphasizes gross types of immorality and evil-doing: temple-robbing, kidnaping, swindling, and so forth (see 348d 5–8). On Thrasymachus' view, to perpetrate such acts is to do injustice; not to commit them is essential to being just. Similarly, when Glaucon, for the sake of the argument, extols injustice, he finds it apt to relate the story of Gyges' ancestor, a man who seduced his king's wife, murdered the king, and usurped the kingdom; Glaucon then alleges that no one who enjoyed the impunity of Gyges' progenitor would "persevere in justice and endure to refrain his hands from the possessions of others and not touch them . . . [but would] take what he wished even from the market place and enter into houses and lie with whom he pleased, and slay and loose from bonds whomsoever he would" (360b 5–360c 2). Here, again, is a list of acts set forth as incompatible with justice and as constituting injustice. It should be stressed that the examples of unjust acts are presented by Socrates' interlocutors in such a way that it is plain they conceive the commission of any of them as injustice, and not committing any of them justice.[7]

## The Platonic Conception

Although the speeches of Glaucon and Adeimantus at the beginning of Book II give expression to the vulgar conception of justice, elements of the Platonic conception are also prominent in them. Commentators have often recognized that the speeches are vital for an understanding of how Plato conceives justice and for grasping what he tries to establish concerning it.

Glaucon, before his speech, asks Socrates if he really wishes to persuade them that it is in every way better to be just than unjust. The phrase "in every way" (παντὶ τρόπῳ, 357b 1) is then glossed by Glaucon's classification of goods and his and Socrates' discussion of it. The classification appears to be roughly the following: goods valued for their own sake, goods valued for their own sake and their effects, and goods valued only for their effects. The second type of goods is the one better in every way and Socrates says that, if a man is to be happy, he should thus regard justice; that is, value it both for its own sake and for its effects.

Plato's use of the expressions which I have conventionally rendered by the phrase "valued for their own sake" has perplexed readers about the main argument and aroused controversy.[8] The difficulty to which it has given rise is this: on the one hand, Socrates states to Glaucon that justice is to be valued for its own sake as well as for its effects, and Glaucon and Adeimantus stress in their speeches that they want Socrates to praise justice in itself (358d 1–2; 363a 1–2; cf. 367c 5–d 5); on the other hand, throughout the *Republic,* Socrates confines himself to an attempt to show that being just eventuates in happiness and pleasure for the just man; that is, he praises justice solely for what he alleges are its effects. Consequently, it has been charged that Plato, at the start of Book II, misconceived the task he thereafter tried to carry out; that he promised to prove that justice is good both for its own sake and for its effects, but addressed himself only to what he presumed were its effects.[9]

The expressions Plato uses are indeed likely to perplex contemporary readers, but an examination of the contexts in which they occur can help to remove the perplexity. When characterizing the first of the three types of goods, Glaucon says, "Are there not some which we should wish to have, not for their consequences, but just for their own sake, such as harmless pleasures and enjoyments that have no further result beyond the satisfaction of the moment?" The sentence just quoted is Cornford's very free translation of the problematic lines 357b 4–8; it has the merit, in comparison to other translations, of forcibly suggesting that αἱ ἡδοναί signifies activities or objects which produce pleasure, and not the pleasure produced.[10] The clause beginning "that have no *further* result" should suggest that "for their own sake" is not being contrasted with "for (all and) any effects whatsoever" and that, instead, a distinction *among* effects is implicit. This is also suggested by the mention of enjoyment (χαίρειν ἔχοντα, 357b 8), which one would naturally take to be an effect; indeed, if the sole effect of something is pleasure or enjoyment, it would appear to be an instance of the first type of goods in Glaucon's classification.[11]

When Socrates is asked where he places justice in the classification, he replies, "In the fairest class . . . amongst those which he who would be blessed, must love both for their own sake and their consequences."[12] Again, a present-day reader may wonder: how does Socrates conceive the relation of justice, which he places among the second type of goods, to blessedness or happiness? Socrates' remark is difficult, but Glaucon's comment on it is helpful: "That is not the opinion of most people. . . . They place it in the *troublesome* class of good things, which must be pursued for the sake of the reward and the high place in public opinion which they bring but which *in themselves are irksome* and to be avoided."[13] Glaucon's words are clear; according to the many, he is saying, justice in itself, since it is harsh or painful, should be avoided. The troublesomeness and harshness of it, then, are included under the heading "in itself." By analogy, the blessedness or happiness which Socrates thinks being just produces may be placed under the same heading. The need for discriminating the kind of effect intended by the phrases "in itself" and "for their own sake," from those intended by "effects" or "consequences" said *simpliciter,* is plain.

The distinction among effects is clarified by the repeated and virtually identical demands made of Socrates in Glaucon's and Adeimantus' speeches. Glaucon's request at 358b 4–7 is typical (see 366e 5–9; 367b 3–5; 367e 1–5; also 367a 1–8; 367c 5–d 5). He asks to be told the powers (δύναμεις) that justice and injustice, being present in the soul, exert *by themselves*—leaving aside the rewards and effects of both. From these passages it can be seen that Plato conceived of justice as good in itself, a good for its own sake, in terms of the effect which he supposed it exerted within the soul of its possessor. In the same way, he thought injustice an evil in itself. (The expressions literally translated by "for its own sake" and "in itself" might be paraphrased in a less confusing way for present-day readers by the locutions "on its own" and "by itself.") For Plato, *no other* effects of justice and injustice were grounds for characterizing them as good or evil in themselves—

and notably not those effects due to the knowledge or opinion others have of one's justice or injustice.

Glaucon's classification of goods, then, proves quite complex: first, items which by themselves (or on their own) are productive of good and of nothing else; second, those which by themselves are productive of good and, in conjunction with other things, have additional good effects; third, those which by themselves have bad effects but also have good ones which outweigh them.

Obviously, the classification is neither exhaustive nor neat, but if my account of the vexing phrases that occur in it and in Glaucon's and Adeimantus' speeches is correct, then Plato is not open to the charge of having promised to undertake what he never attempts.[14]

Plato's notion of the effects of the powers of justice and injustice in the souls of men is fundamental to the Platonic conception of justice (see 366e 5–6ff.; 367b 2–5). When Adeimantus complains that no one has adequately stated how justice and injustice, because of their powers, constitute respectively the greatest good and the greatest evil in the soul, he is anticipating theses Socrates will expound in Books IV, VIII, and IX. Adeimantus' speech is especially important because it repeatedly expresses Plato's aim of delineating the powers of justice and injustice as powers exerted solely by their existence or presence in the soul (see 366e 5–9). In this connection the word "power," though it correctly translates δύναμις, can prove misleading. For if it is conceived after the model of other uses of "power"—indeed on the model of other uses of δύναμις in Adeimantus' speech (e.g., 366e 2; 366c 4)—it will not be thought a power which *must* be exercised. What Adeimantus asks to be shown, however, is the good which justice inevitably works by its mere existence in the soul. Injustice, likewise, is to be proven an inescapable evil for the soul in which it is present. And these, of course, are the very demands Socrates attempts to meet in Books IV, VIII, and IX.

The most familiar evidence that Plato is intent on characterizing justice and injustice as things which cannot but work good and evil is, of course, contained in the famous similes of Book IV, where the just soul is compared to the healthy body, the unjust to diseased bodies, and the entire ἀρετή, or virtue, of the soul is called a kind of health and beauty and good condition, its contrary, κακία, being termed the soul's disease, ugliness, and enfeeblement (see 444c–e *et circa*).

If Socrates were to succeed in proving that justice by itself cannot but be good for the soul of its possessor, and injustice evil, he still would not be meeting Glaucon's and Adeimantus' challenge; for they ask him to show that justice is the greatest good of the soul, injustice its greatest evil. Further, showing this will not be sufficient unless Socrates thereby shows that the life of the man whose soul possesses justice is happier than the life of anyone whose soul is unjust. The latter is required of Socrates when Glaucon asks him to compare certain lives in terms of happiness. Glaucon envisages a just man's life "bare of everything but justice. . . . Though doing no injustice he must have the repute of the greatest injustice . . . let him on to his course unchangeable even unto death . . . the just man will have to endure the lash, the rack, chains, the branding-iron in his eyes, and finally, after every extremity of suffering, he will be [impaled]."[15] On the other hand, the unjust man pictured by Glaucon enjoys a position of "rule in the city, a wife from any family he chooses, and the giving of his children in marriage to whomsoever he pleases, dealings and partnerships with whom he will, and in all these transactions advantage and profit for himself," and so forth, including a not unreasonable expectation of divine favor.[16] Socrates has to prove that a just man whose condition is that described by Glaucon will still lead a happier life than anyone who is unjust if he is to show that, in terms of happiness, which is the Platonic criterion for the choice among lives,[17] one ought to choose the just life. Again, if Socrates is able to show that an unjust man who enjoys the existence depicted by Glaucon is more wretched than any just man, that will suffice for choosing to reject any unjust life. As Prichard remarked, "Plato certainly did not underrate his task. Indeed, in reading his statement of it, we wonder how he ever came to think that he could execute it."

Some questions present themselves here. Assuming that the reader is acquainted with Plato's characterization of justice as a particular ordering of the parts of the soul, I will discuss these questions very briefly. Could Plato have thought it possible to lead a life which was neither just nor unjust? In Books VIII and IX he ranks kinds of souls according to degrees of injustice in them; might he have held that some souls lack both δικαιοσύνη and ἀδικία? On the Platonic conception of justice, the answer has to be no because, first, Plato is obliged to affirm, concerning numerous actions which may involve no one besides the agent, that they are done either justly or unjustly; for they, too, can alter the ordering, the polity or constitution, of the soul's parts. Secondly and decisively, even if one could avoid all actions that, on Plato's encompassing view, are just or unjust, the soul's parts would nevertheless be ordered one way or another; that is, either justice or injustice would be present (cf. 449a 1–5).

Another question, one often touched upon by H. W. B. Joseph in his *Essays in Ancient and Modern Philosophy,*[18] can be posed as follows. Few persons, if any, are perfectly just or consummately unjust; does Plato really try to maintain that all such intermediate lives are less happy than any perfectly just man's life would be? Since Socrates agrees that there are a variety of good things besides justice,[19] this question might be put by asking whether Plato really thinks that a life which includes an abundance of goods other than justice—but involves some injustice—must be less happy than, for example, the existence of Glaucon's beleaguered though just man. Anyone familiar with the *Republic* will know that this question has to be answered in the affirmative. Plato's consideration of the matter, it should be observed, is developed in terms of his own conception of justice. Thus in Book IV, Socrates states that there is one form of ἀρετή, or excellence, of the soul but limitless ones of κακία, or defect (cf. 445c 5–d 1; also 449a 1–5), four of which are worth special notice; they are the defects responsible for the timocratic, oligarchical, democratic, and tyrannical polities of the soul, the famous discussion of which occupies Books VIII and IX. There, while contending that the man whose soul possesses its ἀρετή, is happier than any man whose soul lacks it, Plato tries to determine which of the four forms of κακία produces the least unhappiness and which the greatest wretchedness. Clearly, what Plato attempts to establish—but again in terms of his own conception of justice—is that any intermediate life, any soul characterized by some degree of injustice, is inferior in point of happiness to the perfectly just, despite any other good things an intermediate life might include; and that the extent to which a soul is unjust is paralleled, *pari passu,* by the misery of the man whose soul it is (cf. 576b–e; 580a–c).

To summarize thus far: I began with the familiar observation that Plato held that the choice between the just life and an unjust life is to be decided by determining which is the happier. I then claimed that this position of Plato's is complicated by the presence in the *Republic* of two conceptions of justice, Socrates maintaining a distinctively Platonic one and Thrasymachus a vulgar one, while Glaucon and Adeimantus give expression to both. After stating the vulgar conception, I discussed some aspects of the Platonic one. In my discussion of the latter I tried to clarify what was meant when Socrates affirmed—and when Glaucon and Adeimantus insisted that he establish—that justice is good for its own sake or good in itself, and injustice evil in itself. Plato, I contended, characterized justice and injustice in these ways because he thought that on their own—or by themselves—they effect the soul's greatest good and greatest evil; this being due, Plato believed, to the powers which they inevitably exert upon the souls in which they are present. I further claimed that, on Plato's view, justice or injustice—one or the other but not both—must exist in every soul, and that the man in whose soul justice exists will be happier than a man whose soul includes any degree of injustice, happiness varying inversely with injustice.

In what follows, I argue that Plato failed to relate the two conceptions of justice adequately and that it is implausible to suppose that the omission, a complex one, can be repaired. Consequently, Plato's conclusions about happiness and justice—as he conceives the latter— prove irrelevant to the dispute between Socrates and Thrasymachus (and Glaucon and Adeimantus, in so far as they, too, are concerned with the happiness of vulgarly just and unjust men).

## The Fallacy

Toward the end of Book IV, Socrates formulates the Platonic conception of the just man: a man, each part of whose soul attends to its business or function, performing no tasks but its own. Further, Socrates says that if an action preserves or helps to produce the condition of the soul in which each of its parts does its own task, one ought to believe the action just and name it so, and believe an action unjust and name it so if it has a contrary effect (see 443e 4–444a 2). In accord with this, Socrates suggests that acting justly is to be understood as acting in a way which will produce the condition of justice in the soul, and that acting unjustly is to be understood as behavior which produces a contrary condition. Glaucon, I take it, is sounding a like note when he affirms that just acts are necessarily productive of justice, unjust ones of injustice (444c 1–3; 444c 10–d 2).

It will be recalled that Thrasymachus, in stating his position, mentioned among unjust acts temple-robbing, kidnaping, swindling, thieving, and so forth. This list, again, was enlarged by Glaucon's mention of sexual relations with whom one pleases, killing, freeing from bonds anyone one wishes, and so forth; that is, acts commonly judged immoral or criminal. The man of whom it was to be proven that his life will be happier than other lives is the man who does not commit such acts.

What Plato tries to establish, however, is that a man each of the parts of whose soul performs its own task, and who conducts himself throughout his days in such a way that this condition will remain unaltered, leads a happier life than any men whose souls are not thus ordered. Regardless of Plato's success or failure in this endeavor, for it to be at all relevant he has to prove that his conception of the just man precludes behavior commonly judged immoral or criminal; that is, he must prove that the conduct of his just man also conforms to the ordinary or vulgar canons of justice. Second, he has to prove that his conception of the just man applies to—is exemplified by—every man who is just according to the vulgar conception. For, short of this last, he will not have shown it impossible for men to conform to vulgar justice and still be less happy than men who do not. Plato had to meet both of these requirements if his conclusions about happiness and justice are to bear successfully against Thrasymachus' contentions and satisfy Glaucon's and Adeimantus' demands of Socrates. There are passages in the *Republic* which show that Plato thought there was no problem about the first requirement; there are, however, no passages which indicate that he was aware of the second. In any event, the fact is that he met neither requirement; nor is it plausible to suppose that he could have met either of them. Before I argue that this is the position as regards the main argument of the *Republic,* some objections which may be raised here should be faced.

For the purposes of this paper, which are the internal criticism and incidental clarification of the main argument of the *Republic,* I am not questioning—what have often been questioned—Plato's conclusions to the effect that men who are Platonically just are happier than men who are not, and that the farther a man's soul is from Platonic justice the more wretched he will be. My object is to show that these conclusions of Plato's are irrelevant to the dispute between Socrates and Thrasymachus and Thrasymachus' sometime advocates, Glaucon and Adeimantus. However, to press both of the requirements that I have stated may seem too stringent. It may be felt that, if Plato's conclusions are granted, he then need fulfill only the first requirement; that is, provide a demonstration that the Platonically just man cannot perpetrate vulgar injustice. For Plato's conclusions, together with such a demonstration, would have the consequence that the happiest men are among those who conform to vulgar justice; thereby, Thrasymachus' position would be refuted. But even granting Plato's conclusions, had he met the first requirement and not the second, he would have left open the possibility of Platonically unjust men who were vulgarly just and yet no happier, perhaps less so, than vulgarly unjust men. Alternatively, it may be thought that the satisfaction of the second requirement—namely, a demonstration that the vulgarly just man is Platonically just—would, together with Plato's conclusions, have sufficed. For it would then follow that no one was happier than vulgarly just individuals; and this, too, would refute Thrasymachus' position. It would, however, leave open the possibility of there being men who were Platonically just, and consequently as happy as anyone else, yet capable of vulgar injustices and crimes. Because of these considerations, both requirements had to be satisfied.

Both explicitly and by implication, Plato distinguished his special conception of justice from the ordinary understanding of morality.[20] Moreover, he repeatedly alleged connections between the two. In Book IV, after Socrates defines the virtues (441c–442d), he and Glaucon agree that the Platonically just man is least likely of all men to commit what would ordinarily be thought immoral acts; and in Book VI, Socrates attributes the vulgar moral virtues to men of a philosophical nature—to men, that is, whose souls are pre-eminently ordered by Platonic justice (484a–487a). Doubtless, then, Plato thought that men who were just according to his conception of justice would pass the tests of ordinary morality. But although Plato more than once has Socrates say things to this effect, he nowhere tries to prove it. Attempts to show that Platonic justice entails ordinary morality are strikingly missing from the *Republic*; Plato merely assumes that having the one involves having the other. The assumption, moreover, is implausible. On Plato's view, the fulfillment of the functions of the soul's parts constitutes wisdom or intelligence,[21] courage, and self-control; and if these obtain, justice, according to Plato, also obtains. Intelligence, courage, and self-control are, however, *prima facie* compatible with a variety of vulgar injustices and evil-doing. Neither as usually understood nor as Plato characterizes them are those virtues inconsistent with performing any of the acts Thrasymachus and Glaucon mention as examples of injustice. In this regard it is tempting to assert that the most that can be said on behalf of Plato's argument is that crimes and evils could not be done by a Platonically just man in a foolish, unintelligent, cowardly, or uncontrolled way.

In Books VIII and IX, where Plato sketches the degeneration of the

politics of city and soul, the motives he uses to characterize the timocratic, oligarchical, and democratic types of soul are motives which,
especially when strong, may lead to vulgar immorality and crime. But
Plato, it should be noted, does not state or even suggest that it is inevitable for them to do so. By contrast, his account of the tyrannical soul,
the opposite extreme from the Platonically just, is replete with the description of crimes that men who have tyrannical souls commit (573e–
576a); their immorality and wickedness, aggravated if they become
actual tyrants, is said to pertain necessarily to them (580a 1–7). However, the suggestion that men with souls of a timocratic or oligarchical
or democratic kind are prone to perform immoral acts of course fails
to satisfy the first requirement for Plato's conclusions to be relevant.
And if it were granted that men whose souls are tyrannical are somehow necessarily evil-doers, this still would not meet the requirement.
That is, neither separately nor conjointly do the theses of Books VIII
and IX about other types of soul exclude the possibility of men whose
souls are Platonically just committing what would ordinarily be judged
immoral acts. Any supposition to the effect that the theses of Books
VIII and IX were meant by Plato to establish the claim that vulgarly
unjust acts can be performed only by men whose souls lack Platonic
justice is unconfirmed by the text of those books;[22] in any case, Books
VIII and IX contain neither proof nor intimation of a proof for that
further thesis.

The first requirement, then, is left unfulfilled. Plato merely has Socrates reiterate the implausible assumption a demonstration of which was
needed. The second requirement, it will be recalled, is a proof that the
vulgarly just man is Platonically just. While there are passages in the
*Republic* which indicate that Plato thought there were no difficulties
about the first requirement, the position is not even this favorable in
regard to the second: he nowhere so much as assumes that men who
are just according to the ordinary conception are also Platonically just.
Indeed, there is no reason to suppose that this was his belief; but the
omission of a claim to that effect within the framework of his argument
cannot but seem surprising. Plato abundantly represents Thrasymachus, Glaucon, and Adeimantus as questioning the happiness of ordinarily just, moral men. It seems incontrovertible that when they ask to
be shown how justice, because of its power, constitutes the greatest
good of the soul, Glaucon and Adeimantus are taking for granted that
the souls of vulgarly just men will enjoy the effects of justice. Nonetheless, an examination of Socrates' reply to Glaucon and Adeimantus (an

examination, that is, of Book II, 367e to Book X, 612b) fails to uncover any claim whose import is that vulgar justice entails Platonic justice.

A remark I quoted earlier may seem capable of being drafted into Plato's service here. After Socrates and Glaucon agree that the Platonically just man is the least likely of all men to commit vulgar injustices, Socrates says, "And is not the cause of this to be found in the fact that each of the principles within him does its own work in the matter of ruling and being ruled?" (443b 1–2). <u>Socrates is here stating that the cause of the Platonically just man's vulgar justice is precisely that he is Platonically just.</u> Perhaps someone might be tempted, on the basis of the remark, to think that Plato was suggesting that Platonic justice is a necessary condition for vulgar justice. There is, however, no warrant for extending the remark in this way. Although Plato sometimes speaks of an item as the cause (αἰτία) of something where it seems that he thinks of it as a necessary condition of it (for example, when he speaks of the "forms" as causes at *Phaedo* 100c–d *et circa*), his uses of αἰτία are by no means always of this kind. Nor do I see any reasons for thinking he is so using it at 443b 1–2. A more likely construction of those lines would take them as equivalent to the claim that Platonic justice is sufficient to insure vulgar justice; that is, as equivalent to the implausible assumption, a proof of which is my first requirement.

Apart from the fact that Plato never states that being vulgarly just entails being Platonically just, one may wonder if such a claim is at all plausible. It does not seem to be; for instance, scrupulous, rulebound men of the very type evoked by Plato's portrait of Cephalus at the beginning of the *Republic* provide examples of men who are vulgarly just but whose souls lack Platonic justice, and men with timocratic souls might provide additional Platonic counterexamples to the claim that vulgar justice entails Platonic justice.

My criticism of Plato's argument, it is worth observing, is unaffected by considerations of how he understood happiness (εὐδαιμονία) or blessedness (μακαριότης); and, again, my criticism is independent of the success or failure of his attempts to establish the happiness of *his* just man. Had Plato succeeded in showing that the happiest or most blessed of men are those who are just according to his conception of justice, and that the farther a man is from exemplifying Platonic justice the more unhappy he will be, Plato still would not have shown either that Platonic justice entails vulgar justice or the converse. That is, he would still have to relate his conclusions to the controversy which, plainly, they are intended to settle.

In conclusion, a speculation: it concerns one of the possible philosophical motives for Plato's conception of δικαιοσύνη. In the first interchanges of the *Republic,* the existence of exceptions to moral rules of conduct is emphasized. Plato has Socrates more than once assert—both of telling the truth and paying back or restoring what one owes—that it is sometimes just to do these things, sometimes unjust (ἐνίοτε μὲν δικαίως, ἐνίοτε δὲ ἀδίκως ποιεῖν, 331c 4–5; cf. 331c 1–332a 5 entire). Partly on this basis, partly because of similar passages in other dialogues, I believe it likely that Plato held that there are allowable exceptions to every moral rule, or virtually every moral rule, of conduct.[23] What is more, I believe that Plato was so impressed by what he took to be permissible exceptions to moral rules of conduct that his certainty of the existence of those exceptions, together with his certainty that no defining logos could have any exceptions, led him to—or confirmed him in—the view that rules of conduct do not constitute anything essential to morality or justice. This, I believe, was one of the principal motives for his characterization of δικαιοσύνη, a characterization not in terms of conduct and the relations of persons, but in terms of the relations of parts of the soul.

## Notes

1. "Justice," "injustice," etc. are notoriously unsatisfactory translations of many occurrences in Plato's dialogues of δικαιοσύνη, ἀδικία, and their relevant cognates. My use of the conventional translations does not, however, affect the claims of this paper. I am indebted to Mr. Gerald Barnes and Prof. Marshall Cohen for helpful discussion of some of the points I have tried to make.

2. To my knowledge, the last detailed criticism of both Plato's procedure and conclusions is to be found in H. A. Pritchard's inaugural lecture, *Duty and Interest* (Oxford, 1928), and in the title essay of the same author's posthumously published collection, *Moral Obligation* (Oxford, 1949).

3. Richard Robinson, *Plato's Earlier Dialectic* (2nd ed.; Oxford, 1953), p. 51.

4. It is widely held that Socrates' professions of ignorance have to be discounted to some extent. For instance, Plato often—if not always—must have thought that the "absurdities" he had Socrates elicit really were absurdities. For an example in *Rep.* I, see 333e 1–2 *et supra.*

5. See, e.g., 344e 1–3; 345a 2–7; 352d 5–6; 347e 2–4ff.; as these lines, together with the contexts in which they occur, show, the formulations in terms of an advantageous or profitable or better life are intended as equivalent to

the formulation in terms of happiness. See also 392a–c; 420b–c; 427d; 472c–d; 484a–b; 544a; 545a–b; 578c; 580 *ad fin.*

6. 442d 10–443b 2; I have excerpted the passage from Shorey's translation in the Loeb Classical Library (Cambridge, Mass., Vol. I, 1937; Vol. II, 1942). Except where otherwise indicated, I use Shorey's translation.

7. This statement of conditions for ἀδικία and δικαιοσύνη exhausts the notion of justice of Socrates' host, the scrupulous and fearful Cephalus; that Polemarchus shares much of the ordinary understanding of morality (and, unlike Thrasymachus, remains largely committed to it) is shown by the manner in which he reacts when Socrates reduces one of his positions to the absurd consequence that being just requires a "kind" of stealing (κλεπτική τις). See 334b 3–7. The few examples of injustice that Adeimantus gives are among those mentioned by Thrasymachus and Glaucon.

8. E.g., αὐτὸ αὑτοῦ ἕνεκα ἀσπαζόμενοι (357b 6); αὐτό τε αὑτοῦ χάριν ἀγαπῶμεν (357c 1); αὐτά ... ἑαυτῶν ... ἂν δεξαίμεθα ἔχειν (375c 8). For a compilation of the troubling expressions, see J. D. Mabbott, "Is Plato's *Republic* Utilitarian?," *Mind,* N.S. XLVI (1937), 469–470.

9. A quarter of a century ago, M. B. Foster criticized Plato on this score (M. B. Foster, "A Mistake of Plato's in the *Republic*," *Mind,* N.S. XLVI [1937], 386–393). J. D. Mabbott replied, claiming that Plato does try to prove justice good for its own sake, or a good in itself *(op. cit.)*. Foster, in answer to Mabbott, modified his criticism of Plato, saying that the vexing expressions made merely for a verbal ambiguity, "two different (and mutually inconsistent) ways of expressing what he [Plato] nevertheless conceived always as the same thing." According to Foster, Plato always meant to be claiming that justice is valuable because of its effects. Foster continued to maintain, in my belief rightly, that Plato did not try to prove justice a good in itself, or good for its own sake—in the sense which those qualifying phrases usually bear at present. See M. B. Foster, "A Mistake of Plato's in the *Republic*: A Rejoinder to Mr. Mabbott," *Mind,* N.S. XLVII (1938), 226–232. See n. 14 *infra.*

10. F. M. Cornford (trans.), *The Republic of Plato* (New York, 1945), p. 42. Cornford's translation of τὸ χαίρειν (357b 7) as "enjoyments" is, at best, doubtful. (The occurrence of the phrase at 357b 7 poses, I admit, a difficulty—though hardly a decisive one—for my contentions in this section.) If, contrary to Cornford and following most translators, αἱ ἡδοναί at 357b 7 is taken to mean pleasure(s) rather than what produces it, the conclusion of Plato's sentence presents a considerable obstacle: since ταύτας in καὶ μηδὲν εἰς τὸν ἔπειτα χρόνον διὰ ταύτας γίγνεται ἄλλο ἢ χαίρειν ἔχοντα refers to αἱ ἡδοναί, it will have to be understood as pleasure which produces enjoyment, i.e. pleasure. Plato would then implausibly have to be understood as thinking that pleasure produces pleasure.

11. For a surprising yet likely example, cf. 584b.

12. A. D. Lindsay (trans.), *The Republic of Plato* (New York, 1957), p. 44, 358a 1–3.

13. *Ibid.,* 358a 4–6; my italics.

14. Even Foster's charge of verbal ambiguity (cf. n. 9 *supra*) should be dismissed. It imports into Glaucon's and Adeimantus' speeches a possibly anach-

ronistic interpretation of "good for its own sake" and "good in itself," one in which those phrases mark a contrast with things that are good because of their effects, even when the good they produce is happiness or pleasure. As I have argued, Glaucon's and Socrates' remarks show that Plato did not intend this contrast. See 367c 5–d 2, where Adeimantus places justice among ἀγαθὰ γόνιμα τῇ αὐτῶν φύσει; cf. Adam's conjecture *ad loc.*, and Foster, in *Mind,* N.S. XLVI (1937), 392–393.

15. Excerpted from 361c 3–362a 2; cf. the entire passage, 360e 1–362a 8.

16. Compare 613c 8–614a 3.

17. See the passages cited in n. 5 *supra.* Cf. also Foster, in *Mind* (1937), 387, and (1938), 229, 231–232; A. W. H. Adkins, *Merit and Responsibility, A Study in Greek Values* (Oxford, 1960), pp. 264, 283 ff., especially 290–291.

18. Pp. 76, 80–81, 140–141, 153–154.

19. See, however, *Rep.,* 491c–495a, 505a ff., 521a.

20. In addition to the passage cited in note 8 *supra,* see 517d–e and 538c–539d.

21. Because "wisdom," the orthodox translation of σοφία, is the name of something intimately connected with justice and morality as they are ordinarily understood, I suggest, as an alternative, "intelligence"; whatever Plato intended by his employment of σοφία toward the end of Book IV, one is not entitled to assume without argument that a man who possesses it will be ordinarily just or moral. There is some warrant for using "intelligence" because, in at least one relevant passage, Plato employs φρόνησις interchangeably with σοφία. See 433b 8 *et circa.*

22. As I have stated, at other places in the *Republic* Plato makes unsupported claims tantamount to the assertion that if one's soul is Platonically just, one will be vulgarly just, and this of course implies that, if vulgar injustice is done, it is done by men whose souls lack Platonic justice.

23. Cf., e.g., the vexed passage, *Phaedo* 62a 1–7 *et circa; Symposium* 180e 4–181a 6; 183d 3–6. The remarks in Pausanias' speech in the *Symposium* are, of course, of dubious value as evidence for Plato's own views. For further discussion of the point and additional references, see G. Santas, *The Socratic Paradoxes and Virtue and Happiness in Plato's Earlier Dialogues* (unpublished Ph.D. dissertation, Cornell University, 1961), p. 68 *et passim.*

# 2

# The Psychology of Justice in Plato

*John M. Cooper*

One important merit of the recent spate of articles addressing the *Republic's* central thesis, that all and only those who are just lead flourishing, fulfilled lives, is to have directed attention anew to Plato's moral psychology—specifically to the links Plato tries to forge between the love for knowledge and understanding and the aversion to (at any rate) much of what would ordinarily be counted as unjust treatment of other people.[1] It has rightly been seen that the core of Plato's response to Thrasymachus' challenge lies in this novel—even paradoxical—thesis about the nature of what a contemporary theorist would call "moral motivation." In this paper I want to examine directly and on its own account Plato's theory of the just person's psychology, leaving aside for the most part the controversies that have loomed so large lately about his justification for using the word "just" (δίκαιος) to describe the person whose psychology this is. The state of mind Plato describes has not, I think, been adequately represented in the recent literature, and my interest is more in what kind of person this is whom Plato calls just, than in whether he is correct in calling him that. My discussion will direct attention more than has been usual in this context to the *Republic's* metaphysics, and less to its political and moral theory, narrowly conceived. I hope thereby to illuminate somewhat the Platonic conception of human perfection and to bring out both the close links between the psychology and the metaphysics of the *Republic* and some of the often unnoticed consequences that Plato's metaphysics has for his psychological theories.

## I

Plato develops his account of the psychology of the just person in two principal stages. The later stage, found in *Republic* V–VII, is the more important for present purposes, but before turning to that I must take up briefly the earlier account of book IV. Plato's argument in the later books cannot be understood properly except in conjunction with the book IV account, aspects of which it is intended to fill out, and some of the recent literature on book IV contains misconceptions about the argument there that must be cleared away before we can proceed.

From the beginning of *Republic* IV it is taken for granted that to be just is to be in a psychological state which shapes and directs one's voluntary actions, one's choices and one's preferences over a very wide range of practical concerns. Plato, for reasons we need not go into now, takes it that such a complex state cannot be adequately understood by treating it as a disposition to exhibit any single, or even any complex set of, independently and nonquestion-beggingly specifiable sorts of action. Justice must be characterized instead in internal, psychological terms, as a condition of a person's action-, choice- and preference-producing apparatus, specified by reference to interrelationships among the different elements of this apparatus itself. So, having fixed these elements as three, reason, aspiration[2] and appetite, Plato concludes that justice is the condition of a person in which each of these three plays always and only a certain single role, one for which it is naturally suited. Reason, on its own and without interference from the others, determines how it is best for the person to be and act; aspiration identifies with reason's directives, regarding them as objects to strive for and making the person dissatisfied with himself if through his own fault they are not attained; and appetite, restrained and moderated by reason and aspiration, drives him on toward pleasures of eating, drinking, sex and other bodily gratifications when and as, and only when and as, reason approves. When each of these three psychological elements performs just its assigned job, then, Plato holds, the person in that psychological condition is just; and if in any way or to any degree these elements fail to do their jobs, or attempt to do anything else, such a person is not just. It does not follow, of course, that he is *un*just. As Socrates admits (472b7–d2), it may well turn out that no one fulfills these conditions perfectly; still, the definition is no less correct and no less useful for that, since we are free, for all practical purposes, to count as just those who sufficiently nearly resemble the person so defined. If it can be shown that only a perfectly just person is truly well-off, and lives a fulfilled life, then the more nearly anyone approximates to this internal condition the closer he will come to leading the perfectly flourishing human life: we need perfect models of just and unjust persons so that "however we find them to be as regards flourishing or its reverse, we will necessarily have to agree also that whoever of ourselves is most like them will have a share [of flourishing] most like theirs," 472c7–d1.[3] Strictly, then, only the person who fully attains precisely this psychological condition is just.

Even so, it is obvious enough that Plato has presented no sufficiently determinate theory of justice until he explains more fully what the role of reason is to be and how it is to go about performing it. He explains at some length in books III and IV what functions the other two parts are to perform, but with the simple idea, which is all I have enunciated so far, that reason is to rule—to determine what is to be done and to put these determinations into effect—one has at best a formal criterion from which no substantive choices and preferences can be derived. Plato is deliberately vague in book IV on this point, since he is not yet in a position to define the role of reason more precisely; but he is not nearly so vague even in IV as he is sometimes thought to be. For in the full statement of what the function of reason is, Plato says not merely that reason is to rule but that it is to rule *with wisdom:* "Does not it belong to the rational part to rule, being wise and exercising forethought on behalf of the entire soul, and to the principle of high spirit to be subject to this and its ally?" (441e4–6, tr. Shorey). And a little farther on he characterizes wisdom: "But [we call an individual] wise by that small part that ruled in him and handed down these commands, by its possession in turn within it of the knowledge (ἐπιστήμη) of what is beneficial for each and for the whole, the community composed of the three" (442c5–8, tr. Shorey). So a person's reason is not doing its job unless three conditions are met: first, it *knows* what it is best for him to do; second, it makes all its decisions in the light of this knowledge; and third, its decisions are effective.[4] The main contribution of books V–VII is indeed to work out a theory of what this knowledge consists of; but already in IV Plato is explicit that unless one's reason has this knowledge, whatever exactly it amounts to, it is not performing its work fully and adequately.

It follows from what has been said so far that on Plato's account no one is just, strictly speaking, who does not have *knowledge* of what is best to do. True belief is not sufficient for an individual's justice in the

*Republic,* nor, I think, though this is a more complicated question, for any other virtue of individuals.[5] It is true that Plato conspicuously defines a *city's* courage (429a–430c) in terms of the deep-dyed belief (not knowledge) of the soldier-class in the correctness of the laws and institutions of the city they serve. But it is noteworthy that he denies that this condition of belief makes the soldiers themselves brave, except in a qualified sense: it makes their city brave, but it gives them, as Socrates cautions, only "civic bravery" (πολιτικὴ ἀνδρεία, 430c3), not bravery *tout court.* It makes them consistently do the things one expects of brave citizens—they are fearless and selfless soldiers and police officers—but they are far from having the philosopher's pervasive strength of character, that will not let one rest content until one has achieved the fullest possible understanding of what is good for oneself and why it is so.[6] Similarly the city's justice is defined as the condition in which each class sticks to its own social work (432d–435a), but this does not mean, nor does Plato anywhere suggest, that people who do stick to their social work thereby show themselves to *be* just. They do what is just, but whether they *are* just is obviously not settled by pointing to their behavior alone. "Doing one's own social work" is presented only as a description of just action. It is not presented as part of the definition of the condition of justice itself—except, of course, the justice of a city, which is a different matter entirely.[7] Here Plato does not even allow an analogue of "civic bravery," and for a very good reason: in defining the city's justice he has said nothing about the internal condition(s) of the citizens, which cause(s) them to act justly, so he has not provided any ground here, as he has in the case of bravery, for attributing even a reduced form of the virtue to the individuals themselves. Once these points are duly noted, one sees that Plato consistently restricts justice, as a virtue of individuals, to those who possess within themselves *knowledge* of what it is best to do and be.[8]

## II

Clearly, then, one cannot know what the just person according to Plato is like until one has some grasp, at least, of the nature and substance of this knowledge. For a person's considered conception of how it is best to be and act inevitably colors his attitudes to himself and to other people, as well as establishing or altering more particular attachments and antipathies—and especially so in the case of someone who is so structured that there is no possibility of opposition or resistance to the effective and total adoption of the recommendations of his reason. And if one wants to know what the state of mind of Plato's just person would be, one will have to know something about how he thinks and feels in these respects.

In book IV itself, as already remarked, little is said about what the just person knows. It is noteworthy, however, that the wisdom he is said to have is described merely as knowledge of what is advantageous to himself (442c5–8). Yet earlier in the book the same name, σοφία, is given to the knowledge, possessed by the rulers of the ideal city, "which takes counsel about the city as a whole as to how it would best order its relations to itself and to other cities" (428c12–d3; cf. 429a1–3). Unless Plato is guilty here of a gross equivocation, he must suppose that it is one and the same knowledge that knows both these things.[9] No doubt part of his reason for supposing this derives from his conviction that it is only in cities that human beings realize their full nature; but there is a more general reason as well. For both of these accomplishments essentially involve knowledge of what is good (for the city, for the individual); and you cannot, Plato thinks, know any such particular good without knowing the good-itself: "Whoever cannot mark off in his discourse the form of the good, separating it from all other things . . . you will say knows neither the good-itself nor any other good" (534b8–c5). To be sure, merely knowing the good will not by itself suffice—at any rate not for knowing how best to run a city. This is why Plato insists that before coming to know the good his rulers must spend fifteen years getting experience in city management (539e2–5). Still, the only part of what either sort of person knows that counts, on a strict view, as knowledge (the sort that encompasses understanding, of why things are the way they are and how they ought to be) is knowledge of the good-itself. Without this, all the experience in the world would be useless. So what Plato describes in book IV now as knowledge of how one ought to live oneself, now as knowledge of how a city should conduct its affairs, is in the end nothing less than knowledge of the μέγιστον μάθημα [highest study], the good-itself.

Thus we are led directly up to the central metaphysical theories of the *Republic*. This part of the dialogue is extremely difficult to interpret, since Socrates himself refuses to speculate about what the good-itself might be (506b2–e5) and for the most part offers only the treacherous analogies and parables of sun, line and cave to convey those aspects of it that he *is* willing to hazard an opinion on. But without claiming to offer any proof that this is what Plato means, and avoiding scholarly controversy so far as possible, I risk the following summary of what is relevant in Plato's views on the good-itself for our present inquiry.

First, pending a qualification to be entered directly, the good-itself is a good thing, over and above the good things of this world:[10] over and above, that is, both individual good things like particular persons and events, and such things as a quiet, studious life or a cool drink on a hot day which one might speak of as good things, though they are not individuals but classes or kinds of individuals.[11] Unlike these other good things, however, it is not merely a good something-or-other, or good as such and such, or good for so and so or from such and such a point of view. To use Aristotelian language, one could say its essence is to be good; it is not, like every other good thing, essentially something else (a meal, a person) that, for one reason or another, happens to be good (is accidentally good).[12] Its goodness is not, therefore, diluted and compromised by being mingled with and made dependent on other features of things, as is true of every other good. Thus its goodness is pure, as that of no other good is. Furthermore, it is the only perfect good. Every other good, being good only in some respect or relation or from some point of view, is also not so good, or even quite bad, in some other ways.[13] No other good can possibly be as good as this one: the very best imaginable human life, for example, will still not be as good as this is, and so not as good as it is possible to conceive something as being.

Given the purity of the good-itself, and the impurity of every other good, it should be apparent why Plato says that one cannot know any other good except by knowing this one. Knowledge here, as usual in Plato, is taken to entail understanding, so that to know, e.g., a good life is not just to know which life is good, and from what points of view or in what circumstances, and so on, but precisely to understand what this goodness itself is that one attributes to it with these qualifications. To understand that, however, is to conceive a good that stands apart from all such qualifications—in short, to form one's conception of goodness on the good-itself.

Given the perfection of the good-itself, and the imperfection of every other good, it is apparent why Plato insists that adequate practical thinking requires constantly keeping this good uppermost in one's mind. Everyone wants what is best, but the only sure criterion of goodness in any other thing is the degree to which it approximates the goodness of this perfect good. Any other criterion of goodness, based, say, merely on some conception of human needs and interests, cannot fail to be inadequate, since it must represent as the ideal, as the final achievement, something that cannot be that. Clarity and truth require that all partial standards be seen and treated as such.

So much for what one might call the functional properties of the good-itself. How about its substance or nature? Here Socrates is deliberately least informative. One may, however, render this curious entity more concrete by thinking of it somehow or other as a perfect example of rational order, conceived in explicitly mathematical terms: a complex, ordered whole, whose orderliness is due to the mathematical relationships holding among its parts. This is, I think, implied by the mathematical nature of the higher education that Plato prescribes in *Republic* VII (524d ff.) as preparing the way for dialectic, which itself culminates in the knowledge of this entity, and by the role which he assigns to knowledge of the good as completing and supporting the mathematical sciences of arithmetic and geometry (511c6–d1, 533b6–d1).[14] It should be recalled that the last stage of the preliminary studies, mathematical harmonics, already encompasses the idea that certain numerical relationships are in themselves harmonious and itself provides some explanation for why they harmonize (531c3–4); notice, too, that Socrates recommends the study of music for this reason especially, saying that this makes it "useful for the investigation of the beautiful and the good" (c6–7).[15] Thus mathematics and philosophy merge at their borders, and mathematics itself is capable, on Plato's account, of handling and partially explicating evaluative notions.

## III

If this account of the good-itself is right, what must be the state of mind of the person who has a firm grasp on it? First of all, as Plato emphasizes in many places, he must be a lover of learning (a φιλομαθής). This is so, to begin with, because only someone who felt a natural affinity for reading and thinking and abstract discussion and had learned to value these things more highly than almost anything else could ever have persevered through the rigorous course of training that must be undergone to achieve it, with the attendant restriction of bodily gratification and curtailment of other sorts of pleasant pursuit. This knowledge is obviously not easily won, and if justice requires hav-

ing it, and only a studious sort of person, who cares relatively little for
other pursuits in comparison with intellectual ones, can achieve it, then
no one can be just who is not that kind of studious person. This argument depends, of course, on somewhat doubtful causal connections,
and it is worth noting that much the same conclusion follows more
directly and firmly from the very nature of what the just person according to Plato knows. He knows the good-itself and therefore whatever
he values he values strictly in the light of a comparison between that
thing and the good. Whatever exhibits more fully and perfectly the sort
of rational order that the form of the good possesses as its essence he
values more highly than other things. Naturally, it would be rash to
claim to know how he would rank things in the light of this knowledge.
But it does seem inevitable that he would find in intellectual work generally, and contemplation of the good-itself in particular, the most
nearly adequate instances of rational order in the natural world. This is
so because pure, i.e., theoretical, rational thought is to the greatest
degree possible completely determined by the requirements of rational
order itself: by contrast, desires, material objects and everything else
that is a mixture or combination of thought and bodily things and
events, even when they do exhibit rational order, must remain a joint
product of reason and something else. What such good things are like
is largely determined, not by the demand for orderliness, but by the
nature of these things themselves. The best pure thinking, on the other
hand, is almost wholly the product of rational orderliness itself. Thus
the contemplation of the good, and in lesser degree all other abstract
scientific thought, since in these activities the impulse for rational
order confronts less in the way of alien material to work upon, must
be the most perfect earthly embodiments of good; and just men and
women would know this and make this knowledge effective in their
own lives. Hence they would prefer this kind of thinking to everything
else; in it they would be closest to the good-itself, the only perfectly
good thing there is.

On the other hand, it does not follow that they would always choose
to live a contemplative's life, retired among their mathematical books
and constantly engaging in philosophical discussions. Perhaps one
would choose this if all he cared about was *his* realizing the good so
far as possible. But a just person is a devotee of *the* good, not *his own*
good; and these are very different things. Knowing the good, what he
wants is to advance the reign of rational order in the world as a whole,
so far as by his own efforts, alone or together with others, he can do

this. He recognizes a single criterion of choice: What, given the circumstances, will be most likely to maximize the total amount of rational order in the world as a whole? And here he has a wide arena for possible activity. He can not only impose rational order on his own soul, thinking rational thoughts and satisfying rationally controlled appetites of his own; he can help to bring rational order to the souls of other individuals, and to their social life. To be sure, under certain conditions (for example, perhaps, those characteristic of Plato's own time: cf. 496c5–e2) he might find it rational not to work for the improvement of anything except himself. If conditions make it impossible for his efforts to bear fruit, then his time would be wasted in interesting himself in others: the reign of rational order would not thus be advanced, or not significantly enough to compensate for the loss of pure thinking the world would have to suffer in consequence of his taking time off from his studies. On the other hand, conditions need not always be so bad as that. There may be others intelligent enough to reach the higher intellectual realms themselves and willing to learn from him how to achieve them; and society itself may be ready, if he and others who know the truth work together, to accept their recommendations for its improvement. Under such conditions it would seem that the interests of rational order would be better served by his devoting himself, some of the time, to private teaching and to cooperation with other intellectuals in bettering the condition of mankind generally—in addition, of course, to doing a substantial amount of philosophical work of his own. This combination of activities, it seems plausible to say, would under such conditions constitute his best answer to the question: How can I maximize the total amount of rational order in the world as a whole?

Hence I believe Plato is perfectly entitled to the answer his Socrates gives to Glaucon's complaint (519d8–9) that it is unjust to make those who in the ideal city have reached the goal of intellectual culture leave off intellectual work and spend some of their time putting their knowledge to practical use in the improvement of the lives of others. Socrates answers, in part, that, on the contrary, it would not be fair of them to refuse, seeing that they have themselves exploited the city's institutions for their own intellectual benefit (520a6–c1): and, Glaucon now agrees, just people, such as these men and women are, will not refuse to do what is fair (δίκαια γὰρ δὴ δικαίοις ἐπιτάξομεν, e1). In saying this Socrates is transparently appealing to common sense principles of justice, which he elsewhere (see 538d6–539a1, esp. the implications of e6, τὰ ἀληθῆ μὴ εὑρίσκῃ) rejects as not true. But there is no cause for alarm, since the purer principles Plato himself has been espousing lead to the same conclusion. That these philosophers are just means, on Plato's account, that they know the good-itself and act always with a view to advancing rational order in the whole world. And given the conditions prevailing in the ideal state it does seem very reasonable to think that they would, on their own principles, opt for the mixed political and intellectual life which Socrates insists on.

On the other hand, it is right to emphasize the other part of Socrates' reply to Glaucon as well. For, he insists, they will go down into the cave unwillingly (ὡς ἐπ' ἀναγκαῖον, as Glaucon puts it, 520e1; cf. 540b4–5), that is to say not thinking that (of all things!) the good is to be found in the activities of ruling (cf. 521a5–6, b4–5) and recognizing that there is a life better than the political one (520e4–5, 521b9). They deliberately and freely (520d6–7) choose a life for themselves that is less good than a more singlemindedly intellectual life, of which however they are individually capable. The life they renounce is better because, taken just by itself, the activities it contains exhibit, on balance, a greater amount of rational order than do the combination of activities in the alternative. Furthermore, this life can be said to be in general the ideal best for any human being. There is no activity that comes closer to perfect embodiment of the good than contemplation, with understanding, of the good-itself and the other forms; and given, as Plato makes very clear, that human beings can come into existence who can engage in this activity more or less uninterruptedly, it follows that no other human life could be so good as this one. Hence if the degree of the philosopher's εὐδαιμονία [happiness, flourishing] is judged by comparison with this ideal, Plato's philosophers will settle for a less flourishing existence than they might have had (519e1–520a4; cf. 420b4–8, 465e4–466a6). On the other hand, as previously noted, a true philosopher never concerns himself merely with his own good. His ultimate end is to improve not just the small part of the world that is constituted by his own life, but the whole of it, this part taken together with all the rest. So if a philosopher opted, under the conditions Plato envisages, to ignore everyone else in order to make his own life realize the good more perfectly and fully, he would fail to achieve the goal he was aiming at as nearly as he might have done. And if the degree of one's εὐδαιμονία [happiness, flourishing] is measured by how close one comes to realizing one's ultimate end, such a philosopher would be less εὐδαίμων [happy] than he would have been by living the mixed political and intellectual life Socrates and his interlocutors were urging.

And if one further supposes, as Plato certainly does, that human nature is such that left to themselves most people would always lead *very* disordered lives, it seems fair to say that any philosopher who ever opts for the mixed life will actually be more εὐδαίμων [happy] than any who opts for the purely intellectual life: any philosopher would always *prefer* the mixed life, and he would recognize any situation in which it was rational for him to choose a life of pure contemplation instead as one where external conditions alone, by preventing his efforts on others' behalf from bearing fruit, forced him to settle for less than he had wished to achieve on behalf of the good-itself. So, as Socrates intimates (420b4–5), his philosophers, making the choice to spend some of the time in the cave, but most of it in the world above, would be the happiest and most flourishing men there ever in fact can be.

This shows beyond any reasonable doubt that Plato's just man is no egoist, in any acceptable sense of this term. Not only does he not do everything he does out of concern for his own good, he never does anything for this reason. Even where he acts to benefit himself, recognizing that he does so, his reason for acting is that the good-itself demands it. That *his* good demands it is strictly irrelevant. By the same token, at no time does he act to benefit others out of regard for them and concern for *their* good, just because it is theirs. Again, he confers all benefits out of regard for the good-itself, not out of regard for these more immediate human beneficiaries. As Plato makes clear, the philosopher' turns to this work with regret, ὡς ἐπ' ἀναγκαῖον, and not with any independent attachment to these activities themselves or to those at whose good they are directed. For him there is no pleasure or interest in them for their own sakes. This is, I think, the direct consequence of the role played in Plato's theory by the form of the good. It is the ultimate object of pursuit, yet lies outside the world. Hence no worldly thing or activity can, because of its own properties, because of what *it* is, interest the just man; anything interests him only as a means of coming nearer to the good-itself. Certainly this must be true for most ordinary human activities and interests, involving as they do the expression of appetites and emotions. To this rule there is a single exception, the activity of rational contemplation itself. Since that is the summit of human experience anyone who takes pleasure in it and loves it for its own sake will not be in danger of compromising his pursuit of the ultimate end itself. Because the just person's decision whether to use, or continue to use, his knowledge for the benefit of others is contingent on factors outside his control, he must avoid developing sentiments of attachment to other people and to the normal round of social and political life. But there is no possibility that someone who can contemplate the forms with understanding could ever be forced by circumstances to give up this activity entirely. This worldly attachment, therefore, is firm in a way that no other can be. This means that though the just man in Plato is no egoist, and no altruist either, but a sort of high-minded fanatic; still, his fanaticism is such as to allow him permanent and deep interests in one part of his own good, whereas he cannot similarly have any permanent and deep attachment to any other person's good. This is the only concession that one must grant to the common charge that Plato's just man is a covert, or not so covert, egoist.

I said a moment ago that all this is the consequence of the role played in Plato's theory by the form of the good. Aristotle was right, I think, to insist most emphatically that there is no such thing as a good-itself and that even if there were one ought not to direct one's practical thinking at it as ultimate end. At any rate, the consequence of this insistence is something his own moral sensitivity seems to have made him very reluctant to give up: by placing the object of ultimate pursuit *in* the world Aristotle is able to make room for a wide variety of ordinary human pursuits, interests and attachments as themselves permanent constituents of the final good.[16] He could therefore present a moral psychology that corresponds much more closely than Plato's does to ordinary moral experience. No doubt Plato would not regard this as a defect in his own theory or a point in favor of Aristotle's; but the fact itself is worth reflecting on.

## Notes

1. See especially Richard Kraut, "Reason and Justice in Plato's *Republic*," in E. N. Lee *et al.* (eds.), *Exegesis and Argument* (Assen, 1973).

2. For the idea for this rendering of the Greek θυμοειδές I am indebted to J. C. B. Gosling, *Plato* (London, 1973), ch. III.

3. On the same principle Plato justifies the moral and political subjection of everyone else in his ideal state to the philosophers: by being so subject they approximate as closely as is possible for them to the state of soul possessed by the philosophers, and so also to the condition of flourishing enjoyed by them. See 590c–d.

4. Thus it is clear that Plato does not work even in *Rep.* IV with what Kraut calls the "non-normative" conception of reason's rule (Kraut, *op. cit.*, pp. 208–211).

5. This has been denied by Gregory Vlastos, "The Argument in the *Republic* that 'Justice Pays'," *The Journal of Philosophy.* vol. 65 [1968], pp. 665–674, and its revision and expansion, "Justice and Happiness in the *Republic*" in Gregory Vlastos (ed.), *Plato II* (Garden City, 1971), pp. 66–95; see esp. the latter, pp. 92–94.

6. See 503b7–504d3: to give the best possible account of the virtues one must take a longer route than was taken in describing them in book IV, one which makes explicit reference to knowledge of the good. Notice especially 503e: we require as rulers those who do not shy away like cowards (ἀποδειλιάσει) in the face of difficult intellectual tasks (and, to the same effect, 535b5–9); see also the martial and gymnastic metaphors of 534b8–c3.

7. Vlastos concedes this point in the later version of his paper ("Justice and Happiness in the *Republic*," *op. cit.*, p. 79), but insists that according to Plato a city can be just only if its citizens are just. A moment's reflection shows this to be an extraordinary view for anyone to hold, and especially so for Plato who, as we have seen, very clearly requires wisdom and knowledge of anyone who is just: surely he cannot have slipped even temporarily into allowing *all* the citizens of his city to have this knowledge? In fact the passage Vlastos cites for this view (435e1–436a3) says nothing of the kind. It does not say that in general "moral attributes," as Vlastos has it, come to be predicated of a city only by the antecedent possession of the same attributes by its inhabitants. Plato's point is a more limited one, in accordance with his aims in the passage in which it occurs. Socrates is suggesting, as he will presently argue, that each of us contains three psychological elements corresponding to the three classes of the state. An indication of this, he thinks, is the fact that whole nations are commonly thought to have predominant characters (ἤθη, e2)—the Scythians, for example, to be high-spirited, the Athenians devoted to learning and the Phoenecians fond of money. These characters must attach to these nations by transference from their members (and given that the three characters in question seem to suggest the prominence of the ends of one or another of three distinct parts of the soul, this usage therefore implies that human beings do have the three distinct parts in question). What is true of such predominant national characters need not be true of other properties, not even all "moral attributes"; and Plato nowhere says it is (544d–545b, the only other passage where any similar point is made, applies it to the same restricted set of attributes as we find in this passage). So far as the moral virtues are concerned, as I argue in the text, Plato says different things about different ones: wisdom belongs to the city because the rulers are wise (cf. the repeated emphasis on ἐπιστήμη, 428b6, c11, d8, e8, 429a1–3), bravery because the soldiers have a qualified form, at least, of bravery; justice and moderation, however, though they belong to the city in each case because of *some* property of the citizens, do not devolve upon it from the citizens' being even in a qualified way just and moderate. This seems to me a perfectly sensible view; it is, in any event, for better or worse, what Plato thought.

8. Hence for Plato only accomplished philosophers can be just. Things would have been different, and better, if like Aristotle he had conceived of a kind of practical knowledge substantially independent of the use of theoretical

and scientific powers. He was precluded from doing this by the status of the good-itself in his theory; see below, sect. III.

9. Aristotle, *NE* VI, 1141b24–25, ἔστι δὲ καὶ ἡ πολιτικὴ καὶ ἡ φρόνησις ἡ αὐτὴ μὲν ἕξις, τὸ μέντοι εἶναι οὐ ταὐτὸν αὐταῖς, κτλ, simply reformulates in his own terminology this view of Plato's about these forms of σοφία.

10. I do not follow Vlastos in interpreting Plato's claims that the *F*-itself is *F* as in most cases predicating *F*-ness only of the *F* things of this world—at any rate this move cannot be made with the good-itself. See his "The Unity of the Virtues in the *Protagoras*" and "An Ambiguity in the *Sophist*" in his *Platonic Studies* (Princeton, 1973).

11. I owe a debt here to N. R. Murphy, *The Interpretation of Plato's Republic* (Oxford, 1951), ch. VI, and to J. C. B. Gosling. "*Republic* Book V: τὰ πολλὰ καλά, etc," *Phronesis*, vol. 5 (1960), 116 ff., though my interpretation is not identical, I think, with any of the various ones they seem to have in mind.

12. Hence it is misleading to say, as I just did, that it is a good *thing*. "Good" belongs to it in much the way that "man" does to me, and it would be misleading or nonsensical to call me a man thing: that would invite the inappropriate question, "Man *what?*" So the good is a *good*, but, Plato will insist (to Aristotle's exasperation, cf. *Post. An.* 83a30–35), not a *good thing*.

13. For a defense of this interpretation of the perfection of Platonic forms, see Alexander Nehamas, "Plato on the Imperfection of the Sensible World," *American Philosphical Quarterly*, vol. 12 (1975), pp. 105–117.

14. It also accommodates those later reports of a lecture *On the Good* that, to the surprise of some of its hearers, had to do with mathematics and little else (cf. Aristoxenus, *Harm.* 2.20.16–31.3).

15. On this see Gosling, *Plato, op. cit.,* ch. VII.

16. Cf. my *Reason and Human Good in Aristotle* (Cambridge, Mass., 1975), esp. ch. II, and "Friendship and the Good in Aristotle," forthcoming in *The Philosophical Review.*

# 3

# Plato's Totalitarianism

## C. C. W. Taylor

Though the topic of this paper was originally suggested by Popper's attack on Plato in *The Open Society,* my main concern is not to take sides in the great debate prompted by that celebrated critique.[1] My aim, rather, is expository. I shall first attempt to distinguish three principal varieties of totalitarianism and then try to see how close the fit is between any of those varieties and the political theory of the *Republic,* which is the Platonic text with which I shall be mainly concerned.

Totalitarian states are characterised by a coincidence of two features, authoritarianism and ideology.[2] By authoritarianism I understand a system in which the ordinary citizen has no significant share, either direct or indirect, in the making of political decisions. Ancient tyrannies and some modern colonial regimes are or were authoritarian in this sense. But a typical tyranny was not totalitarian, since another necessary condition, viz. ideology, was lacking. By an ideology I understand a pervasive scheme of values, intentionally promulgated by some person or persons and promoted by institutional means in order to direct all or the most significant aspects of public and private life towards the attainment of the goals dictated by those values.[3] Ancient tyrannies had, as far as our evidence suggests, no ideology; the principal aim of the tyrant was to preserve power and status for himself and his family and dependents, and while, as in the Sicilian tyrannies of the fifth century B.C., public resources were devoted to the maintenance of that end by such means as building of temples and participation in athletic festivals, there is no indication that tyrannical governments attempted to direct private life for public ends.[4] The clearest example of an ancient Greek state which did have an ideology was Sparta, which, interestingly enough, was not authoritarian on my definition, since its magistrates were elected and their enactments subject to some degree of control by the citizen body. (Authoritarianism is, of course, a matter of degree, but I shall not attempt to pursue that question in this paper.) A state may be authoritarian and have an ideology without being totalitarian, if the locus of political power is distinct from the organisation which directs the ideology, as in medieval Western Europe, where authoritarian monarchies co-existed, often uneasily, with the ideology of the Roman Catholic Church. The identity of the locus of political power and the source of the ideology is what I mean by the 'coincidence' of athoritarianism and ideology; coincidence is therefore to be distinguished from mere co-existence.

It can hardly be disputed that by these criteria the ideal state of the *Republic* is a totalitarian state. It is, of course, an instance of extreme authoritarianism. All political decisions are made by the guardians without any reference to the citizen body. The guardians, moreover, are neither elected nor removable from office by popular vote. Politically, their power is absolute; the only control over them is itself ideological, in that they are under an absolute moral obligation not to allow any deviation from the system of education by which the ruling ideology, and therefore acceptance by all of the political system, is passed on from one generation to the next (424b). That the ideal state has an all-pervasive ideology is also indisputable. The context just cited provides a good example: innovations in music and poetry (i.e. in education) gradually spread to affect people's character and behaviour, their personal relations and finally laws and constitutional forms 'until in the end they overthrow everything both public and private' (424d–e). Here is a perfect example of that seamless web of aesthetics, etiquette, education, morality and politics which is typical of an ideological society (cf. Puritan commonwealths in England and America, or the official policy of the Soviet Union). And finally the locus of political power is identical with the source of the ideology, viz. the intellect of the guardians. The knowledge of the Good which is the most precious possession of that intellect determines the content of the ideology, which in turn provides the justification for the power which that intellect exercises via its knowledge of how the Good is to be realised.

It is, therefore, uncontroversial that the ideal state of the *Republic* is a totalitarian state. Where there is room for dispute is on the question of what kind of totalitarian state it is. The significance of that question will become apparent when we make the three-fold distinction of kinds of totalitarianism mentioned at the outset. The basis of that distinction is a distinction in the values which the ruling ideology seeks to promote, and hence in the crucially important differences in the relative values assigned to the goals and well-being on the one hand of the state and on the other of the individuals who compose it.

a) In the first kind of totalitarianism the purposes and well-being of individuals are totally subordinated to those of the state. The well-being of the state is defined in terms of such goods as power, prestige and security, and the ideology requires that the citizens shall bend their energies to the promotion of those ends for their own sake. In so far as the promotion of individual well-being is itself an aim of the state, that is simply because, the citizens being essentially a resource to be exploited for the benefit of the state, it is prudent for the state to husband that resource, just as it is prudent for a slave-master to see that his slaves are well-fed, well-housed and generally content. Orwell's Oceania is a totalitarian state of this extreme kind,[5] and Nazi Germany comes close to providing a non-fictional example, though the necessity of enlisting the loyalty of the citizen to support the regime gives Nazi propaganda a character which partly assimilates Nazism to the second form of totalitarianism.

b) Here the aims of the state are defined as before, and are paramount as before. In terms of the ideology, however, the welfare of the individual is not a resource to be fostered as a means to, and if necessary sacrificed for, the good of the state. Rather the good of the individual is identified as his/her contribution to the good of the state. To confer the greatest benefit on an individual is to cause that individual to be in the best condition of which he/she is capable. But the best condition for any individual is the condition of maximum contribution to the good of the state. Hence in requiring total commitment to the achievement of the well-being of the state the state itself *ipso facto* promotes the well-being of the individual. This form of totalitarianism may rest on a view of the individual as essentially part of an organic social unity, and therefore as an entity whose proper functioning, and hence its good condition, is defined as its contribution to the well-being of the whole.[6] The ideologies of Fascism in general and Nazism in particular present a debased version of this view, in which the individual transcends his particular limitations by identification with nation or race and achieves personal grandeur via the aggrandisement of the latter through the machinery of the state.[7] In this form of totalitarianism the welfare of the individual has intrinsic value, not merely instrumental value as in the first form. But this value, though intrinsic, is not ultimate; it is derivative from the identification of the good of the individual as his contribution to the good of the state, which is the ultimate good.

c) In the third form of totalitarianism the priority is reversed. The function and aim of the state is simply to promote the welfare of its citizens, that welfare being defined independently in terms of such individual goods as knowledge, health and happiness. The good condition of the state is thus defined as the state of maximum well-being for the citizens; as in b) both individual good and the good of the state are of intrinsic value, but here the good of the individual is ultimately valuable, that of the state derivatively. This form of totalitarianism, then, is a form of paternalism. Citizens of a state of this kind are subjected to totalitarian authority for their own good; the justification for that subjection is their inability to achieve the good for themselves, whether through intellectual incapacity, individual weakness of character or collective political ineptitude.

The distinction of these three kinds of totalitarianism is of some interest, both in the abstract and with reference to Plato. In the abstract the three theories rest on different metaphysical assumptions and are, therefore, open to challenge on different grounds. The paternalist theory is a humanist, teleological theory of a familiar kind; it treats recognisable, individual human goods as paramount and evaluates social institutions in terms of their efficacy and efficiency in producing them. Its dubious features are its denial of autonomy as itself a constituent of human welfare, and its claim that some individuals are entitled to wield absolute political power in virtue of possessing knowledge of what is good for themselves and for others, a claim which is contestable both on the metaphysical ground that it is dubious whether such knowledge is possible and on the moral ground that, even if possible, it is doubtful whether it confers political authority. This theory can claim to be individualist in that it gives primacy to the good of individuals, though it is opposed to individualism in its denial of political freedom, self-expression and self-determination. At the other extreme *1984*-style totalitarianism is anti-individualist in a much more damaging sense, viz. that it assigns to the individual only instrumental value. Moreover, its ascription of ultimate value to such features of the state as power and prestige, once the connection of such features with individual good is severed, seems totally mysterious. The individual is required to sacrifice his own interests for the sake of these things, yet without being given anything that can be recognised as a reason for doing so. This 'theory' is then, not merely anti-individualist and anti-humanist, but ultimately anti-rational, resting on a blind worship of power and on a hidden appeal to coercion rather than reason. Theories of the second type attempt to remedy these deficiencies by the identification of the good of the individual with that of the state, but at the cost either of introducing highly questionable metaphysical assumptions about the nature of both, or of slipping into sheer intellectual dishonesty in passing off something quite distinct from the individual's interest as his 'real' or 'higher' interest.[8]

It is, therefore, crucial for critics and defenders of Plato to determine which of these kinds of theory is closest to the theory of the *Republic*. Popper's position is clear: though he does not explicitly allude to the classification sketched above, he regards Plato as a totalitarian of the first, extreme kind, and the oral fervour of his polemic springs from his indignation at what he sees as Plato's basic anti-humanism. He asserts that for Plato *'(t)he criterion of morality is the interest of the state'* (p. 107, his italics),[9] that the interest of the state (i.e. the best state) is 'to arrest all change, by the maintainance of a rigid class division and class rule' (p. 89) and that 'the individual is nothing but a cog (sc. in the state machine)' and hence that 'ethics is nothing but the study of how to fit him into the whole' (p. 108).[10] This is not the place for a detailed discussion of Popper's attack on Plato's alleged historicism, but this much must be observed without more ado. Popper seems to attribute to Plato the absurd view that the interest of the state *consists in* its immunity from change. That that view is absurd needs no argument. It is one thing to believe that all change is for the worse; but that view, silly though it is (and it is certainly not one which Plato held, see below), at least presupposes an independently specifiable good state from the standpoint of which change can be seen as deterioration. But the view that change is as such bad because it is a process away from a prior state commits one who holds it to the view that any earlier state is better than any different later state just because it is earlier.[11]

In fact it is obvious that Plato accepted neither that absurd view nor what I have called the silly thesis of universal pessimism, viz. that by some prior criterion of value all change is deterioration. To take the most obvious case, the freeing of the prisoners in the cave from their chains and their journey to the sunlight, while a process of change, is not a process of deterioration. Nor did he think that the course of human history is one of continuous deterioration; e.g. the account of the recreation of civilisation after the flood at the beginning of *Laws* III is not an account of degeneration.[12] Obviously, the reason why the ideal state is to remain stable is not that stability is itself the good for a state or even a good at all, but because the ideal state is perfect (*teleōs agathēn*, 427e); hence any change must necessarily be deterioration. It is perfect in that it is so constructed as to fulfil, as well as the human condition allows, the function of the state. It is clear that Plato's insistence on the changelessness of the ideal state *admits* the claim that the function of the state is to promote the good of the citizens. Whether that was in fact his view of its function is what we have now to consider.

As a prelude to that discussion it is worth recalling some features of the structure of the *Republic* which are so familiar as perhaps to escape notice. The central theme of books II–X is Socrates' response to the challenge of Glaucon and Adeimantus to show that *dikaiosunē* [justice] is something worth having, an intrinsic good to its possessor, independently of any good consequences which it is instrumental in producing. The suggestion that it is something good, not for the agent, but for something or someone else is after all the thesis that it is *allotrion agathon* [the good of another] which Thrasymachus had urged against Socrates and which, all parties agree at the beginning of book II, has not been adequately refuted. Now suppose that Plato were an extreme totalitarian as Popper alleges. In that case surely his proper response to Glaucon and Adeimantus would be as follows:

> Of course justice is *not* an intrinsic good for the just individual. Justice, in the case of the individual, is simply the virtue of fitting into one's proper place in the state machine, and is good purely instrumentally, in so far as it promotes the good condition of that machine, i.e. its stable functioning. Individual justice is, then, *allotrion agathon,* the *allo* [other] in question being the *polis* [city] itself. But besides, and of incomparably greater value than the justice of the individual is the justice of the *polis,* that state of the *polis* in which every individual fulfils his/her proper social role, i.e. the role such that his/her filling it best preserves political stability. That form of justice is an intrinsic good for its possessor, but its possessor is the *polis,* not the individual.

It will immediately be obvious how far that reply diverges from the reality of the text. First, justice for the individual is not the virtue of filling one's proper social role. Plato indeed argues that that will flow from one's possession of justice (441d12–e2), but justice itself is that

inner condition of psychic harmony in which each of the principal elements of the personality performs its proper role. And that inner state
is argued to be an intrinsic good for its possessor, first via the analogy
with health at the end of book IV (444a–445b), and then in the comparison of lives in book IX, where the life of psychic harmony is argued to
be the only life which is fully desire-satisfying and truly pleasant. Plato,
then, accepts the challenge to show that justice is constitutive of *eudaimonia* [happiness] for the individual and structures the whole of the
work to meet it, whereas if he were a consistent and honest totalitarian
he would dismiss the challenge as based on a misconception. The
question of honesty cannot be discussed independently; since our only
access to Plato's intentions is via his text, it is obviously futile to suggest
that he really intends to espouse extreme totalitarianism, but attempts
to disguise that intention by pretending to argue that individual justice
is good for the just individual. For the only evidence which could be
adduced in favour of that claim is evidence that at other places in the
text Plato defends extreme totalitarianism, and that that thesis is the
dominant one, i.e. evidence that the passages arguing for the benefits
of justice to the individual are inconsistent with the (alleged) central
thesis of extreme totalitarianism.

Where, then, do we find the alleged dominant thesis maintained or
argued for in the text? Despite, or perhaps because of the emotional
intensity of Popper's polemic he is remarkably short on documenta-
tion. It is an astonishing fact that ch. 6 of *The Open Society*, vol. I, which
contains the kernel of his argument, does not refer directly to a single
passage of the *Republic* which even looks as if it supports extreme
totalitarianism. The alleged total subjection of the individual to the
state is proclaimed on the basis of three passages of the *Laws*, 739c ff.,
923b ff. and 942a ff. The second and third of these can quickly be set
aside; in 942a ff. the principle that no one should think of acting for
him or herself without the orders of a leader is enunciated as part of a
code of military discipline, and therefore has no implication that in
general the individual's good is subordinated to that of the state. In
923b ff., in a passage regulating the making of wills, the legislator states
that, since property belongs, not to an individual, but to a *genos* [fam-
ily] and ultimately to the *polis*, the testator cannot bequeath it at pleasure, but in such a way as best to serve the interests of *genos* and
*polis*, to which those of the individual must be subordinate. This plainly
allows and perhaps even suggests the contrast between the interest of
all and the interest of one rather than that between the interest of the

individual and the interest of the group, where the latter is conceived, as the extreme totalitarian thesis requires, as independent of the interests of the individuals composing the group. This leaves us with 739c ff., where Plato, apparently referring to the ideal state of the *Republic,* praises the total communism which characterises it, the abolition of the family and private property

> and by every means the total abolition of what is private *(idion)* from their life, to such an extent that as far as possible even what is naturally private is in a way common, so that their eyes and ears and hands seem to see and hear and act in common, and they praise and censure in unison, all liking and disliking the same things.

This picture of the elimination of private life and private feeling is indeed forbidding, but it does nothing to support the thesis that Plato is here supporting extreme totalitarianism, for he continues (d6–e1):

> that sort of city, whether inhabited by gods or several children of gods (is such that) in living that sort of life they inhabit it *euphrainomenoi,* i.e. enjoying themselves.

Popper omits that sentence, thereby conveying the entirely false impression that in this passage Plato advocates the suppression of individuality for a collective good, when he quite plainly, though paradoxically, says that the suppression of individuality brings the pleasantest life for the individual, such a blessed life indeed that it can plausibly be compared to that of a god.[13]

In fact the strongest support for Popper's thesis in the text of the *Republic* is the well-known passage from the beginning of book IV (420b–421c, cited by Popper in note 35 to chapter 5, but not discussed) where Socrates says that our aim is founding the ideal city is not to make any one class *(ethnos)* especially *eudaimōn* [happy], but as far as possible to make the whole *polis eudaimōn.* On the extreme totalitarian interpretation *polis* must be understood as 'state', i.e. as an organisation conceived as distinct from the individuals who compose it, and the aim of the founder of the ideal *polis* is to promote the wellbeing of that organisation (conceived by Popper as its stability) in total independence from the welfare of its members. This interpretation has, I believe, been refuted by Vlastos,[14] who points out that in this passage the contrast is not between the interest of the abstract organisation and that of the individuals who compose it, but between the interest

of the whole *polis,* i.e. the whole community, and the sectional interest
of any particular class within that community.[15] Vlastos also points out
that when Socrates refers back to this passage at 519e–520a, where he
is explaining why the guardians are to be required to sacrifice their
personal interest in uninterrupted intellectual activity in order to spend
fifteen years in government, he describes the *nomos* [law] which requires them to do so as 'not being concerned that one particular sort
*(genos)* of person shall do especially well, but contriving to bring this
about in the whole *polis,* fitting the citizens together by persuasion and
compulsion, making them give one another the benefit which each is
capable of conferring on the community *(to koinon)*'.

This insistence that the aim of the organisation of a *polis* is to ensure
that the citizens co-operate for their mutual advantage, and in particular that those in possession of political power must aim to benefit those
subject to them, picks up two themes stated earlier in the work. Socrates had argued against Thrasymachus that if government is a *technē*
[craft], i.e. a rationally ordered activity, its aim must be to promote the
welfare of the governed (341d–342c). Of course, book I being an aporetic prelude to the whole work, we should be cautious about taking
claims made there as definitive statements of Plato's views; but at least
the onus is on someone who thinks that that view is repudiated in the
later parts of the work to provide evidence of repudiation, whereas
519e–520a counts against that hypothesis. Then the organisation of the
primitive *polis* in book II is unambiguously attributed to the necessity
for co-operation in satisfying first the basic need for survival and then
the desire for a modicum of material goods (369b–372a).[16] The primitive *polis* is, then, an organisation set up by individuals to secure for
themselves a share of *eudaimonia* [happiness], understood at its most
basic level as a materially tolerable life. As the work develops, this conception of *eudaimonia* is superseded by the more sophisticated conception of *eudaimonia* as psychic harmony, i.e. of the fully worthwhile
life as consisting in the integration of the personality in the pursuit of
the most intrinsically desirable goals. But the conception of the aim of
the *polis* remains constant. The ideal as distinct from the primitive *polis*
is not, indeed, instituted by its own citizens; for the unphilosophical
individual, while capable of the primitive conception of *eudaimonia,*
is not capable of the more sophisticated conception, since he is incapable of grasping what the highest intrinsic goods are. Hence it has to be
set up externally, by an authoritarian, philosophic legislator. But his
aim in setting up the ideal city is continuous with the aim of the cre-

ators of the primitive city, viz. the maximisation of *eudaimonia* for the citizens.

It is clear, then, that Plato is not an extreme totalitarian, since the whole structure of his theory requires that the *polis* is an organisation devised with the paramount aim of promoting individual *eudaimonia*. But that formulation raises the crucial question 'Whose *eudaimonia?*'. Is the aim of the foundation of the ideal state the promotion of the *eudaimonia* of all its citizens, or only that of the guardians? If the latter, then while Plato may be humanitarian as far as the guardians (including for this purpose the auxiliaries) are concerned, he is still an extreme totalitarian as far as concerns the members of the productive class (who are by far the most numerous element in the state, 428e), since he regards them, not as individuals whose interests are to be fostered, but merely as a resource to be utilised as the promotion of the guardians' *eudaimonia* requires. The point is strongly urged by Popper:

> The workers, tradesmen, etc., do not interest him at all, they are only human cattle whose sole function is to provide for the material needs of the ruling class. (p. 47)

This accusation can be supported by the following argument. The function of the *polis* cannot be the promotion of the *eudaimonia* of all its citizens, for only the guardians, and to a lesser degree the auxiliaries, are capable of *eudaimonia*. *Eudaimonia* is constituted by psychic harmony, the integration of the personality under the control of the intellect, itself directed by knowledge of the Forms. But the members of the third class are incapable of providing that intellectual control, and are therefore incapable of true psychic harmony and hence of *eudaimonia*.[17] They are valuable, then, not for their own sake but merely instrumentally, as necessary for the functioning of the organisation whose aim is the *eudaimonia* of the guardians.

A possible response would be that Plato is nonetheless committed to holding that the *eudaimonia* of the *polis* is constituted by the *eudaimonia* of the individual citizens by his acceptance at 435e of the general principle that the characteristics of communities are logically derivative from those of individuals 'for they could not have come from anywhere else' (e3). Hence, it might be claimed, just as the Thracians are a warlike people just in virtue of the fact that all or most individual Thracians are warlike, so the ideal city is a *eudaimōn polis* just in virtue of the fact that all or most of its citizens are *eudaimones*. But that would be wrong; Plato does not in that passage make the absurd claim that for any predicate *F*, *F* applies to a *polis* in virtue of the application of *F* to the individuals composing the *polis*.[18] His claim is the more restricted one that the psychological typology *(eidē te kai ēthē)* [parts and characteristics] which defines the classes of the ideal state, *to logistikon* [reason] etc., requires that those characteristics apply in the first instance to individuals; thus the spirited element in a *polis* is that element composed of predominantly spirited individuals. Plato is far from maintaining that a city's being *F* requires that all or most citizens be *F*; for any particular value of *F* it will be a matter for special investigation whether the city's being *F* is compatible with none of the citizens being *F* (as in the case of 'large' or 'beautiful'), or whether it requires that some but not necessarily all should be *F* (as with 'courageous' (429b) or 'wise' (428e)), or that all should be *F* (as with *sophron* [temperate] (432a)). The application of any predicate is subject to the requirement (435b) that the predicate should apply to *polis* and individual 'in virtue of the same *eidos* [part]', i.e. that the features of an individual in virtue of which that individual is *F* should be the same as those in virtue of which an *F polis* is *F*. This applies to *eudaimōn* as to any other predicate. Now for the individual *eudaimonia* is constituted by psychic harmony; given the integration of the personality under the direction of knowledge of the Good the individual requires nothing more to make his/her life supremely worth having. By the principle of 435b1–2, therefore (the 'analogy of meaning', as Williams calls it, op. cit.), the *eudaimonia* of the *polis* is constituted by its social harmony, i.e. by the harmonious integration of its social classes under the direction of the knowledge of the Good supplied by its intellectual element, the guardians. And the difficulty remains that *that eudaimonia* appears to require that the majority of the citizens should *lack* individual *eudaimonia. Eudaimōn* seems to be an adjective with this special feature, that according to Plato's theory *'Polis P is eudaimōn'* is not merely compatible with 'most citizens of *P* are not *eudaimones*' (as is the case with e.g. *'Polis P* is courageous'), but actually entails it.

The concept of a *eudaimōn polis* seems thus to contain a crucial ambiguity. Vlastos' reply to Popper requires that a *eudaimon polis* is a happy community, i.e. a community all of whose members enjoy a maximally worthwhile life; he has, I believe, shown that when Plato says that the legislator's aim is *eudaimonia* for *holē hē polis* [the whole city] that is what he means. But the analogy of meaning requires that the *eudaimōn polis* is the harmonious state, i.e. the maximally integrated state directed via the intellect of the guardians towards the realisation of the good. And the central difficulty for Plato's theory appears to be the fact that these two conceptions of the *eudaimōn polis* are not merely distinct but incompatible. So we have the familiar paradox of the ideal state,[19] expressed in terms of *eudaimonia;* true *eudaimonia* requires an ideal individual, but a community of ideal individuals would not be an ideal community.

Plato's theory may seem to provide a ready answer to this difficulty. The conception of the harmonious state outlined above presupposes the prior conception of the good to be realised. And what is that good? Nothing other than the maximisation of individual *eudaimonia.* Hence the two conceptions of the *eudaimōn polis* are not in conflict, since the function of the harmonious state is precisely to realise the happy community. To the objection that that cannot be, since the harmonious state requires the absence of *eudaimonia* in the majority of its citizens, Plato's reply is clear. The goal of the *polis* is the production of as much individual *eudaimonia* as possible. But the majority of people are not capable of *eudaimonia* on their own; since they are incapable of grasping the Good, they cannot provide for themselves that impetus towards it which is a necessary condition for psychic harmony. Left to themselves they will be a prey to their lawless lower impulses, and will therefore sink into an uncoordinated chaos of conflicting desires. The nearest they can get to *eudaimonia* is to submit to direction by the intellect of someone else. The best state for an individual is, of course, to be able to provide this direction for himself; but failing that (as it does fail in most people's case) it is better for him to submit to another's direction towards the good than to succumb to the tyranny of his own undisciplined desires. That is to say, as Vlastos reminds us (op. cit.), it is better for him to be a slave to a master who has his ultimate good at heart than to be a slave to his own lower nature (590c–d). Indeed, since what everyone ultimately wants is his/her own good, the authoritarian organisation of the ideal state is precisely designed to give everyone what they really want, as opposed to the satisfaction of particular desires, which frustrate the attainment of that goal (cf. *Gorgias,* argument with Polus). Hence, though Plato does not make the point explicitly in the *Republic,* the 'idealised slavery'[20] which is the condition of the producers in the ideal state is necessary for the achievement of their genuine freedom, viz. the ability to get what they really want.

The combination of Plato's metaphysics and his pessimistic moral psychology seems thus to offer a compellingly neat solution to the difficulty we have been discussing. There is an objective good for the individual, which everyone wants to achieve, but which most are incapable of achieving by their own efforts, since its achievement requires a grasp of the nature of that good of which most are incapable. Hence society must be so organised that the direction towards that good is provided by a ruling elite with the power to direct themselves and others towards the good which they alone grasp. The *eudaimōn polis* is thus the perfectly organised *polis,* and the criterion of its perfect organisation is its realising, to the maximum extent possible, given the ineliminable fallibility of human nature, each individual's potential for personal *eudaimonia.* Hence Plato's theory, while admittedly totalitarian, is straightforwardly paternalistic, thereby absolving him from the charge of anti-humanitarianism which is at the heart of Popper's attack.

As an account of Plato's intentions this seems to me right, but I think that the solution it offers is too neat. For it mentions an objective good for the individual, identified as psychic harmony, the integration of the personality under the direction of the intellect. And the direction of the intellect is to be understood as the systematic pursuit of a goal or goals apprehended by the intellect as supremely good. But what are these goals, or what is this goal? It plainly will not do to say that the goal is psychic harmony itself, since psychic harmony is defined via the apprehension and pursuit of some goal. Nor will it be helpful to say that the goal is the Form of the Good. For that raises the question of how the individual is supposed to pursue and to realise the Form of the Good. To that question only two answers seem possible. The first is that the individual realises the Form of the Good by contemplating it. But in that case psychic harmony and hence *eudaimonia* are beyond the reach of the non-philosopher, and we have no alternative to accepting the version of extreme totalitarianism in which the non-philosophers achieve the best they are capable of by enabling the philosophers to contemplate the Good and thereby to achieve *eudaimonia.*[21] The other alternative is that the individual realises the Form of the Good by being an instance of it, i.e. by bringing it about that his/her personality is in the best possible state. But this merely reinstates the original question; what goal or goals must the intellect direct the individual to pursue? The problem is not peculiar to Plato; any form of paternalism presupposes an answer to this question, which it cannot, therefore, itself supply. But the fundamental weakness of paternalism is that it assumes without justification that autonomy, i.e. self-direction in the light of the agent's own scheme of values, is not itself part of the best possible state for an individual. To put the point in Platonic terms, what prevents it from being the case that the philosopher's knowledge of the Form of the Good shows him that the good cannot be realised in rational agents unless autonomously, and therefore that the perfect organisation of society demands that opportunities for autonomy be maximised? This suggestion cannot be refuted by the familiar observation that individuals may make autonomously bad choices both of particular actions and of ways of life, and hence that autonomy is a dispensable means to the production of an independently specifiable good. For the objection is not that a life's being autonomous is a sufficient condition of its being a good one (in which case it would be contradictory to describe someone as having overall made an autonomous choice of a bad life), but that it is a necessary condition. This allows that a life's being good requires that it realise a plurality of values, one of which is autonomy; the questions of the relative weighing of those values, and hence of the possible extent of trade-off between them, are of course further questions.

It might be replied that the producers in the ideal state are autonomous, since, knowing that the philosophers know what is best for them, they freely and indeed gladly accept their direction (e.g. 432a, 433c–d). This reply points up the incoherence in Plato's treatment of the producers. Either they have a coherent scheme of values, and are capable of organising their lives in the light of it, or left to themselves they are merely a prey to their uncoordinated, short-term bodily desires. In the latter case they can provide no direction to their lives, and must therefore be externally directed for their own good; but since they can make no autonomous choices at all, *a fortiori* they cannot autonomously choose to be directed by the guardians. If, on the other hand, they can direct their own lives in the light of their values, why do they need to be subject in every detail of their lives to the control of the guardians? Then, assuming that the producers are capable of autonomy, how do the guardians know that a life whose nearest approximation to autonomy consists in willingly accepting the direction of another is a better life than one in which autonomy has a central place? They certainly do not know that just in virtue of knowing that there are objective moral truths. For it may be an objective moral truth that autonomy is a central moral value. There is no inconsistency in an objectivist's assigning a central or indeed supreme value to autonomy, just as one may believe that while there are objective truths to be discovered, say, in philosophy, the aim of the activity is to *discover* them, not just accept them passively. The highest value, then, attaches to their independent discovery, but failing that it is better to arrive independently at erroneous views than to believe the truth purely on the word of someone else.

Plato is not, then, an extreme totalitarian, as Popper alleges. His theory is paternalist, as Vlastos shows, and in common with other varieties of paternalism conceals a crucial evaluative gap. He needs to show that an adequate conception of a good life need not include any substantial measure of autonomy, but he makes no attempt to do so. Indeed he shows no sign of awareness of the problem. His failure to provide a plausible independent specification of the good life may easily lead a hostile critic to the view that he is in fact a totalitarian of the second type, who pays lip-service to the individual while identifying his good with his contribution to the perfectly organised state. This would be unjust to Plato, since it is clear that at least in intention he subordinates the perfectly organised state to the happy community. But it points to the central problem of paternalism, that of distancing itself from tyranny, and in that Plato is no more successful than his many successors.

## Notes

1. This is a revised version of a paper read at the 1984 meeting of the Society for Greek Political Thought, held at the London School of Economics. (The coincidence of date and venue irresistibly suggested the topic.) I am grateful to all who took part in the discussion, especially to Julius Tomin, whose personal experience reminds us that the importance of the subject is not confined to the theoretical sphere.

2. I do not purport to offer a precise definition of totalitarianism, but merely to give a characterisation of the phenomenon sufficient for the purpose of this paper. For discussion of the question whether a definition is possible, of the marks by which totalitarian regimes may be recognised and much else of interest beyond the scope of this enquiry, see Leonard Schapiro, *Totalitarianism* (Macmillan, London and Basingstoke, 1972).

3. 'The Fascist conception of the state is all-embracing, and outside of the state no human or spiritual values can exist, let alone be desirable.' ([Mussolini], article on Fascism in *Enciclopedia Italiana,* quoted by Schapiro, op. cit., p.49).

4. Cf. A. Andrewes, *The Greek Tyrants* (Hutchinson, London, 1956).

5. 'The party seeks power entirely for its own sake. We are not interested in the good of others; we are interested solely in power. Not wealth or luxury

or long life or happiness; only power, pure power. . . . We are different from all the oligarchies of the past, in that we know what we are doing. All the others, even those who resembled ourselves, were cowards and hypocrites. The German Nazis and the Russian Communists came very close to us in their methods, but they never had the courage to recognize their own motives. They pretended, perhaps they even believed, that they had seized power unwillingly and for a limited time, and that just round the corner there lay a paradise where human beings would be free and equal. We are not like that. We know that no one ever seizes power with the intention of relinquishing it. Power is not a means, it is an end. One does not establish a dictatorship in order to safeguard a revolution; one makes the revolution in order to establish the dictatorship.' (George Orwell, *Nineteen Eighty-Four* (Penguin edition, Harmondsworth, 1954), p. 211).

6. 'Since the state is mind objectified it is only as one of its members that the individual himself has objectivity, genuine individuality and an ethical life.' (Hegel, *Philosophy of Right,* tr. Knox, pp. 155–6, quoted by Schapiro, op. cit., p. 81).

7. '[Totalitarianism] appears to make the state swallow the individual, and to absorb into authority completely the liberty that should be set against every authority that limits it . . . But one might say just the opposite; for in this conception the state is the will of the individual himself in its universal and absolute aspect, and thus the individual swallows the state, and since legitimate authority cannot extend beyond the actual will of the individual, authority is resolved completely in liberty. . . . the true absolute democracy is not that which seeks a limited state but that which sets no limit to the state that develops in the inmost heart of the individual conferring on his will the absolutely universal force of law.' (Gentile, *Genesis and Structure of Society,* tr. Harris, p. 179, quoted by Schapiro, op. cit., p. 35).

8. Cf. Isaiah Berlin, 'Two Concepts of Liberty', sect. II, (in Berlin, *Four Essays on Liberty* (Oxford University Press, London, Oxford and New York, 1969).

9. All quotations from Popper are from *The Open Society and Its Enemies,* vol. I (Routledge, London, 5th (revised) edition, 1966).

10. The statement that the individual is nothing but a cog in the state machine is the antecedent of a conditional, but the context makes it clear that Popper accepts its truth.

Cf. p. 98 '. . . it is the purpose of the individual to maintain the stability of the state'.

11. Popper is apparently led to his view that for Plato all change is deterioration by his belief that since Forms are prior to their changeable instances all change is change from a condition of maximum resemblance to the Forms to a lesser degree of resemblance, i.e. (since Forms are paradigms of perfection) all change is deterioration. 'The perfect and good Forms or Ideas are prior to the copies, the sensible things, and they are something like primogenitors or starting points of all the changes in the world of flux. This view is used for evaluating the general trend and main direction of all changes in the world of sensible things. For if the starting point of all change is perfect and good, then change can only be a movement that leads away from the perfect and good; it

must be directed towards the imperfect and the evil, towards corruption.' (pp. 35–36).

This account rests on a misunderstanding of the notion of priority. Forms are prior to their instances in various ways; temporally (being eternal, they exist before any particular instance comes to be), causally ($F$ things are $F$ in virtue of participation in the Form of $F$) and ontologically (for most values of $F$ there can be no $F$ things if there is no Form of $F$, but the Form of $F$ does not have to have instances). But none of these sorts of priority implies that Forms are starting-points of change; moreover, not only is there no evidence to support the latter claim, but there is conclusive evidence against it, e.g. in the doctrine of the *Phaedo* that things come to have certain properties by Forms coming to be in them (e.g. 102d–e). Things which become $F$ obviously become more like the Form of $F$, not less like it as Popper's account requires.

The myth of the *Politicus* does indeed describe a cosmic process of degeneration, in which the inherent disorderliness of matter inevitably leads to a gradual loss of the order originally imposed by the *Demiourgos*, necessitating periodic divine intervention to restore the original order. This may be merely a metaphor for the permanent tension between rational order and recalcitrant matter which is a fundamental principle of Plato's cosmology. But even assuming that Plato believed in cosmic degeneration, counterbalanced by periodic divine intervention, that gives no support to Popper, since such cosmic degeneration is clearly compatible, and was recognised by Plato as being compatible, with social and political development (274c–d). See next note.

12. 'So surely . . . thousands upon thousands of states have come into being, while at least as many, in equally vast numbers, have been destroyed? Time and again each has adopted every type of political system. And sometimes small states have become bigger, and bigger ones have grown smaller; superior states have deteriorated and bad ones have improved.' (676b–c, tr. T.J. Saundera, *Plato, The Laws* (Penguin, Harmondsworth, 1970)).

Against Popper's contention that '(a)ccording to the *Republic*, the original or primitive form of society, and at the same time, the one that resembles the Form or Idea of a state most closely, the "best state", is a kingship of the wisest and most godlike of men' (p. 39), Plato says explicitly at 499c–d that the question of whether the ideal state ever existed in the remote past is, like the question whether it now exists in some remote part of the world, irrelevant to his present undertaking, which is to show the conditions under which it could come into being.

13. Plato twice uses the verb *euphrainesthai* to describe the reaction of a divine being to something which pleases it, once of the *Demiourgos* rejoicing in the creation of the world (*Tim.* 37c) and once of a goddess pleased by acts of worship (*Laws* 796b–c).

14. 'The Theory of Social Justice in the *Polis* in Plato's *Republic*', in H. North ed., *Interpretations of Plato* (Brill, Leiden, 1977).

15. Ordinary Greek usage does not encourage a sharp distinction between the *polis* conceived as an abstract organisation, the state, and the *polis* conceived as an organised community. Greek *poleis* were regularly referred to via the names of their peoples, as 'the Athenians', 'the Spartans' etc.; this usage is

standard in the historians and in official documents (see e.g. R. Meiggs and D. Lewis, *A Selection of Greek Historical Inscriptions* (Clarendon Press, Oxford, 1969)). In the case of Athens we find the two forms 'the Athenians' and 'the Athenian people' *(ho dēmos tōn Athēnaiōn,* e.g. Meiggs and Lewis, op. cit., nos. 47, 52, 56).

16. This is summed up at 372a1–2 by the statement that justice and injustice are to be found in these people's treatment of each other, where the word translated 'treatment' *(chreia)* also has connotations of use and need.

17. Vlastos argues (in 'Justice and Happiness in the *Republic*', sect. VIII, in Vlastos ed., *Plato,* vol. II (Garden City, N.Y., 1971), reprinted in Vlastos, *Platonic Studies* (Princeton, 1973)) that the lower classes in the ideal state have psychic harmony, and therefore *eudaimonia,* because it suffices for psychic harmony that the elements in the personality should be directed by true belief as to what is best, which the lower classes have. It is true that at 429b–c courage, which is the special virtue of the auxiliaries, is defined as the power of retaining in all circumstances the <true> belief about what is to be feared, while the *sōphrosunē* [temperance] of the city consists in the agreement *(homodoxia)* of all classes on who is to rule (433c; cf. 432a, where the crucial word is 'harmony' *(sumphōnia)).* Vlastos concedes (ibid., n. 72) that true belief which is not produced by education is not seen by Plato as sufficient for psychic harmony, being described as 'brutish and slavish' at 430b. But while the auxiliaries clearly share the elementary education outlined in books II–IV, and therefore qualify for the appropriate level of true belief, there is no indication that the producers do so; that education is repeatedly described as directed to the formation of future guardians (e.g. 378c, 387c; other citations are given by Guthrie, *A History of Greek Philosophy,* vol. IV (Cambridge, 1975), p. 455, n. 2), while those who have been trained in it are better men than 'the shoemakers, who are trained in shoemaking' (456d8–10), which implies that the producers are confined to a purely technical education (cf. G.F. Hourani, 'The Education of the Third Class in Plato's *Republic*', *Classical Quarterly* xliii (1949)). The producers, then, can have no understanding of what goodness is or what the best life is for an individual or a community. They can be said to have true beliefs about these things only in the minimal sense that they believe (truly) that what the philosophers say about them is true, and it is hard to see how Plato's account gives them any reason to believe even that. Vlastos is in the paradoxical position of insisting that the intellect of the producers is both sufficiently developed to have genuine control over their lives, and therefore to ensure psychic harmony, and so weak as to require them to be enslaved to the guardians for their own good.

18. On the absurdity of the general claim see Bernard Williams, 'The Analogy of City and Soul in Plato's *Republic*', in this volume.

19. Cf. R. Demos, 'Paradoxes in Plato's Doctrine of the Ideal State', *Class. Quart.* N.S. vii (1957).

20. Vlastos, 'The Theory of Social Justice', p. 28.

21. It will not do to suggest that non-philosophers approximate to contemplation of the Good by having true beliefs about it which they take on trust from the philosophers; the gap is too great to allow talk of approximation to cut any ice.

# 4

# The Analogy of City and Soul in Plato's *Republic*

### Bernard Williams

In making the first construction of the city, there is an assumption that it should be able to tell us something about δικαιοσύνη [justice] in the individual: we look to the larger inscription to help us read the smaller one, 368D. But, as Plato indeed implies, the larger inscription will help with the smaller <u>only if they present the same message.</u> What is Plato's reason for expecting the same message? Basically, it is that δίκαιος [just] applies to both cities and men, and that it signifies one characteristic: "So the just man will not differ at all from the just city, so far as the character of justice is concerned, but will be like it" (καὶ δίκαιος ἄρα ἀνὴρ δικαίας πόλεως κατ' αὐτὸ τὸ τῆς δικαιοσύνης εἶδος οὐδὲν διοίσει, ἀλλ' ὅμοιος ἔσται, 435B). That there should be some kind of analogy between cities and men in respect of their being δίκαιος would seem to be a presupposition of asking the question "what is δικαιοσύνη?" and expecting one answer to it.

Indeed at 434E Plato says that when we transfer what we have said about the city back to the man, we may find that it does not work out; but the moral will be that we should go back and try again and "perhaps by looking at the two side by side and rubbing them together, we may make justice blaze out, like fire from two sticks. . . ." Plato clearly has a fair confidence that this technique will work: his confidence is in what I shall call the *analogy of meaning.*

At 435E, however, he takes what is in fact a different tack. Proceeding there to the division of the soul, he seems at first sight to be backing up the "analogy of meaning." "Are we not absolutely compelled to admit that there are in each one of us the same kinds and characteris-

49

tics as there are in the city? For how else could they have got there? It would be ridiculous to imagine that among peoples who bear the reputation for being spirited . . . the spirited character in their states does not come from the individual citizens, etc." This looks as though it means that we call a city, people, etc. "spirited" because most or all of its individual persons can be called "spirited"—and for certain terms, this style of account is very reasonable.

But for such terms (the three examples that Plato gives at 435E correspond, it is worth noting, to the three elements of his analogy), so far from having something that backs up the previous principle of finding a common characteristic in virtue of which both cities and men are called so-and-so, we have something that defeats it. For if we say that "F" is applied to the city just because it is applied to the men, we have already explained how the term can be applied to both cities and men, and to go on from there to look for a similar explanation of how "F" applies to men is at least pointless, since the phenomenon which set off the search for the analogy in the first place, viz. the fact that "F" applies to both cities and men, has already been explained. If, moreover, the rule for applying "F" to cities is taken as itself the common λόγος [account] that we were looking for, then we have not just pointlessness but absurdity, since the common λόγος [account] will have to be something like "x is F if and only if x has constituent parts which are F," which leads to a regress. Thus the argument at 435E, so far from backing up the "analogy of meaning," defeats it.

Plato in any case does not seem to think that every term which can be applied to both cities and men obeys the rule of 435E. Thus at 419A ff. (the beginning of Book IV), answering Adeimantus' objection that the guardians get a thin time of it, Socrates says that a city's being sublimely happy does not depend on all, most, the leading part, or perhaps any, of its citizens being sublimely happy, just as a statue's being beautiful does not depend on its parts being severally beautiful. This contradicts the principle of 435E, and certainly contains a truth. Leaving the importantly, and indeed deeply, contentious case of "happy," we can certainly agree that a large crowd of sailors is not necessarily a crowd of large sailors, while an angry crowd of sailors, on the other hand, is a crowd of angry sailors. So what Plato has here are two classes of term: one class ("angry," "spirited," etc.) obeys the rule of 435E, which we may call *the whole-part rule;* while the other class ("large," "well-arranged," etc.) does not.

However, Plato does not proceed along the lines of this distinction.

Rather, for an indeterminately large class of terms, possibly including δικαιοσύνη [justice] he wants to say both:

(a) A city is F if and only if its men are F;

and

(b) The explanation of a city's being F is the same as that of a man's being F (the same εἶδος [form] of F-ness applies to both).

The combination of these, as we have already seen, could lead to a regress, but Plato avoids this by holding (a) only for the city-man relation, and not for the relation of the man to any further elements—that is to say he does not take (a) as itself identifying the λόγος of F-ness. Thus "F" does not occur again in the explanation of what it is for a man to be F: at that stage, it is reduced to something else. Thus the explanation of a man's being δίκαιος , and the λόγος of δικαιοσύνη in general, are alike given us by the formula

(c) Each of the elements (λογιστικόν [reason], θυμοειδές [spirit], and ἐπιθυμητικόν [appetite]) does its job.

which of course implies

(d) λογιστικόν [reason] rules.

Applying (a) to the particular case of δικαιοσύνη, we get

(e) A city is δίκαιος [just] if and only if its men are;

while at the same time, for a city as for a man, we have the requirement that its being δίκαιος [just] consists in (c)'s being true. But what does (c) mean of a city? For like cities, the elements of cities consist of men: and how are the characters of these elements to be explained? Here it seems the whole-part rule must certainly apply—it was, we remember, with reference to these characteristics that Plato introduced us to it. We shall have

(f) An element of the city is logistic, thymoeidic, or epithymetic if and only if its men are.

But the δικαιοσύνη [justice] of a city, as of anything else, consists in (c)'s being true. So in order to be δίκαιος [just], a city must have a logistic [rational], a thymoeidic [spirited], and an epithymetic [appetitive] element in it. Since it must have an epithymetic element, it must, by (f), have epithymetic men: in fact, it is clear from Plato's account that it must have a majority of such men, since the lowest class is the largest. So a δίκαιος [just] city must have a majority of epithymetic men. But an epithymetic man—surely—is not a δίκαιος man; if he is not, then the city must have a majority of men who are not δίκαιοι [just], which contradicts (e).

This contradiction is, I believe, powerfully at work under the surface of the *Republic*. Remaining still at a very formal and schematic level, we get another view of it by asking what follows if we accept (e) and also take the analogy between city and soul as seriously as Plato at some points wants us to. Since the men are δίκαιοι [just], of each man (d) will be true, and λογιστικόν [reason] (no doubt in some rather restricted way) will be at work in each member even of the lowest and epithymetic class. Some minimal exercise of λογιστικόν [reason] would seem to be involved in bringing it about that each man sticks to his own business, which is the most important manifestation of social δικαιοσύνη [justice]: though it is very notable that Plato repeatedly uses formulations abstract and impersonal enough to prevent such questions pressing to the front. (A very striking example of this is at the point where δικαιοσύνη [justice] is first, after the hunt through the other cardinal virtues, pinned down. At 433C–D we have a reference to the beneficent effects of the φρόνησις [wisdom] of the guardians, but by contrast with this, "that which is in" [τοῦτο . . . ἐνόν] even slaves, artisans, women, etc., and which makes the city good, is represented not as a characteristic of theirs, but merely as a *fact*, that each minds his business [ὅτι τὸ αὑτοῦ ἕκαστος εἷς ὢν ἔπραττε καὶ οὐκ ἐπολυπραγμόνει, 433D4–5]. Clearly, this fact cannot be "in" these people—the question is, what has to be in these people to bring about this fact.)

But now if the epithymetic class has in this way to exercise some λογιστικόν, and this helps it to stick to its tasks, recognise the rulers and so forth, and if we read this result back through the analogy to the individual soul, we shall reach the absurd result that the ἐπιθυμητικόν [appetite] in a just soul harkens to λογιστικόν [reason] in that soul through itself having an extra little λογιστικόν [reason] of its own. Recoiling from this absurdity, we recognize that in the individual soul, the ἐπιθυμητικόν [appetite] cannot really harken; rather, through training, the desires are weakened and kept in their place by λογιστικόν [reason], if not through the agency, at least with the co-operation, of θυμοειδές [spirit]. If with this fact in our hand we come back once more across the bridge of the analogy to the city, we shall find not a δίκαιος [just] and logistically co-operative working class, but rather a totally logistic ruling class holding down with the help of a totally thymoeidic military class, a weakened and repressed epithymetic class; a less attractive picture. The use of the analogy, it begins to seem, is to help Plato to have it both ways.

Does Plato intend us to accept the proposition (e), that the citizens of the δίκαιος [just] city are themselves δίκαιοι [just]? The question is not altogether easy. The passage 433–4, from which I have already quoted the most notable evasion, manages to create the impression that the answer must be "yes" without, so far as I can see, ever actually saying so. An important contributory difficulty here is the point which has been often remarked, that the earlier account of σωφροσύνη [temperance] has left δικαιοσύνη with not enough work to do, so that it looks like merely another way of describing the same facts. In the case of σωφροσύνη [temperance] he comes out and says that it is a virtue of all citizens (431E–432A); but the route to this conclusion has several formulations which make even this seem shaky (431B–D, particularly: "the desires in the many and vulgar are mastered by the desires and the wisdom in the few and superior"). The tension is always the same. The use of the analogy is supposed in the upshot to justify the supreme rule of a logistic element in the city, where this element is identified as a class of persons; and it justifies it by reference to the evident superiority of a soul in which the logistic element controls the wayward and chaotic desires. But this will work only if the persons being ruled bear a sufficient resemblance to wayward and chaotic desires—for instance, by being persons themselves controlled by wayward and chaotic desires. And if they are enough like that, the outcome of Plato's arrangements will be less appealing than first appears.

Suppose, then, we give up the proposition that all or most people in the δίκαιος [just] city are δίκαιοι [just]; thus we give up the whole-part rule for δικαιοσύνη [justice]. We might, at the same time, put in its place something rather weaker than the whole-part rule, which we might call *the predominant section rule:*

(g) A city is F if and only if the leading, most influential, or predominant citizens are F.

The effect of using (g) with δικαιοσύνη [justice] is of course to cancel
any implication that the citizenry at large are δίκαιοι [just]—it merely
gives us something that we knew already, that the guardians are
δίκαιοι [just]. But the importance of (g) is in no way confined to the
case of δικαιοσύνη [justice]—it is a rule which Plato appeals to often,
and particularly in his discussions of the degenerate forms of city in
Book VIII. It is in the light of the *predominant section* idea that we
should read the reiteration of the whole-part idea which introduces
those discussions at 544D. If we look at some of the things that Plato
says about the degenerate cities, this will lead us back again to the just
city, and to the ineliminable tension in Plato's use of his analogy.

With the degenerate cities, it is clear in general that not all the citizens are of the same character as the city, and there are references to
citizens of a different character. The tyrannical city is, not surprisingly,
that in which there is most emphasis on the existence of citizens different in character from the tyrant: 577C "the whole, so to speak, and the
best element is dishonourably and wretchedly enslaved"; cf. 567A,
568A "the best people hate and flee the tyrant." In other kinds of city,
there may be a minority of citizens of a character inferior to that of the
city as a whole: there may be a few men of tyrannical character in cities
where the majority is law-abiding (575A); if few, they have little influence, but if there are many, and many others who follow their lead,
then they produce a tyrant (575C). We can notice here that even in a
tyranny there is a requirement that a substantial and influential section
of the citizens should share the character of the city. Again, at 564D we
are told that the "drones" are already present in an oligarchy, but in a
democracy they become the leading element (τὸ προεστὸς αὐτῆς).

The democracy, however, presents a special difficulty. Plato says that
the distinguishing mark of a democracy is that it is the state in which
one finds men of every sort (παντοδαποί, 557C), and like a garment
of many colours it is decorated with every sort of character (πᾶσιν
ἤθεσιν, ibid.). Having said this, it would be impossible for Plato to say
that all the citizens were "democratic" men as described at 561D *al.*—
always shifting, without expertise in anything, prepared to indulge any
ἐπιθυμία [appetite], etc. Nor should it be easy for him to say that the
majority are such men. Yet this is precisely what he has to say. The
"predominant section" rule says that the character of the state is derived from that of the ruling citizens. In the cases where the rulers are
few, this will not necessarily imply much about the character of other
citizens, for the few may hold their power by force, threats, etc. (as in

the case of the tyrannical state, already considered: and cf. 551B, the origin of the oligarchy). Plato says that a democracy will also come into being by threat of force, 557A—but this is merely vis-à-vis the ruling oligarchs. A democracy is a state in which the many rule, and if it gets its character from that of its rulers, then the majority must have a "democratic" character. This, on the face of it, sorts none too well with the claim that the democratic state will particularly tend to contain all sorts of character—the "democratic" character seems in fact to be a special sort of character. Moving between the social and the individual level once more, Plato seems disposed to confound two very different things: a state in which there are various characters among the people, and a state in which most of the people have a various character, that is to say, a very shifting and unsteady character.

These people, moreover, are the same people that constitute the lowest class in the δίκαιος [just] city; so we are led back once more to the question we have already encountered, of how, consistently with Plato's analogy and his political aims, we are to picture their quiescent state when λογιστικόν [reason] (in the form of other persons) rules. It may be said that in the difficulties we have found about this, we have merely been pressing the analogy in the wrong place. The essential analogy here might be claimed to be this: just as there is a difference between a man who is controlled by λογιστικόν [reason] and a man who is controlled by ἐπιθυμία [appetite], so there is such a difference between states, and to try to infer the condition of the epithymetic class when it is ruled from its condition when it is not ruled is like trying to infer the condition of a man's ἐπιθυμίαι [appetites] when *they* are ruled from their condition when they are not. What we are concerned with (it may be said) is the healthy condition of man or city, and relative to that the difference between a good and a bad state of affairs can be adequately—and analogously—explained for each.

Such attempts to ease out the difficulties only serve to draw attention to them. For, first, certain things *can* be said about the ἐπιθυμίαι [appetites] when they are "ruled." For instance, there is the notable difference between a man who has his ἐπιθυμίαι [appetites] under control, so that he does not act on them except where appropriate, but for whom they are nevertheless very active, so that control is the outcome of struggle and inner vigilance; and a man whose λογιστικόν [reason] has achieved inner peace. That inner peace, again, might be of more than one kind: some ἐπιθυμίαι [appetites] might be mildly and harmoniously active, or there may have been some more drastically ascetic achievement—*solitudinem faciunt, pacem appellant* [they make a desert and call it peace] could apply to inner peace as well. But these differences, read back into the political case, precisely revive the earlier problems. Inner peace is what Plato must want, but that in the political case requires the allegiance of the epithymetic element, and we are back to the question of how we are to picture that being secured. Again, a difference between the barely self-controlled man and the man of inner peace is that the first has some ἐπιθυμίαι [appetites] which the latter does not have—if a man has inner peace, then some ἐπιθυμίαι [appetites] he will have eliminated or never had. But does the difference between the good city and democracy then lie partly in the emergence in the latter of extra and more violent epithymetic persons? If so, then Plato has to explain why the working class even in the good city has to be thought of as though they were already potentially such persons. If not, we are faced with the original problem once more, of what it was in those potentially violent persons that kept them in their place in the good city.

Let us suppose that it is the inner peace model that Plato has in mind, and that it is achieved through the exercise of λογιστικόν [reason], on a modest scale, by the individuals in the working class. (They might have been said to possess some measure of ὀρθὴ δόξα [right opinion], if that were not inconsistent with the eccentric theory of knowledge which the *Republic* presents.) If their individual λογιστικόν [reason] helps in keeping the workers in their place, then (as we saw earlier) the analogy is no longer in full working order, since that feature cannot be read back into the soul without absurdity. But let us waive that point, and ask what has to be presupposed to keep even the remnants of the analogy going for Plato's purposes. It is not enough that in its economic function, the role of the lowest class should bear some analogy to the role of the ἐπιθυμίαι [appetites] in individual life. For if we stick merely to the nature of certain roles or functions, no argument will have been produced against the view of Plato's democratic enemy, that those roles or functions can be combined with the business of ruling. Criticism of Plato often concentrates on his opinion that ruling is a matter of expertise; but he needs more than that opinion to reach his results in the *Republic,* and has to combine with it a set of views about what characteristics and talents generally co-exist at the level of individual psychology. In that area, he has to believe not only that λογιστικόν [reason] comes in two sizes (as we might say, regular size and king size), but also that the talents and temperament that make good

soldiers go with thymoeidic motivations, and the talents and temperament that make good workers go with epithymetic motivations.

Of these, the former looks plausible enough—indeed, soldierly temperament and thymoeidic motivation are perhaps necessarily connected (that is a question we shall come back to). Again, logistic
supremacy and fitness to be a guardian are of course for Plato necessarily connected. But how about epithymetic motivation and fitness to be
a δημιουργός [craftsman]? Not even Plato at his loftiest can have believed that what actually qualified somebody to be a cobbler was the
strength of his ἐπιθυμίαι [appetites]. The most he can have thought is
that the sort of man who made a good cobbler was one who had powerful ἐπιθυμίαι [appetites], and this is also the least he can think, if he
is to keep any of the analogy going and justify the subordinate position
of cobblers by reference to their epithymetic disposition. So what we
have to believe, it seems, is that cobblers are characteristically men of
powerful passions—of more powerful passions, indeed, than soldiers—who nevertheless have enough rational power to recognize the
superiority of philosopher kings when there are philosopher kings, but
become unmanageably volatile when there are no philosopher kings.

There have been those who thought that the working classes were
naturally of powerful and disorderly desires, and had to be kept in their
place. There have been those who thought that they were good-hearted and loyal fellows of no great gifts who could recognize their natural
superiors and, unless stirred up, keep themselves in their place. There
can have been few who have thought both; Plato in the *Republic* comes
close to being such a one, even though we can recognize that his heart,
and his fears, lie with the first story. His analogy helps him to combine
both stories, in particular by encouraging us to believe in an outcome
appropriate to the second story from arrangements motivated by the
first.

What about θυμοειδές [spirit] and the military class? Here there is a
slightly different kind of tension in the structure. At no point, we must
remember, does the structure present a simple contrast of the psychological and the political, for on both sides of that divide we have two
sorts of thing: elements, and a whole which is affected by those elements. On the political side we have classes, and a state which is affected by which class is predominant among them (hence the
"predominant section rule" we have already looked at); the theory is
supposed to yield both an analysis and a typology of states. On the
psychological side, we have "parts of the soul," and persons in which

one "part" or another is dominant; this yields, first, a classification of motives within the individual, and, second, a typology of character. The difficulties we have just been considering, about the epithymetic class, are generated across the political-psychological boundary, in the relations that Plato finds between, on the one hand, the working class and a state dominated by that class, and on the other hand, epithymetic motivation and a character dominated by such motivation. In the case of the θυμοειδές [spirit], the most interesting difficulty (it seems to me) breaks out earlier, in the relations between the type of motivation that is represented by this "part of the soul," and the type of character that is produced by its predominance. Once the type of character is established, the political consequences follow, granted Plato's general outlook, fairly easily. Indeed, it is just the appropriateness of those consequences that seems to dictate the connection of ideas on the psychological side; whatever may be the case elsewhere in the *Republic,* here the political end of the analogy is dictating certain features of the psychological end.

I shall not attempt here any general discussion of the divisions of the soul, which, particularly with regard to the distinction between λογιστικόν [reason] and ἐπιθυμητικόν [appetite], is a large subject of great independent interest;[1] I shall make only some remarks about θυμοειδές [spirit]. When it first appears, it already has a rather ambivalent role. On the one hand, it seems to be something like *anger,* and we are told, in distinguishing it from λογιστικόν [appetite], that it is manifested by children (441A) and animals (441B), and we are reminded of the Homeric figure who reproached his own anger. However, right from the beginning it takes on the colour of something more morally ambitious (as we might put it) than mere anger or rage; the case of Leontius and other examples (439E–440E) take it rather in the direction of noble indignation, and we are told (440E) that rather than class it with ἐπιθυμητικόν [appetite], we should rather say that "in the strife [στάσει, a significantly political word] of the soul it takes arms on the side of λογιστικόν [reason]." If θυμοειδές [spirit] merely represented anger this would indeed be a surprising psychological claim.

The claim is indeed weakened a little at 441A, when it is said that θυμοειδές [spirit] acts as ἐπίκουρος [servant] to λογιστικόν [reason] "if it has not been corrupted [διαφθαρῇ: it can scarcely mean "destroyed"] by bad upbringing." But the concession is not adequate. For so long as there is any conflict at all—and if there is not, the question does not arise—it clearly is possible for anger to break out, not merely against λογιστικόν [reason], but on the side of ἐπιθυμητικόν [appetite] against λογιστικόν [reason]. What is more interesting than that psychological platitude is the fact that Plato reveals elsewhere that he is perfectly well aware of it, and indeed in a passage where he is defending exactly the same doctrine as in the *Republic*. In the image of the chariot and the two horses in the *Phaedrus*, when the black (epithymetic) horse bolts, the white (thymoeidic) horse helps the (logistic) charioteer to bring it to a halt; and when the black horse is finally stopped, it turns on its companion and "abuses it *in anger*" (μόγις ἐξαναπνεύσας ἐλοιδόρησεν ὀργῇ, 254C). Mere anger, Plato's dramatic realism reveals, can always side with the devil. The thymoeidic element in the soul is from its inception more than mere anger, or indeed any other such motive which there might be good reason on purely psychological grounds to distinguish from ἐπιθυμίαι [appetites] (a drive to self-destructive risk-taking, for instance).

It is to be understood, rather, by working backwards from the character which is determined by its dominance, a character which is in turn to be understood in terms of a form of life: the military or competitive form of life which it was a standard thought to contrast with the life of contemplation on the one hand and the life of gain on the other (cf. Aristotle *EN* I.5.1095b17, with, in particular, *Rep.* 581C), a contrast embodied in the Pythagorean saying about the three sorts of people that come to the Games (Iamblichus *De Vit. Pythag.* 58). In this contrast of types of character there is also a political or social thought, of course, and that is why, as I suggested earlier, Plato has great ease in adjusting psychology and politics in the case of θυμοειδές: as the passage in question makes explicit (440E–441A, 440D), politics is there at its introduction. Ἐπιθυμητικόν [appetite] has an independent psychological foundation, and Plato makes a lot of it and of its psychological relations to λογιστικόν [reason] in the individual, as a type of motivation. With that, I have argued, there are grave obstacles to Plato's reading back into the city what he needs for his political conclusions, obstacles to some extent concealed by his use of the tripartite analogy.

## Notes

1. For a very brief suggestion on this matter, see my "Ethical Consistency," in *Problems of the Self* (Cambridge, 1973), p. 169.

# 5

# Inside and Outside the *Republic*

*Jonathan Lear*

## I. Introduction

An engaged reader of the *Republic* must at some point wonder how—or if—it all fits together. There seems to be jumbled within that text a challenge to conventional justice, a political theory, a psychology, a metaphysics, a theory of education and a critique of art, music and poetry. A brilliant work; but is it an integrated whole? A just republic, for Plato, turns out to be a harmonious, though differentiated, unity; and so the question can be rephrased: is the *Republic* a just *Republic*? Most of the illuminating discussions of the *Republic* can be seen as attempts to answer this question. I would like to suggest that this prob-lem of unity arises in a particularly acute form for modern readers, because we are disposed to see the *Republic* as existing in bits. For we tend to conceive of psychology as the psychology of the individual. Since Plato, in the *Republic,* is concerned with the constitution of the individual psyche, it is easy for us to assume that his psychology is revealed in that account.[1] But this omits what, I believe, is the most distinctive aspect of Plato's psychology: a dynamic account of the psy-chological transactions between inside and outside a person's psyche, between a person's inner life and his cultural environment, between *intra*psychic and *inter*psychic relations.[2] If we ignore these dynamic transactions, we cannot understand even individual psychology. We miss what, for Plato, holds a person together—and also what holds Plato together. For if one assumes that psychology is individual psy-chology, the *Republic* will then look like it is composed of various bits—among them, a psychology and a political theory—and there will inevitably be a question of how they fit together. In Plato's psychology, as I understand it, this question should not arise. For *psyche*-analysis and *polis*-analysis are, for Plato, two aspects of a single discipline, psychology, which has at its core the relation between inside and outside. What holds the *Republic* together is Plato's understanding of what holds people and polis together.

In this paper I shall concentrate on two topics that lie at the heart of the *Republic*. First, there is the analogy between city and psyche. Plato thought that there were important structural isomorphisms between city or polis and psyche, and thus that he could use discoveries about one to prove results about the other. It is now widely accepted that Plato uses this analogy to fudge his arguments. Plato, so the charge goes, uses a vague analogy fallaciously, and he is thereby able to hide a fundamental tension which underlies his ideal polis. That is, he disguises the repressive relation between the ruling class and the ruled by an illegitimate comparison with the structure of the psyche. I shall argue that these criticisms look valid because Plato's psychology is not well understood.

Second, Plato's critique of the poets has inspired a wealth of deep and imaginative discussion,[3] but all of it has tended to concentrate on two questions: what is the effect of poetry on us?; and what is the moral value of art? Plato's argument is intriguing because, roughly speaking, we tend to think that art is good for us, while Plato argues that it is bad. Modern psychoanalysts and psychologists often think that art offers a kind of psychic salvation; while Plato treats acquaintance with Homer and the great Greek tragedians as a psychological catastrophe. And so we are led, like bees to nectar, to find a flaw in Plato's argument or, less often, to reevaluate our own aesthetics. Perhaps it is this fascination which has blinded us to the fact that we have been living on a restricted diet of questions. There are other questions, central to Plato's psychology, which as far as I know have not been asked, let alone answered. For example: who, psychologically speaking, are the poets? What, from a psychological point of view, are the poets doing in making poetry? And what is Plato doing, psychologically speaking, in banishing the poets? These are questions which, I think, tend to be obscured by assuming psychology to be the study of the individual psyche, but they come to the fore when psychology is taken to span across the boundary of an individual's psyche. For we will then see poetry as coming from some psyches and entering others, and the question naturally arises: what, from a psychological perspective, is going on?

My hope is that the discussions of the polis-psyche relation and of poetry will illuminate the approach to Plato's psychology that I am advocating, and help to confirm it. As a byproduct, I hope we shall also see the *Republic* as more unified than it is often taken to be.

## 2. Internalization

At the beginning of Book II, Socrates takes up the challenge, which will occupy the rest of the *Republic,* to describe justice and injustice as an "inherent condition inside the psyche" (τίνα ἔχει δύναμιν αὐτὸ καθ' αὑτὸ ἐνὸν ἐν τῇ ψυχῇ . . .).[4] Although he proposes to look first at justice writ large in the polis,[5] in fact Socrates turns almost immediately to the psyche. For he begins his construction of the ideal polis with a discussion of the education of young children. And he justifies this by saying that "the beginning of any project is most important, especially for anything young and tender. For it is then that *it takes shape and any mold one may want can be impressed upon it*" (. . . πλάττεται καὶ ἐνδύεται τύπος, ὃν ἄν τις βούληται ἐνσημήνασθαι ἑκάστῳ . . .).[6] If we carelessly allow children to hear any old stories, he says, they may *"take into their psyches"* (λαμβάνειν ἐν ταῖς ψυχαῖς) beliefs that are contrary to those they should hold as adults.[7] Nursemaids and mothers must be allowed only to tell certain stories to their children and so *"shape their psyches"* (πλάττειν τὰς ψυχάς). Children should not be allowed to hear the classic tales of warring gods because the young cannot distinguish what is allegorical from what is not, and the opinions they form at that age tend to be unalterable.[8] For Plato, humans enter the world with a capacity to absorb cultural influences. The young human psyche is like a resin, able to receive the impress of cultural influences before it sets into a definite shape. And it is clear that, for Plato, the stakes are high. The goal of achieving a well-governed polis depends on there being no one in the polis either asserting or hearing any tales which suggest that God is the cause of anything bad.[9] Plato believes these tales will shape the character of the future citizens.[10] Mothers must not be allowed to terrify their children with bad tales about gods sneaking about in disguise, "for at the same time as they blaspheme the gods, they make their children cowardly".[11]

If, for example, one is an honor-loving person, one should be brought up on stories of brave men doing brave deeds so as to fear slavery more than death;[12] one should be allowed to play at and later imitate only the deeds appropriate to a guardian "lest from imitation they take (ἀπολαύω) the reality";[13] one should be brought up in a rigorous program of music and gymnastics that reinforce the honor-loving part of one's psyche;[14] and taken out even as a youth to observe battles:[15] so that when one is grown, it is through the activities of guardianship that one achieves happiness.[16] If this program of education and culture is successful, the qualities appropriate to guardianship should *"settle into one's character and into one's nature"* (. . . εἰς ἔθη τε καὶ φύσιν καθίστανται . . .).[17] Plato seems to be saying that through proper imitations from youth, one actually constitutes oneself as a certain type of person. Whether one develops into a noble and brave person, at one extreme, or a base coward, at the other, depends significantly on the myths one has heard from youth, the education one has received, the models one has been given to imitate. Leaving divine inspiration aside, Plato thinks that were it not for this training, one would not develop the character or nature of a guardian.[18]

The *Republic* is a study in the health and pathologies of cities and psyches. And the conditions of city and psyche are interdependent. The variety of pathologies of the psyche, for example, depends on the person taking in pathological structures from the culture. Culture penetrates so deeply, that a fractured polis will produce a fractured psyche. For Plato, it is only the ideal polis that can properly be called a polis or a city.[19] Other actual cities or poleis are only apparently such. In fact, each lacks sufficient internal unity to count as *a* polis: each is, in truth, many poleis or, more properly, polis-parts.[20] But, Plato argues, for every pathological polis there is a corresponding pathology of the psyche.[21] The conclusion of the syllogism is that a pathological psyche is not, in fact, *a* psyche, but various psychic parts. So, for example, just as an oligarchy is not *a* polis, but two parts, a rich part and a poor part,[22] so an 'oligarchical psyche' is in fact two psychic parts: a ruling part and a ruled.[23] For Plato, there is not sufficient integration in the functioning of the parts for them to count as a genuine unity, a psyche. Indeed, even among the oligarchical person's appetites there will be division and faction.[24] Being thrifty and acquisitive, the oligarchical person will satisfy only his necessary appetites and "enslave" his other appetites.[25] Because of his "lack of culture", his unruly and unnecessary appetites spring up in him, but they are "forcibly restrained" (βίᾳ κατέχει) by the better part.[26] The oligarchical person is, says Plato, διπλοῦς τις, someone double.[27] For Plato, being double is a way of not being an integrated person: it is a divided and conflicted existence.[28] In fact, the pathologies of psyche Plato examines turn out, strictly speaking, to be studies in the failures to become a psyche.[29]

By now it should be clear that, for Plato, satisfying the human need for culture is a process of taking cultural influences into the psyche. Let us call this process, whatever it is precisely, *internalization.* Although Plato did not have an articulated theory, he did think that imitation *(mimesis)* was a paradigmatic means of internalization. It is youthful imitations which settle the shape of one's character and nature.[30] That is why musical education is preeminent: "because rhythm and harmony *permeate the inner part of the psyche* (. . . καταδύεται εἰς τὸ τῆς ψυχῆς . . .), bring graciousness to it, and make the strongest impression, making a man gracious if he has the right kind of upbringing; if not, the opposite is true."[31] And it is clear that Plato thought that internalization was a largely unconscious process. Guardians should not be brought up among images of evil lest they "little by little collect all unawares a great evil in their own psyche" (. . . κατὰ σμικρὸν . . . λανθάνωσι κακὸν μέγα ἐν τῇ αὐτῶν ψυχῇ).[32] One cannot change the modes of music, Plato says, without upsetting fundamental constitutional laws;[33] and it is clear that the causal route of this destabilization proceeds via internalization. For lawlessness, Plato says, easily creeps into music without our noticing and, "having little by little settled in there it *flows into the characters* and pursuits" of people (. . . κατὰ σμικρὸν εἰσοικισαμένη ἠρέμα ὑπορρεῖ πρὸς τὰ ἤθη τε καὶ τὰ ἐπιτηδεύματα).[34] And so, in our education and rule of children, one should not let them be free until "a constitution is set up inside them just as in the polis" (. . . ἐν αὐτοῖς ὥσπερ ἐν πόλει πολιτείαν καταστήσωμεν).[35]

For Plato, we are culture-vultures: we 'feed' our psyches by internalizing cultural influences. That is the psychological point of culture; and it is why education and upbringing, on the one hand, and the shaping of culture, on the other, play such a predominant role in the *Republic*. It would seem, then, that *internalization is a fundamental psychological activity.*[36] The fact that we are so dependent on internalization for our psychological constitution, makes us susceptible to cultural luck. Our ultimate dependency is manifest in the fact that we internalize these influences before we can understand their significance. We are dependent on culture for the constitution of our psyches, but on what does culture depend? How is culture itself shaped and formed?

## 3. Externalization

Plato suggests that culture is formed by an inverse process of psychological activity, moving outwards from psyche to polis. For example, Plato says, "there must be as many types of character among men as there are forms of government. Or do you suppose that constitutions spring from the proverbial oak or rock and not from the characters of the citizens (ἐκ τῶν ἠθῶν τῶν ἐν ταῖς πόλεσιν), which as it were, by their momentum and weight in the scales draw other things after them."[37] And character, Plato says elsewhere, is inherent in the psyche.[38] The same forms, he says, will be found in the polis *and in the individual psyche* (τὰ αὐτὰ ταῦτα εἴδη ἐν τῇ ψυχῇ ἔχοντα),[39] and the shape of the polis has to be understood as deriving from the shape of the psyche:

> . . . we are surely compelled to agree that the same forms and character-types are in each of us just as in the polis (τὰ αὐτὰ ἐν ἑκάστῳ ἔνεστιν ἡμῶν εἴδη τε καὶ ἤθη ἅπερ ἐν τῇ πόλει). They could not get there from any other source. It would be ridiculous if someone supposed that spirit-edness has not come to be in polis from individuals who are reputed to have this quality . . . or that the same is not true of the love of learning . . . or the love of money.[40]

It would seem, then, that for a significant range of psychopolitical predicates F,

> (EK) If a polis is F, there must be some citizens whose psyches are F who (with others) have helped to shape the polis.

This is easiest to see in the case of the just polis.[41] It will be shaped by the philosopher-king, whose thoughts are directed towards realities.[42] And though he will try to shape the city according to a divine paradigm,[43] he does so by first imitating these eternal realities fashioning himself as far as possible in their likeness (. . . ταῦτα μιμεῖσθαι τε καὶ ὅ τι μάλιστα ἀφομοιοῦσθαι).[44] It is by associating with the divine order that the philosopher himself becomes ordered and divine, insofar as that is possible for humans.[45] The philosopher, Plato suggests, has a paradigm of the internal realities inside his psyche (. . . ἐν τῇ ψυχῇ ἔχοντες παράδειγμα).[46] Although there is no existing ideal polis on earth—and thus no ideal cultural template to internalize—there is a paradigm of it in heaven, and a person studying it can constitute himself (ἑαυτὸν κατοικίζειν) its citizen.[47] Only after the philosopher has shaped his own psyche by internalizing divine order is he then able to shape the polis according to what has now become the order in his psyche.[48]

Let us call *externalization* the process, whatever it is, by which Plato thought a person fashions something in the external world according to a likeness in his psyche. Then, for Plato, the polis is formed by a process of externalization of structures within the psyches of those who shape it. And, more generally, *externalization is a basic psychological activity*. For Plato suggests that cultural products in general are externalizations. Good rhythm, harmony, and diction, for example, should follow and fit good speech (εὐλογία); and speech, in turn, follows and fits the character of the psyche (ὁ λόγος . . . τῷ τῆς ψυχῆς ἤθει ἕπεται).[49] In painting and all artistic works, weaving, embroidery, architecture, the making of furniture, harmony and grace are closely related to and an imitation of good character (. . . ἀγαθοῦ ἤθους, ἀδελφά τε καὶ μιμήματα).[50] And character, as we have seen, is inherent in psyche.

Notoriously, Plato believes that education must begin by telling young children false tales.[51] These myths are distinguished from unacceptable myths and legitimated, first, because there is truth in them,[52] but, secondly, because that truth is a reflection of a truth in the poet's psyche. A falsehood which is merely a falsehood in words (τό γε ἐν τοῖς λόγοις [ψεῦδος]) "is an imitation of something in the psyche, a later reflection", (μίμημά τι τοῦ ἐν τῇ ψυχῇ ἐστι παθήματος καὶ ὕστερον γεγονὸς εἴδωλον) which is therefore not completely untrue.[53] It is precisely because this merely verbal falsehood is an externalization of something true within the poet's psyche, that it can be used, with caution, as a medicine.[54] By contrast, falsehood in the psyche, falsehood taken as truth (ὡς ἀληθῶς ψεῦδος), is what people hate most of all.[55] This is ignorance in the psyche (ἡ ἐν τῇ ψυχῇ ἄγνοια). Though Plato does not say so explicitly in this paragraph, the implication is that unacceptable myths and poems are externalizations of this real falsehood (τὸ τῷ ὄντι ψεῦδος).

And so it seems that in the ideal polis, after we internalize our cultural roles by a process of education, we then externalize them in our social roles. It is by a process of internalization and externalization that we are able to conform to the rule of each performing his own task. Incoherence is avoided because Plato's is a developmental psychology. Internalization is primarily going on in unformed youths, externalization is going on primarily in adults who have already formed themselves through prior cultural internalizations. Psyche and polis are mutually constituted by a series of internalizations and externalizations, with transformations occurring on both sides of the border.[56] We tend to think of the economic model in psychology as concerned with the distribution of a fixed quantity of energy—and, indeed Plato lends support to this model since he believes that when a person's desires incline strongly towards something, they are correspondingly weakened for other things.[57] However, if we consider Plato's psychology as a whole, it would seem that a more promising economic model would be of trade across a border. Plato's psychology is basically one of interpsychic and intrapsychic trade. What is being traded across a boundary is not unformed energy, but psychological products. They are crafted both outside and inside an individual's psyche and they are traded back and forth across the boundary of the psyche. Once inside, they become citizens of a more or less federated republic and are subject to the vicissitudes of intrapsychic conflict, before being externalized again across the border.

Plato decides first to look for justice writ large in the polis because, he says, he will then be able to read the small print of the individual psyche.[58] By now it should be clear that he is not relying on a mere analogy of polis and psyche, but on an isomorphism which must hold due to the way we function psychologically. Psyche and polis, inner world and outer world, are jointly constituted by reciprocal internalizations and externalizations; and the analogy is a byproduct of this psychological dynamic.

## 4. The Analogy of Psyche and Polis

One way to see the virtue of an interpretation is to see how the *Republic* looks without it. In his classic essay, "The Analogy of City and Soul in Plato's *Republic*", Bernard Williams offers the most penetrating critique we have of Plato's analogy.[59] According to Williams, Plato's argument is incoherent, and the analogy disguises a fundamental tension in his account of psyche and polis. If Williams is right, the *Republic* is a brilliant mess. In this section, I would like to try to rescue the analogy from Williams' critique by attending to the psychological principles which underlie it.

The analogy, for Williams, is founded on two principles. First, there is *the whole-part rule*:[60]

(a) A city if F if and only if its men are F.

Second, there is the *analogy of meaning*:[61]

(b) The explanation of a city's being F is the same as that of a man's being F (the same *eidos* [form] of F-ness applies to both).

Although it appears that these two principles support each other, Williams argues that is not so: the whole-part rule in fact "defeats" the analogy of meaning:

> For if we say that "F" is applied to the city just because it is applied to the men, we have already explained how the term can be applied to both cities and men, and to go on from there to look for a similar explanation of how "F" applies to men is at least pointless, since the phenomenon which set off the search for the analogy in the first place, viz. the fact that "F" applies to both cities and men has already been explained. If, moreover, the rule applying "F" to cities is taken as itself the common *logos* [account] that we were looking for, then we have not just pointlessness but absurdity, since the common *logos* [account] will have to be something like "x is F if and only if x has constituent parts which are F", which leads to a regress.[62]

However, Plato does not in fact think that F is applied to a polis "just because" it is applied to its citizens. Even if he were committed to principle (a) (or some variant),[63] the principle cannot fully capture Plato's intentions. For the principle describes a formal relation between polis and citizens, whereas Plato believes the formal relation holds in virtue of causal-psychological transactions. Plato's point (at 435E) is not that a spirited polis, say, is spirited simply in virtue of having spirited citizens, but in having spirited citizens who are successful in shaping the polis in their image. And so, one has not "already explained" how spiritedness can be applied to both polis and psyche. Plato has not yet given us the explanation: he is showing us where to look for one. He is saying that there is an externalizing psychological relation from citizen to polis. The explanation of what it is that makes either polis or man spirited lies in the future. So far Plato has only given us the methodology of a research project, one based on his psychology. If this is a general point which holds for significant psychopolitical predicates, it is not pointless to move from an explanation of, say, justice in the polis to an explanation of justice in the psyche. If a just polis is an externalization of just citizens who shape it, it would be reasonable to work one's way backwards down this externalization to learn about the psyches of these citizens. This reasoning can occur before one has any idea what the structure of justice is.

To be sure, Socrates does say that a just person and a just polis will be alike in respect of the form of justice; and he defends this claim by appeal to a semantic principle: "things called by the same name are alike in respect to which the name applies".[64] This is the basis for William's principle (b). Yet even if Socrates accepts this semantic principle, there remain questions about it: e.g. why should such a semantic principle hold?; why does it hold in the realm of psychopolitical predicates?; given that it does hold, how could it be legitimate to call a certain sort of person and a certain sort of polis just? Again, the semantic principle is the beginning not the end of a research project. Only a few sentences after he introduces it, Socrates explains that a wide range of political characterizations of the polis are to be understood as externalizations of the same qualities from within the psyches of the historically significant citizens.[65] I read this not simply as making a psychological-causal point about the relation of the polis to its citizens, but also as providing a psychological grounding of the semantic principle, at least within the range of psychopolitical predicates. The semantic principle is introduced in the course of a dialectical inquiry, and it therefore remains open to further explication and defense. It also remains vulnerable to future emendation and revision. It should not be treated as an obvious axiom forever beyond criticism or inquiry. The psychological principles of internalization and externalization help us to understand why the semantic principle might hold in spite of the fact that there are a range of predicates which apply both to polis and to psyche.

Principles (a) and (b) do not, therefore, give us Plato's reason for thinking there to be an isomorphism between polis and psyche. The isomorphism depends on psychological relations Plato believed to hold between inside and outside. If justice, for example, can be found outside (in the polis) it must have come from inside (i.e. it must be a causal outcome of just men shaping the polis according to their conception of justice). Given the psychologically dynamic relations between inside and outside, a weak version of a whole-part rule will follow as a corollary.[66] And so, there is neither regress nor absurdity in Plato's argument, for there is no reason to think that he has thus far given us the common *logos.* It is often thought that Plato uses his analogy to derive his psychology: that by simply claiming the analogy and looking at the structure of the polis, he derives his psychology. But once we see that psychology is not just individual psychology, we can see that the situation is pretty much the reverse: his psychology is used to legitimate belief in isomorphism.

Williams thinks that there is a "contradiction . . . powerfully at work under the surface of the *Republic.*"[67] The contradiction lies in the fact that if we apply principle (a) to the case of a just polis we get that

(a') a polis is just if and only if its men are

but a just polis will have a majority of appetitive (epithymetic) persons, who, by the analysis of justice ought to be doing their proper jobs. But an appetitive person is not a just one; and that must contradict (a'). By now it should be clear that Williams is not entitled to attribute (a) to Plato, but at most

(a'') If a polis is F, then some its men are F[68]

and so he is entitled to derive not (a') but

(a''') If a polis is just, then some of its men are just;

and this generates no contradiction.[69]

But it is clear that Williams thinks there is a contradiction here which goes beyond the validity or invalidity of this formal argument. For, he reasons, the appetitive (epithymetic) class must exercise some reason *(logistikon)* of its own, even if it is only in the service of obeying its rulers, sticking to its tasks, etc.

> But now if the epithymetic [appetitive] class has in this way to exercise some *logistikon,* and this helps it stick to its tasks, recognize the rulers and so forth, and if we read this result back through the analogy to the individual soul, we shall reach the absurd result that the *epithymetikon* [appetitive part] in a just soul harkens to the *logistikon* in that soul through itself having an extra little *logistikon* of its own. Recoiling from this absurdity, we recognize that in the individual soul, the *epithymetikon* cannot really harken; rather, through training, the desires are weakened

and kept in their place by *logistikon*, if not through the agency, at least with the co-operation of *thumoeides* [the spirited part]. If with this fact in our hand we come back once more across the bridge of the analogy to the city, we shall find not a *dikaios* [just] and logistically co-operative working class, but rather a totally logistic ruling class holding down with the help of a totally thymoeidic military class, a weakened and repressed epithymetic class; a less attractive picture. The use of the analogy, it begins to seem, is to help Plato to have it both ways.[70]

Plato's commitment to the analogy, according to Williams, forces him into absurdities both within the realm of politics and of psychology. That is the way it will look if one takes the analogy to be *merely* an analogy. If, by contrast, we view the isomorphism as a manifestation of internalization and externalization, it seems we can use the 'analogy' to form a clearer idea of how Plato understood psychological structure. This is important because Plato identifies the distinct parts of the psyche via each part's ability to enter into fundamental conflictual relations with the other parts.

Psychological structure is delineated most obviously in intrapsychic conflict. The question then is: how are we to understand psychological structure in the absence of conflict? Instead of assuming we know what psychic parts are and using the analogy to derive absurdities, let us use Plato's principles of internalization and externalization to try to find out more about what it is to be a psychic part. In the just polis, the appetitive class does have to exercise some reason of its own, to stick to its tasks, recognize its rulers and so forth. What intrapsychic condition (of a member of the appetitive class) might have this socially harmonious behavior as an externalization?[71]

Plato believes this requires a certain type of intrapsychic harmony appropriate to an appetitive person. This requires that the appetitive part of his psyche harken to reason in that psyche. The question is how one might avoid the absurdity of the appetitive part needing to have a little extra logistikon of its own. Not surprisingly, we need to understand the psychic part as having been formed by previous internalizations. Plato, as is well known, divides appetites into necessary and unnecessary.[72] The necessary appetites are either unavoidable (e.g. for basic nourishment) or they are for things which do us some good. Unnecessary appetites, by contrast, are both avoidable by proper training from youth and they lead to no good (or even to bad). In an ideal polis, then, an appetitive person will be brought up so as not to have unnecessary appetites. That is why, in contrast to his pathological cousin, the oligarchic man, he does not need to hold them down by force.[73] Due to his education, there is nothing in him which requires forcible restraint. Such a person will only have appetites for the bare necessities of life and for things which genuinely do him good. In the well-ordered polis, Plato says, each class will enjoy the happiness that suits its nature.[74] Assuming that the things that do a person good are the things that give him the happiness that suits his nature, in Plato's vision[75] the appetitive person in a well-ordered polis should have just those appetites which the polis gives him the opportunity to satisfy.

The appetitive part has thus been shaped to be responsive to reason in the psyche. The idea that appetite needs extra reason of its own derives from the thought that appetite "cannot really harken"; and this thought in turn flows from taking the conditions in which the psychic parts are isolated to be the essential conditions in which they must operate. We identify the appetitive part by seeing it functioning in opposition to reason. If this is the way it must operate then, of course, appetite cannot harken to reason. And one can be tempted to make this inference by the thought that this is the way appetites must be.[76] On this picture all domination by reason would ultimately have to be repression, and Plato's alleged distinction between the oligarchical person and the appetitive person in the just polis will look like propaganda.

Moreover, if a psychic part must be the way it is when it is originally isolated, it is natural to identify appetitive persons with the appetitive parts of their psyches. For since, on this assumption, the appetitive part can have no real commerce with the other psychic parts, there seems to be no other option for appetitive persons than to be driven by their appetites. This conflicts with the claim Plato makes about the difference between the oligarchical psyche and that of the appetitive person in the just polis; but again this will look as if it is Plato's problem. However, once we recognize internalization and externalization as basic psychological activities, we can see that the psychic parts can be shaped, and thus that the conditions under which we first identify them need not be the conditions under which they operate. This allows us to see that an appetitive person need not simply be someone driven by the appetitive part. And once we see that psychic parts need not always be functioning in the conflictual ways in which they are first identified, we can then grant culture a greater role in psychic formation than would otherwise be thought possible.

Consider, for example, the appetitive person or money-lover: how did his appetites ever come to love *money?* Money is the paradigm cultural artefact: it has no existence *hors de culture.* So if the appetites can be directed onto money, it would seem that culture can permeate and inform the lower elements of the psyche.[77] The appetitive personality will organize his personality around his appetites; and a paradigm, for Plato, is the money-lover who devotes himself to the pursuit of wealth: reason will be directed instrumentally toward figuring out ways of satisfying this desire, he will feel honor in achieving wealth-related goals, and there is a peculiar pleasure in achieving them.[78] The pursuit of wealth, then, is setting the overall agenda for this person's projects, and honor and reason are disciplined to serve this outlook. But within this schema there is room for the oligarchical personality, the democrat, the tyrant and (as I shall argue) the poet, all of whom are appetitive types. 'Appetitive' is thus a genus of personality organization and the variety of species is due to the fact that internalization can inform the appetitive part of the psyche.[79]

It might at first seem paradoxical that, on the one hand, the appetitive part is the ruling principle of an appetitive person,[80] while, on the other, the appetitive person should believe along with everyone else that reason should rule.[81] Plato is trying to have it both ways, but, within the framework of his psychology, he can get away with it. The appetitive person thinks that the peculiar pleasures available to his way of life are the best,[82] and, since the appetitive part rules in his psyche, his reason will be directed towards figuring out ways to secure those pleasures. But given that this appetitive person has been brought up to have just the appetites which the well-ordered polis can satisfy, his reason ought to be telling him that the best way to satisfy his appetites is to harken to the reason manifest in the laws of the philosopher-king.

In the temperate polis, Plato says, the same belief about who should rule will be inside both the rulers and the ruled (ἡ αὐτὴ δόξα ἔνεστι τοῖς τε ἄρχουσι καὶ ἀρχομένοις . . .).[83] This belief helps to constitute the reason of the appetitive person in the just polis. Ironically, it is because the reason in his psyche is subservient to the appetitive part that the appetitive person submits himself to the rule of reason in the polis. Just as the appetitive person will abjure junk food for healthy bread and relishes, so he will abjure junk bonds for municipal bonds. And all the while he will be telling himself, correctly, that this is the really good investment for himself and his family. This is how the appetitive person's role in a well-ordered polis looks from an appetitive perspective. On the one hand, his reason is focused on securing gain; on the other he concludes that the best way to do this is by following the rule of reason in the polis. This would not have been possible if he had not been brought up in such a way as to internalize appropriate cultural influences and get rid of unnecessary appetites. Yet for all that he remains basically an appetititve type: organizing his life, values and thoughts around production and acquisition. For him, justice is basically a matter of doing and getting one's own.[84] Temperance in the polis is like "a certain harmony" which "spreads throughout the whole".[85] But if temperance spreads throughout the whole, it must spread through the whole of the whole. That is, there would not be genuine harmony in the polis if the psyche of an appetitive citizen were at war with itself. Plato does not believe the appetitive person has the *virtue* of temperance, but in a well-ordered polis, due to well-crafted internalizations, such a person will be well disposed to temperance, both inside and outside himself.

So too for the honor-loving members of society: Each will commend the distinctive pleasures of the honor-achieving life as the best,[86] and will try to organize his life and character around this pursuit. In a just polis, honor-lovers will be educated to hold fast to the laws, and to fear only those things which the lawgivers think are fearful.[87] These people will be brought up to be soldiers: they will be educated so as to be free of unnecessary appetites and to have their other appetites disciplined to the pursuit of honor. Their reason too will be directed towards honor, but they will have been educated so as to understand that the way to achieve true honor is to defend and safeguard the law (laid down by the philosopher-rulers).[88] Therefore, although honor is the fundamental principle of this person's life, on that very account he will, when brought up in a just polis, believe that reason should rule. Whatever one thinks about Plato's prescription for attaining health, one must, I think, acknowledge that his conception of a healthy, harmonious psyche is not just a dodge to cover up an irresolvable tension, but a natural consequence of his psychology.

The analogy between polis and psyche is a manifestation of the fact that there are important structural similarities between interpsychic relations and intrapsychic relations. But, for Plato, these structural similarities are themselves a manifestation of important psychological transactions, back and forth, between interpsychic and intrapsychic. This is true in sickness as in health. If we examine Plato's tale of political decline, we see that the degeneration occurs through a dialectic of internalization of pathological cultural influences in individuals which provokes a degeneration in character-structure (as compared to the previous generation) which is in turn imposed on the polis, which thus acquires and provokes deeper pathology.[89] Plato does not merely want to show that the same neurotic structure can exist in both psyche and polis, but that the pathology in each helps to bring about pathology in the other. This has not been easy to see, I suspect, because Plato's conception of pathology is not well understood.

It is, for example, easy to read his accounts of the rise of the democratic polis and the emergence of democratic man as two parallel accounts which have only a structural analogy in common. In fact, Plato traces a sophisticated interaction between polis and psyche that helps to account for both. Consider, for example, Plato's account of the rise of democratic man.[90] He emerges from an oligarchic family, the values and goals of that family being set by the father who is himself a manifestation of an oligarchic personality. The oligarchic father is thrifty and frugal; he has organized himself around the pursuit of wealth, and tries to instill this same structure in his family.[91] He has been able to keep his unnecessary appetites in check, but because he has not had a proper upbringing, because he has not experienced or internalized true culture, these appetites must be held in place by the only means available to him: brute force. This is a man whose personality is held together by forcibly holding down an inner world of unruly appetites. He presents a good face to the world, but in fact exists in two bits.[92] The emergence of the democratic man is, roughly speaking, the return of the repressed in the next generation.[93] The oligarchic father creates in his family and immediate social environment a micro-culture, a template for internalization, which embodies contradictory demands. On the one hand, there is the demand *inside* his family for frugality so as to accumulate wealth. There is some suggestion that this demand on its own is self-contradictory. For to pursue wealth is to organize the family around the appetites; and Plato does say there is a tendency to spoil the children.[94] Yet to insist on frugality is to hold those appetites in check. The appetites are thus simultaneously encouraged and forcibly restrained. The only way the father knows how to instill frugality is by force. Having failed to internalize a more harmonious psychic structure, forcible restraint is the only means at his disposal: and he imposes it on his family as well as on himself. Thus the child is brought up in a miserly fashion without real education.[95] But, on the other hand, the oligarchical father encourages prodigality *outside* his family.[96] By lending others money and encouraging wastefulness, he hopes eventually to acquire their property. These people, made poor, will eventually revolt and usher in democracy.[97]

Here we see how the oligarchic father, by pursuing his own ends, recreates on the interpsychic stage of his family and immediate social environment a model of his own intrapsychic relations. His son, having his appetites both encouraged and held down, becomes an interpsychic correlate of the appetites within the father. However, as a member of the outer world, the son is open to other polis influences. The oligarchical father encouraged prodigality outside the family, but Plato's point is that this prodigality cannot, finally, be kept outside. The prodigal youths, encouraged by the oligarch, are an externalization and interpsychic correlate to the unnecessary appetites within the oligarch's psyche. Because the son's appetites have been both encouraged and held back, he is susceptible to appetitive influences around him. "Just as the city changed when one faction received help from like-minded people outside, so the young man changes when help comes from the same type of appetites outside to one of the factions within himself."[98] But these appetites outside are also offspring of the father. It is these appetites—whose pedigree goes back to the father—which are reinternalized in the intrapsychic battle within the son. For a while, a struggle rages both inside and outside his psyche. The father lends his influence to aid the internalized repressing forces, the young thugs on the block egg the appetites on.[99] But this is a struggle which the appetites have to win, because this youth never had the opportunity to internalize good cultural structures. When the appetites come knocking on the door of his psyche, they find no one is at home.[100] The psyche is easily reshaped, and a "democratic man" is born.

There is a problem, though, about the relation of the democratic polis and the democratic man. The democratic polis is one which contains every sort of character, like a garment of many colors.[101] However, as Williams points out, the democratic man is described as always shifting, following the appetite of the moment, without any expertise.[102] And here Williams tightens the noose:

> A democracy is a state in which the many rule, and if it gets its character from that of its rulers, then the majority must have a "democratic" character. This, on the face of it, sorts none too well with the claim that the democratic state will particularly tend to contain all sorts of character— the "democratic" character seems in fact to be a special sort of character.

> Moving between the social and the individual level once more, Plato
> seems disposed to confound two very different things: a state in which
> there are various characters among the people, and a state in which most
> of the people have a various character, that is to say, a very shifting and
> unsteady character.[103]

Surely a society of many colors does not require that each of its members be a patchwork quilt. Have we finally reached the true absurdity
of Plato's analogy? I don't think so. That a polis allows and even prides
itself on the fact that it has various sorts of character[104] is, for Plato, a
manifestation of the fact that it does not have a firmly established sense
of better and worse. There can be no agreed or enforced set of values,
beyond tolerance: thus the political possibility of various types. It is as
though citizens are allowed to decide for themselves what will constitute their own goods. However, for Plato, this is not a serious psychological possibility: humans need a socially grounded culture to
internalize.[105] A person may decide, say, to be a politician, but such a
decision is superficial and eminently shakeable by external events. By
historical luck the person may succeed at the appearance of state-craft,
but Plato's point is that this is thin stuff. And so, even in democracy's
finest hour, when it appears a many-colored fabric, full of different individuals each performing their own tasks, Plato's point is that this cannot be more than appearance. For although at that moment the
citizens will not all be shifting characters, they will all have characters
which are shift*able*. Thus their characters are unsteady, however firm
they may appear.
    Williams concludes:

> There have been those who thought that the working classes were natu-
> rally of powerful and disorderly desires, and had to be kept in their place.
> There have been those who thought that they were good-hearted and
> loyal fellows of no great gifts who could recognize their natural superiors
> and, unless stirred up, keep themselves in their place. There can have
> been few who have thought both; Plato in the *Republic* comes close to
> being such a one. . . .[106]

This thought is amusing, but not absurd. Indeed, if one takes the role
of internalization seriously, it would seem to follow that in one political
environment the working class will be a disorderly mob that has to be
kept in its place, while in another it will consist in good-hearted fellows
who recognize their superiors. Again and again, what presents itself as

an absurdity dissolves once one takes seriously the idea that humans are dependent on internalization for acquiring psychological structure.

The initial appearance of absurdity depends once more on assuming that psychic parts are invulnerable to cultural influence. If the appetitive part must be in the conflictual relation with reason in which it is originally identified, then the working class will have to be a direct manifestation of contentious appetite. If intrapsychic conflict is unavoidable, then, given the analogy, so is political conflict. It will then look, just as it does to Williams, that when the obfuscating mask is pulled away we will see that Plato's just polis has the same repressive structure that Plato himself diagnoses in oligarchy. And, I think, it is tempting to go along with Williams' argument in part because Plato's ideal polis does look to us as though it has repressive features.[107] But the point of the present argument is not to rescue Plato's polis, it is to understand the psychological basis of the isomorphism. Once one sees that the isomorphism is not a mere analogy, but is grounded in internalization and externalization, one sees that there is room to influence the shape and content of the psychic parts, and this allows room to influence the specific type of say, appetitive person, which in turn allows room to influence the specific type of appetitive class in the polis. This is hard to see in part because Plato concentrates so much on pathology, and pathological structures are inherently conflictual. Plato's psychology, like Freud's, is "wisdom won from illness".[108] Plato finds himself in a pathological social situation,[109] and, given his psychological principles, he deduces that this pathology is both cause and manifestation of pathology within the psyche. And it is his task to work his way back from the conceptualization of this pathology towards a conception of health.[110] His strategy was to assume a dynamic psychological relation between psyche and polis, and to construct an idealized genealogy of illness.[111]

For Plato, the hallmark of pathology is a lack of harmonious relations between inside and outside. That is one reason why the principles of internalization and externalization have been difficult to recognize. For it is a sign of oligarchy being a pathological structure that it cannot simply be internalized and externalized without further ado. The oligarchical father does externalize the structure of his psyche. And it is such externalizations which shape the oligarchical polis: by encouraging one class to accumulate wealth, the other class to forfeit it. The son, for his part, does internalize the polis influences. But because oligarchy is a pathological configuration, the internalization cannot stably reproduce the psychic structure of the previous generation. The instability is manifest in the inability of inside and outside to maintain a mirroring relation—and in the ensuing failure of the son to grow up in the image of the father. All this in spite of the fact that internalization and externalization are basic psychological activities.[112]

The point of Plato's argument is to show that there is only one relatively stable equilibrium position between inside and outside.[113] Only the just polis and its citizens are so structured that the various internalizations and externalizations will maintain harmony in each and harmony between them. Justice, for Plato, is a certain harmony within the psyche; it is also a certain harmony within the polis.[114] But now we can see that each of these harmonies is possible only if there is a larger harmony—between inside and outside—which encompasses and explains them.[115] Justice when properly understood is each part, inside and outside, doing its own task. That is why it is ultimately misleading to think of there being merely an analogy between polis and psyche.[116] That is how it might look at the beginning of inquiry, but not how it should look at the end. When it is first introduced, the isomorphism may appear to be little more than an argumentative device. But then we, at that stage, are deep in the cave, confronted by what appear to be contradictory arguments about whether justice is good or bad.[117] The remainder of the *Republic* works through these contradictions, and what we come to see is that, roughly speaking, psyche is internalized polis and polis is externalized psyche. What initially appeared as two things which stood in a merely analogous relation come to appear as the internal and external workings of a psychological universe which may exist in various states of harmony or disharmony.

## 5. Poetic Justice

Internalization and externalization also explain why, for Plato, poetry corrupts our psyches. Given our psychology, there are two features of poetry which make it an especially potent drug. First, the music and rhythms with which poetry is expressed pour directly into our psyches.[118] Second, poetry tends to be expressed in imitative style: the characters speak as though from their own first-personal perspectives.[119] In this way, poetry can preserve the first-personal perspective throughout its transmissions.[120] Whether we are poet, performer or audience, we imaginatively take up the perspective of the characters:

even the best of us abandon ourselves and imaginatively take up their feelings.[121] It is as though imitation blurs the boundary between inside and outside. Through imitation we get outside ourselves imaginatively, but psychologically we take the outside in. By pretending to be these characters, we unconsciously shape our characters around them.[122] The mimetic poet, says Plato, sets up a bad constitution in the psyche of each person (. . . τὸν μιμητικὸν ποιητὴν φήσομεν κακὴν πολιτείαν ἰδίᾳ ἑκάστου τῇ ψυχῇ ἐμποιεῖν . . .).[123]

Poetry feeds our psychological hunger to take things in, but it feeds us a diet of fantasy.[124] Its ability to draw us into a world of illusion indicates that it is appealing to a primitive level of mental functioning: Plato calls it "a vulgar part" (τῶν φαύλων τι) of the psyche.[125] For Plato, poetry has a hotline to the appetites.[126] It is able to bypass reason, the faculty which corrects for false appearance,[127] and go straight to the psychic gut. So while reason may tell us to be moderate in our grief, poetry encourages lamentation, excess and loss of control.[128] Poetry thus sets us up for intrapsychic conflict.[129] For poetry encourages "the irrational part" (τὸ ἀλόγιστον) of us to hold on to fantasy in spite of reason's corrections. It establishes a split off part of the psyche to which reason is not accessible. And that is why poetry cannot, for Plato, be just a stage in the developmental cave we work our way through. Other images may generate conflicts that lead us towards reality,[130] but poetic imitations keep us imprisoned at that level. So, on the one hand, poetry promotes intrapsychic conflict; on the other, it keeps us unconscious of that conflict, for the irrational part of our psyche cannot hear reason's corrections. That is why poetry, with its throbbing rhythms and beating of breasts, appeals equally to the nondescript mob in the theatre and to the best among us.[131]

But if poetry goes straight to the lower part of the psyche, that is where it must come from. First, imitation by its very nature encourages poet, actor and audience to go through the same motions. Although imitation is only play,[132] it is in this play that we unconsciously shape our psyches.[133] If poetic imitation sets our appetites in motion, it is reasonable to infer similar motions within the poet. Second, when a part of our psyche is strengthened from outside, it tends to be by an interpsychic manifestation of that very same part of the psyche. So, for example, the budding democrat's appetites are reinforced by the appetitive thugs on the block.[134] The fact that poetry deals in fantasy and the throbbing lamentations of the irrational part of the psyche testifies to its lineage. Third, when Plato in his thought experiment wants to move from a minimal polis to a fevered one, he adds imitators (οἱ μιμηταί): poets, actors, rhapsodes, chorus dancers, theatrical managers.[135] He takes himself to be introducing a pathogen into a healthy organism. And the disease the polis contracts is *pleonexia*: the polis gives itself over to the unlimited acquisition of wealth.[136] Only after the polis is rid of poets who tell tales of gods eating, fighting and deceiving each other, does Plato conclude that he has purged the fevered polis.[137] Introduce the poets and the polis becomes pleonectic, banish them and you cure it. Finally, as we have seen, *logos* [reason] follows and fits the character of the psyche.[138] If poetry is an appetitive falsehood, it must come from an appetitive affection in the psyche. And so it seems that just as law in a good society is an externalization of reason (of the philosopher king (who has already internalized the eternal realities)), so poetry seems to be an externalization of the irrational part (of the poet (who may already have internalized appetitive-poetic elements of culture)).[139]

We can see these appetites in the gods. The gods of the poets spend their time castrating and devouring each other, they are constantly at war, and tend to engage in single-minded pursuit of satisfaction.[140] In short, these gods behave like lawless, unnecessary appetites;[141] and, given Plato's psychology, it seems reasonable to hypothesize that this is just what they are: appetites externalized in Olympus. A moment's reflection will show that there is nowhere else for them to go. Plato calls the lawless appetites "something wild and terrible" (δεινόν τι καὶ ἄγριον) within us.[142] He speaks of Eros as a "tyrant within" (τύραννος ἔνδον) the psyche.[143] Undisciplined appetites are all powerful within, so when they are externalized it makes sense that they should be represented as tremendously powerful. They need a virtually transcendent arena in which to struggle.[144] And so externalization from inside the poet's psyche turns out also to be an inversion: from bottom of the psyche to top of the world. These poetic myths provide a cultural template for youths to internalize, thus inverting their own psyches and, inevitably, the societies in which they live. Children, says Plato, will come to think there is nothing wrong in punishing their father to the limit, in fighting with their family and fellow citizens, if they think they are only following in the gods' footsteps.[145] And it is precisely by those acts, Plato thinks, that the tyrant is born.[146] According to legend, a person who eats human entrails is turned into a wolf; just so, the person who sheds the blood of the tribe by unjust accusations against fellow citizens, who banishes and slays them, has "tasted kindred blood", and is transformed into a tyrant. The tyrant is formed by transgressing the basic norms of human relations. In fact, the tyrant is behaving towards other humans as the Homeric gods behave towards each other. Plato criticizes Euripides for praising tyranny as "godlike" (ἰσόθεον); but he is objecting not so much to the description, as to the fact that it is being used as a form of praise.[147] Tyranny *is* an imitation of the Homeric divine: but there is nothing praise-worthy about that.

This brings us to the most serious charge against the poets: they provide not only an externalization of the appetites, they also provide a *legitimation* of them. That is why the poetic myths are the "greatest lie about the greatest things", "an ugly falsehood".[148] The poets externalize their appetites, but their poetry sends them upwards as well as outwards. When the appetitive gods are re-internalized, it is now with a normative tinge.[149] Since the young are not able to distinguish myth from reality,[150] the tales they hear at their mother's knee provide the means by which the appetites can travel up and infect the norms and values of the developing person. In youth, we begin taking in psychological content and structure, before we know how to distinguish truth from falsity. At a later stage of development, we attempt to take in true beliefs and expel falsehoods.[151] However, if we already have a falsehood inside our psyches, even in mythic form, we will end up taking in more and more falsehood (as though it were true) and getting rid of more and more truth (as though it were false). Introduce this initial virus, and our intake-expulsion machine will start pumping in the wrong direction.[152] That is why having falsehood inside the psyche is what humans loathe most of all.[153] And that, for Plato, is what mimetic poetry introduces: a falsehood taken as truth (ὡς ἀληθῶς ψεῦδος).[154]

Plato is charting the interpsychic and intrapsychic vicissitudes of the appetites. He is following the fate of the poetic trajectory: and what he finds is that the externalized appetites will tend to return, strengthened and legitimated. Poetry thus provides both a legitimation of the appetites, and a cultural template for tyranny. One can see this in Plato's account of the rise of the tyrant. The tyrant is a child of democracy: the son of democratic man.[155] The democratic father is himself a compromise formation, shaped by a thrifty, oligarchical father, who encouraged only the acquisitive appetites, and a 'sophisticated' element which encouraged the unnecessary appetites. The pathology of this solution is again revealed by the instability between inside and outside. The son is brought up in the ways of the father, but is thereby susceptible to lawless influence from outside. It is the "dread magicians" (οἱ δεινοὶ μάγοι) who both whet his lawless appetites and encourage him to expel from his psyche any remnants of shame which would keep the appetites in check. That the intake-expulsion machine is pumping in the wrong direction is testimony to there being a falsehood taken as truth within. And just as, *intra*psychically, the lawless appetites overtook the original, better ones in his psyche, so, *inter*psychically, the tyrant comes to feel justified (ἀξιόω) in taking over his parent's estate; and then going on to rob, punish and enslave family, friends and fellow citizens.[156] In fact, the tyrant re-enacts on the interpsychic stage of the polis the situation that exists inside his psyche: he must expel or get rid of the brave, wise and wealthy, treating them as his enemy.[157] "A fine purgation," Plato says, "and just the opposite of what a physician does with our bodies: for while they remove the worst and leave the best, the tyrant does the opposite."[158] He recreates the polis in the image of his psyche.

And the poet gives him the cultural vehicle by which he can, at least to his own satisfaction, legitimize his acts. Hearing tales about the warring gods, Plato says, children will be encouraged to think this type of behavior appropriate.[159] The gods of the poets are the lawless appetites externalized in Olympus: the tyrant brings this lawlessness back to the polis—sometimes literally. The tyrant is often someone who, because of previous attacks on society, has been banished from the polis.[160] There he remains poised for a triumphant return in the name of democracy; which for Plato is nothing more than a lawless society of appetites. Plato's point is that if you really want to get rid of the tyrant, you also have to get rid of the cultural vehicles that make him look attractive: you must also banish his poetical counterpart. For it is the poets who "draw the constitutions towards tyrannies and democracies".[161]

One might say that the tyrant acts out what the poet only dreams; but, for Plato, both the poet and the tyrant are dreamers, though in slightly different ways. To understand the tyrant, Plato says, we must not settle for his outward appearance, the external pomp and circumstance—we must even strip him of the garb in which tragedy clothes him[162]—and must, in thought, enter into his character.[163] What we find inside is a tyranny of lawless desires.[164] These are the desires we encounter in our dreams, when the rational part of our psyche sleeps, and the wild and animal part wakes up. "There is nothing it will not dare to do at that time, free of any control by shame or prudence. It does not hesitate to attempt sexual intercourse with a mother or anyone else—man, god, or beast; it will commit any foul murder and does not refrain from any kind of food. In a word it will not fall short of any folly or shameless deed."[165] These, of course, are the very deeds with which the gods of the poets occupy themselves. Indeed, the tyrant is a parricide;[166] and parricide is the founding act of Homeric heaven. It is this dream-world that the poets have externalized in Olympus, and which the tyrant has reinternalized. The dreams of the poets enable the tyrant to turn his waking life into a bad dream: a daymare.

Poet and tyrant are essentially dreaming the same dream; indeed, they are bedfellows. From Plato's perspective, poet and tyrant are the same type of person: a Dr. Jekyll and Mr. Hyde of the appetites. Both have organized themselves around their appetites, though they have different strategies for dealing with them. The tyrant keeps his appetites inside: because of them he outwardly enslaves the polis and inwardly is enslaved by them.[167] The poet externalizes his appetites: but there they form a cultural template which, when reinternalized, enslaves us all. Poet and tyrant ultimately enslave us, but while the tyrant enforces external compliance, poetic enslavement reaches inside the psyche and reorganizes it so that we remain unconscious of our slavery.

That is why the poets must be banished from the polis. One might say that Plato is recapitulating the poet's activity, only at a philosophical level. The poets, after all, have externalized their appetites, setting them up outside the polis in a heavenly beyond. What Plato sees is that the 'poetic solution' to the problem of the appetites in fact provokes a psycho-social disaster. The Platonic solution is inspired by his psychological principles. Plato knows that every externalization is fodder for internalization; and his 'final solution' is designed to put an end to this cycle. The important thing for Plato is not to get the poets out of the polis, so much as to get the appetites out of culture. This, he thinks, can be accomplished only by banishing the poets.[168]

Of course, there is plenty of room to doubt whether Plato's solution is called for or whether it would be successful. Does poetry not serve a healthy function? Is poetry not more (or other) than mimesis? Would the banished not find another way to return, if not from poetic heaven, then from beyond the philosophical pale? Is Plato's prescription so removed from anything we have ever experienced that we have no idea what is being prescribed? Rather than try to answer these questions, I shall close by explaining why we have only recently become ready to evaluate Plato's argument from a psychological perspective. Most recent discussions of the psychological value of art rely on an early psychoanalytic conception of the mind. The mind, on this conception, is divided along the lines of repression. The point of therapy was to loosen repression so that the unconscious could express itself, if only in words. In this context the creation and enjoyment of art appeared as another socially acceptable way of expressing unconscious forces. Thus artistic creation and appreciation came to be seen as therapeutic. As psychoanalytic theory developed, it became less concerned with the unconscious per se, and more concerned with the structure of the psyche. The psychoanalytic valuation of art has not kept pace with the development of theory.[169] In fact, Plato's remains one of the few discussions of the psychological value of art within the context of a structural theory of the psyche. Plato's point is that it is not enough to assume that the release of the repressed is a good thing. If one wants to justify art from a psychological perspective, one must understand its role within the context of a structured psyche. And that may require an account of the psychological transactions inside and outside the psyche. This is a challenge which, it seems to me, we are only now ready to take up once again.[170]

## Notes

1. There is even linguistic pressure on us to make that assumption. For although "psychology" is an English word, it comes almost directly from Greek; and while the English word carries the broad connotation of the science of mental activity, its Greek counterpart would be an account or logos of the psyche.

2. In the parlance of contemporary psychoanalysis, it leaves out Plato's object-relations theory. Indeed, it leaves out the possibility of object-relations theory being an element of Plato's psychology. Freud, of course, understood that a person's ego and superego were formed around internalizations of parental figures. In the analytic situation, he concentrated on the intrapsychic configurations of the analysand, but he recognized that these configurations were due in part to interpsychic relations. See e.g. Freud, "Mourning and Melancholia", *The Complete Psychological Works of Sigmund Freud* (London: Hogarth Press, 1957–81) XIV: 249–250; *The Ego and the Id,* XIX: 29–31; and my *Love and Its Place in Nature* (New York: Farrar, Straus and Giroux, 1990; London: Faber and Faber, 1992) chapter 6. For an introduction to post-Freudian object relations theory, see e.g. Melanie Klein, *Love, Guilt and Reparation,* and *Envy and Gratitude* (London: Hogarth Press, 1981, 1984); D. W. Winnicott, *Through Paediatrics to Psycho-Analysis* and *The Maturational Process and the Facilitating Environment* (London: Hogarth Press, 1975, 1982); W. R. D. Fairbairn, *Psychoanalytic Studies of the Personality* (London: Routlege and Kegan Paul,

1984); Margaret Mahler, *On Human Symbiosis and the Vicissitudes of Individ-uation* (New York: International Universities Press, 1967); Otto Kernberg, *Internal World and External Reality*, (New York: Aronson, 1980).

3. See, e.g. Iris Murdoch, *The Fire and the Sun: Why Plato Banished the Artists* (Oxford: Clarendon Press, 1977); G.R.F. Ferrari, "Plato and Poetry", *The Cambridge History of Literary Criticism*, volume 1 (ed. G. Kennedy, Cambridge: Cambridge University Press, 1989); D. Halliwell, *Plato: Republic 10* (Wiltshire: Aris & Philips, 1988); Alexander Nehamas, "Plato on Imitation and Poetry in Republic 10", in *Plato on Beauty, Wisdom and the Arts* (ed. J. Moravcsik and P. Temko, pp. 47–78).

4. II.358B, cp. 366E.

5. II.368D–E; IV.434D.

6. II.377A–B; my emphasis.

7. II.377B.

8. II.378D–E. Cp. V.449D where Plato says that the constitution of the community of women and children makes all the difference to the constitution of the state.

9. II.380B–C.

10. See e.g. III.386A, IV.424E.

11. II.381E.

12. III.387.

13. III.395C.

14. III.411E–412A; IV.424C–D.

15. V.466E–467A.

16. IV.420D–422D; cp. 430A–C; 441E–442C; V.465D–466D.

17. II.395D.

18. Cp. II.366C–D; IV.424E; VI. 492A–493A; 495A–B; 496C; 499B–C.

19. IV.422E.

20. IV.422E–423D.

21. See Books VIII–IX.

22. VIII.551D.

23. VIII.553C–554E.

24. VIII.553C–D; cp.IX.581C.

25. VIII.554A.

26. VIII.554C–D. I do not believe that Plato's conception of "forcible restraint" should be equated with Freud's concept of repression, though there are of course similarities. For Freud, repression is itself unconscious, it is dynamically motivated, and the repressed is unconscious but continues to exercise influence in hidden ways. Plato does not suggest that the "forcibly restrained" is thereby rendered unconscious, or that these intrapsychic struggles must, by nature of the process, occur unconsciously.

27. VIII.554D.

28. Similarly, just as the democratic polis lets a hundred flowers bloom (VIII.557B–C), so democratic man is 'manifold' (παντοδαπός:561E). The timocratic man is a compromise formation: an attempted solution to the conflicting demands of reason and appetite (550A–B). However, that the compromise fails is testified to by the emergence of oligarchic man in the next generation. The

tyrant is just a mess. (I shall discuss the democrat and tyrant below.) For Plato, a human being, looked at from the outside, is only apparently a unity (IX.588C–E); whether each forms a genuine unity depends on the integration of the (potentially) disparate bits of the psyche.

29. Plato says (IV.433D) that in the just polis each person, in performing the task which suits their nature, will be not a multiplicity, but a unity. (See also IV.443E.) This suggests that a healthy polis encourages the development of healthy psyches: people who achieve the degree of psychic unity of which their character-types are capable. Injustice, by contrast, is a kind of civil war both in polis and psyche (IV.444A–B).

30. III.395C–D.

31. III.401D–E.

32. III.401B–C. By contrast, cp. 401C–D.

33. IV.424C.

34. IV.424D.

35. IX.590E.

36. I should stress that I here stipulate "internalization" to mean the process, whatever it is, that Plato thought grounded cultural influence. For an introduction to the concept of internalization as it occurs in the modern psychoanalytic tradition, see e.g. Roy Schafer, _Aspects of Internalization_ (Madison, CT: International Universities Press, 1990); Hans Loewald, "On Internalization" and "Internalization, Separation, Mourning and the Superego", in _Papers on Psychoanalysis_ (New Haven: Yale University Press, 1980); J. LaPlanche and J-B Pontalis, _The Language of Psychoanalysis_ (London: Hogarth Press, 1983) pp. 205–208, 211–212, 226–227, 229–231; B. Moore and B. Fine eds. _Psychoanalytic Terms and Concepts_ (New Haven, Yale University Press, 1990), pp. 102–103, 109–110; R. D. Hinshelwood, _A Dictionary of Kleinian Thought_ (London: Free Association, 1991) pp. 68–83, 319–321, 330–334; Arnold Model, _Object Love and Reality_ (Madison, CT: IUP, 1985).

37. VIII.544D–E. See also IV.435E, quoted below.

38. III.402D. Cp. VI.535B; III.401A; IX.577A.

39. IV.435C.

40. IV.435E–436A; see also 441C.

41. I shall discuss pathological forms of polis in section 4.

42. VI.500B–C.

43. VI.500E.

44. VI.500C. Cp. 484C: They have a paradigm of the reality of things in their psyche. (See also 490B). This is the step which Charles Taylor omits from his account of Plato in _Sources of the Self_ (Cambridge, MA: Harvard University Press, 1989) pp. 121–126.

45. VI.500C–D.

46. VI.484C, 490B. Some such internalization is necessary, Plato thinks, for a person with a philosophical nature to achieve excellence. (VI.492A) This may be through a proper education, but with poor upbringing even a philosophical nature is destroyed and corrupted. (VI.495A–B) Such a person is then capable of the greatest evils, and his only hope is divine inspiration. That is why a person of philosophical nature ought to shun political life in a pathological

polis: he must take care of the "constitution inside himself" (τὴν ἐν αὑτῷ πολιτείαν) and not allow cultural influences to "undo the state of his psyche".

47. IX.592B.

48. Socrates argues that education is not, as the sophists think, a matter of putting knowledge into a psyche, but rather more like turning the eye from the dark (world of becoming) to the light (world of realities). (VII.518B–E) This metaphor may have impeded understanding of Plato's psychology. For Plato is not here saying that internalization does not take place in education, he is rather explaining how internalization comes about. It is more, he thinks, than learning a few sophistical speeches. The point of turning one's gaze towards reality is not just to gawp at it like a bewildered tourist; it is to take reality in, be educated by it.

49. III.400D–E.

50. III.400E–401A.

51. II.376E–377A.

52. II.377A.

53. II.382B–C.

54. II.382C–D.

55. II.382B.

56. I shall discuss the intra- and interpsychic transformations in the following sections.

57. VI.485D. (For the economic model in psychoanalysis, see e.g. Freud, "The Unconscious" XIV.181; *Studies on Hysteria,* II.17, 86, 166–67; "The Neuro-Psychoses of Defense", III.48–49).

58. II.368D–369A.

59. In E.N. Lee, A.P.D. Mourelatos and R.M. Rorty eds., *Exegesis and Argument Studies in Greek Philosophy Presented to Gregory Vlastos, Phronesis:* Supplementary Volume I, 1973 [reprinted in this volume]. This essay has influenced a generation of philosophers, myself included. I turn to it here because I have come to believe, first, that the argument is unsuccessful, second, that in coming to understand why it is unsuccessful we will better understand our own tendency to misread Plato's psychology.

60. Williams derives this from 435E. See "Analogy," this volume, pp. 49–50.

61. Derived from 435A–B.

62. "Analogy," this volume, p. 50.

63. See below.

64. IV.435A–B.

65. IV.435E.

66. Terence Irwin argues that the whole-part rule does not play a role in the argument of Book IV, and focuses instead on Macrocosm-Microcosm rule (MM): the structure of the state is analogous to the structure of the psyche. *(Plato's Moral Theory: The Early and Middle Dialogues* (Oxford: Clarendon Press, 1977), p. 331 n. 29). The MM is true, but it does not give us the psychological principles which ensure its truth. John Cooper also provides criticism of the whole-part rule in "The Psychology of Justice in Plato," *American Philosophical Quarterly* 14, 1977; n. 7, reprinted in this volume.

67. "Analogy," this volume, p. 52; cp. "the ineliminable tension" on p. 54ff.

68. This is the strongest version of the whole-part rule we are legitimately entitled to attribute to Plato.

69. Williams comes close to accepting this when he later adopts the "predominant section rule" which I shall discuss below.

70. "Analogy," this volume, pp. 52–53.

71. Since we have substituted (a''') for (a'), there is no longer reason to believe that everyone in a just polis is just. We therefore look at the psyche of an appetitive-type person.

72. VIII.558D–559C.

73. VIII.554B–E.

74. IV.421C.

75. Cp. IX.576C–D.

76. Essentially the same problem occurs in Freud's discussion of the id. Freud often describes the id as not listening to reason. But he is so describing it in the context of trying to make clear the dynamic structure of neurotic pathology. There is another conception of the id, manifest in his dictum "Where it was there I shall become", which allows the possibility of the appetites harkening to reason. See my *Love and Its Place in Nature,* chapter 6.

77. Of course, there is truth in the claim that money is a means to satisfy bodily appetites (IX.580E–581A), but that is not the whole truth. The oligarchic man, for example, is not using money just as a means to satisfy his bodily appetites: indeed, he keeps these appetites under control precisely because he has developed an appetite for money and property (VIII.553C–554C).

78. IX.580D–581E; cp. VIII.553C–554E.

79. In fact the variation can be much more fine-grained than I have indicated. See the explication by C.D.C. Reeve in *Philosopher-Kings* (Princeton: Princeton University Press, 1988, pp. 5–9, 135–153), a book which I found inspiring and to which I am indebted. I am here both trying to use that account and to show how much it depends on internalization as a basic psychological activity. See also John Cooper in "Plato's Theory of Human Motivation", *History of Philosophy Quarterly* 1, 1984; and Richard Kraut's account of normative rule in "Reason and Justice in Plato's *Republic*", *Exegesis and Argument,* op. cit.

80. IX.581.

81. IV.431D–E.

82. IX.581C–D.

83. IV.431D–E, 433C–D.

84. IV.433E–434A. See Reeve, *Philosopher-Kings* (pp. 246–247).

85. IV.431E–432A.

86. IX.581C–D.

87. IV.429B–430A.

88. IV.429C.

89. Plato, as we have seen, believes a change in musical modes will ultimately upset constitutional laws: it is precisely because lawlessness is internalized with the music that it is subsequently externalized in attacks on established business relations, on the laws and the constitution (IV.424C–E). I shall discuss this further in section 4.

90. VIII.558–562.

91. VIII.554B–555B.

92. VIII.554D.

93. Roughly speaking because, as we have seen, Plato's conception of forcible restraint is not identical to Freud's conception of repression. Yet Plato believes of forcible restraint, as Freud believed of repression, that it is an ultimately unsuccessful means of warding off unwanted desires.

94. VIII.556B–C.

95. VIII.559D.

96. VIII.555C–E.

97. VIII.557A.

98. VIII.559E.

99. VIII.560. Plato's account of faction vs. counterfaction struggling within the psyche bears some similarity to Freud's account of cathexis and countercathexis in a neurotic struggle—although there is no evidence that Plato thought this intrapsychic and interpsychic struggle was unconscious. (Cp. e.g. "Further Remarks on the Neuro-Psychoses of Defense", III:169–170).

100. VIII.560B–C.

101. VIII.557Cff. Quoted by Williams, "Analogy," this volume, p. 54.

102. VIII.561Dff.

103. "Analogy," this volume, p. 54. Note that by now Williams has put in place of the whole-part rule, another which he calls the *predominant section rule*: A city is F if and only if the leading, most influential or predominant citizens are F.

104. VIII.557B–558A.

105. Plato does make an exception for those who have been divinely inspired: e.g. VI.492A, 496C–497A, 499B–C.

106. "Analogy," this volume, p. 57.

107. I suspect that Williams' formal objections to the analogy are fueled by a democrat's suspicion of Plato's conservative political theory: in particular by what he takes to be an ultimately repressive relation between ruling class and ruled. From a democratic perspective the means and organization of society ought to be transparent to all, while Plato advocates feeding the appetitive class a diet of noble falsehoods. It is, of course, beyond the scope of this paper to respond to this type of objection. But I would like to note in passing: (1) Such an objection does not itself constitute an objection to the idea of an isomorphism between polis and psyche. (2) Plato himself issues a challenge to the idea of transparency. One of the motivations for the 'noble falsehood' is that one cannot just assume that, say, the freedom of information act guarantees freedom of information: one has to take into account what the subjective meaning of this (external) information will be. And once one does so, Plato thinks, one can only get this information across if one presents it in certain mythic forms which, strictly speaking, are not true. Each side will think the other is restricting information, one because of the alteration in form, the other because the idea of subjective understanding is being ignored.

108. The phrase is from Thomas Mann's description of psychoanalysis. See "Freud and the Future", *Freud, Goethe, Wagner* (New York: Knopf, 1937).

109. See e.g. VI.497A–B, 496C–D, 488A–489B, 499B–C.

110. Virtue or excellence, Plato says, is a certain sort of health (IV.444D).

111. In a sense Plato has again to recapitulate the poet, only at a philosophical level. Socrates must tell a tale in which the just man is stripped of all the outer trappings and the glittering prizes—which from a conventional perspective are all the rewards there are—are given to the unjust man (II.360E–361D). This, in effect, is what the poets have already done (362E–366A). They have shaped a culture which values only the appearance of justice. By showing that it is nevertheless better to be just, Plato is doing more than showing that justice will triumph even in the worst possible dialectical circumstances. He is trying to show that it will triumph in (what he took to be) the actual situation. From Plato's perspective, his argument has to take this shape if it is to be persuasive, for the worst-case scenario is the way things are. Plato thus starts out with poetic appearance in order to work through to a (non-poetical) conclusion which penetrates beyond surface appearances.

112. So for any pathological structure F*, one should not expect that an F* polis is an immediate and simple externalization of F* citizens. Nor should one think that F* citizens are shaped by a simple internalization of the structure of the F* polis. The whole point of F* being pathological is that no such simple mirroring relation can occur. So, for example, the democratic polis is shaped not only by the degenerate son of oligarchy, but also by the rebellious poor (556C–557A). However, the rebellious poor also had their psyches shaped via internalizations of previous externalizations of the oligarchical rulers. And both they and democratic man—the metaphorical and literal sons of oligarchy— help to shape the democratic polis via externalization of structures in their psyches.

113. And this is built up by what Plato calls a "circle of growth", which seems to be the opposite of the tale of degeneration: "a sound nurture and education if kept up creates good natures in the state, and sound natures in turn receiving an education of this sort develop into better persons than their predecessors . . ." IV.424A–B. Although, of course, Plato thinks that even the ideal polis is subject to eventual decay: VIII.546A–547A.

114. IV.441D–E. See e.g. V.462C–D, 463E, 464A.

115. And thus I think the psychological principles of internalization and externalization can help us to address a long-standing interpretive problem: why did Plato think there was a relation between justice as a condition of the psyche—psychic justice—and conventionally recognized justice? (See e.g. Gregory Vlastos, "Justice and Happiness in Plato's Republic", *Platonic Studies* (Princeton: Princeton University Press, 1981); David Sachs, "A Fallacy in Plato's *Republic*", *Philosophical Review* 72, 1963; Terence Irwin, *Plato's Moral Theory*, (op. cit., pp. 205–206, 331). I address this problem in "Plato's Politics of Narcissism", which I presented at the memorial conference for Gregory Vlastos in May, 1992 and which will appear in a volume dedicated to his memory.

116. In fact, Plato never uses the word "analogy" (ἀναλογία) to describe the relation between polis and psyche, though he is sometimes translated as though he did. See e.g. Paul Shorey's translation of II.368E in the Loeb edition of *The Republic* (Cambridge, MA: Harvard University Press, 1982).

117. The contradictory arguments of Book I bear a significant resemblance to the problems which Plato says are provocative of thought (VII.523–4).

118. III.411; cp. e.g. 395C–D, 401B–D, 413C.

119. III.393B–D.

120. See e.g. Ferrari, "Plato and Poetry", esp. §§1,4.

121. X.605.

122. III.395C–396E, 378D, 398A–B, 401B–402A; X.605–606.

123. X.605B–C.

124. X.598B: *phantasma,* cp. 599A. In fact, Plato says that imitation gives us a fantasy of a fantasy—a second-order fantasy, but this depends on his metaphysical conception of ordinary empirical objects themselves being removed from reality. There are, obviously, important metaphysical objections to tragic poetry and art, but in this paper I am restricting my focus to the primarily psychological objections.

125. X.603A, 605A–B.

126. X.603A–B; cp. 605A–B.

127. X.601B, 602D–603B.

128. X.604–605.

129. E.g. X.604B; cp. 603D.

130. See e.g. VII.523.

131. X.604E–605D.

132. X.602B.

133. X.606B.

134. VII.559E–560. See above, pp. 76–78.

135. II.373B.

136. II.373D–E.

137. III.399E. The purgation is supposed to have occurred as an unconscious byproduct of banishing the poets.

138. III.400D–E.

139. X.604D, 605B, 605E–606B.

140. II.377E–378D. (Should the reader also be interested in the work of Melanie Klein, and wonder what she meant by "part objects", the Homeric gods of which Plato complains are, I think, paradigms.)

141. IX.571B–D.

142. IX.572B.

143. IX.573D; cp. 573B.

144. Compare Freud on the omnipotence of archaic mind: e.g. *Totem and Taboo,* XIII:83–91, 186, 188; "The Uncanny", XVII:240–244.

145. II.378B–C.

146. IX.565D–566B.

147. VIII.568A–B.

148. II.377E.

149. Freud noticed that the superego often speaks with an iddish accent: it tends to take on a harsh, vindictive tone that testifies to some sort of commerce with the id. (See e.g. *The Ego and the Id,* XIX:36, 48–49, 52; "Neurosis and Psychosis", XIX:151–152; *Inhibitions, Symptoms and Anxiety,* XX:115–116.) This was puzzling both because the superego's function is to help keep

the id in place and because it is unclear how this commerce takes place. Plato in fact provides a satisfying explanation of how commerce between id and superego can occur via commerce between inside and outside. This is superior to simply saying that the superego becomes fused with aggression, because it explains how this fusion comes about.

150. II.378D–E.

151. III.412E–413B; II.382.

152. II.382.

153. II.382A–B.

154. E.g. II.382B: Often translated as "veritable lie" or "truthful lie".

155. IX.572C–573C.

156. IX.574A–C; VIII.569B.

157. VIII.567B–C.

158. VIII.567C.

159. II.378B–C.

160. VIII.566A–B.

161. VIII.568B.

162. VIII.557B.

163. IX.577A.

164. IX.577C–E;575A.

165. IX.571C.

166. VIII.569B.

167. IX.577–579.

168. This, I think, provides one of the deeper reasons why Book X comes where it does. It is not just that it has to follow the entire psychology and metaphysics of the *Republic* but that it has to follow Book IX.

169. Nor has the theory of technique. See e.g. Paul Gray, " 'Developmental Lag' in the Evolution of Technique of Psychoanalysis of Neurotic Conflict", *Journal of the American Psychoanalytical Association,* 1982.

170. Drafts of portions of this paper have been given at philosophy colloquia at The University of California, Berkeley; Cornell University, Holy Cross, The University of Colorado, Boulder, and the Legal Theory Workshop at the Yale Law School. I should like to thank the participants for their searching comments. I would also like to thank to Rudiger Bittner, Myles Burnyeat, John Dunn, Christopher Dustin, Cynthia Farrar, John Ferrari, Gail Fine, Raymond Geuss, Terence Irwin, Malcolm Schofield, David Sedley, Timothy Smiley, all of whom read drafts of this paper and offered astute and helpful comments. I am indebted to the National Endowment for the Humanities for a stipend which facilitated the research for and preparation of this paper.

# 6

# The Philosopher and the Female in the Political Thought of Plato

*Arlene W. Saxonhouse*

At the beginning of the fifth book of Plato's *Republic* Socrates offers his radical proposals for the inclusion of women in the guardian class of his just city. The women are to train and exercise with the men as they prepare to become warriors to protect the city. They are to eat and live communally with the men, and when the philosopher-rulers are introduced women are allowed to enter their exalted rank. Though some have accepted the sincerity of Plato's attempts to rescue the female from her low status and sheltered life during the fourth century B.C. in Athens,[1] there are enough questions raised within Book V itself and elsewhere in the dialogue to make us doubt the seriousness of these proposals. While Socrates allows women to enter the ruling class, he affirms that they will always be weaker than men (455e; 456a; 457a).[2] While he argues that they are not by nature necessarily different from men, he calls the plundering of a corpse the work of a small and "womanish" mind (469d). As the discussion proceeds, the presence of women in the guardian class is sometimes forgotten (460ab; 465ab; 467)[3] or Glaucon, hesitant to include them in the army (471d), must be reminded of the participation to which he had agreed earlier (540c). Elsewhere in the dialogue the critical remarks about women are more forthright: they succumb easily to grief while men remain strong (388a; 605e); they are like children in their enjoyment of the multifarious and the multicolored (431c; 557c); they bring about the degeneration of various political systems described in Book VIII. In Book V there is talk of equal participation in the governance of the city, common meals, and common education; yet in Book VIII it is equality and freedom between the sexes that characterize the city degenerating into anarchy and tyranny (563b). Socrates's famous proposals must be read with an awareness of these qualifications.

Since I cannot accept the view that Socrates wishes to emancipate the Athenian woman, I would like in this essay to raise the issue of how and why the female is introduced into Book V. As Socrates attempts to turn women into men by making them equal participants in the political community, he ignores the peculiar natures of each and thus undermines the perfection of the political society in the *Republic*. I shall be concerned with the appearance of women in the *Republic* as they go from courtesans in the early books to the de-sexed and unnatural females of Book V, and once again to the sexual female in Book VI—after eros has been reintroduced into the dialogue with the appearance of the philosopher. We can, I shall argue, gain from an understanding of this development an insight into the Platonic perception of the relationship between politics and philosophy, and how each, like the male and female, is to be allowed to preserve its independent nature. The opposition between women and men becomes a model for the opposition between philosophy and politics; the attempt to equalize both sets of opposites destroys all.

### I. *Republic* V: The Female De-sexed

The women who enter the rank of the guardian class in Book V of the *Republic* are almost without body and, more important, free from eros. They are neither the desired nor the desiring. It is these women whom I shall call the "de-sexed" females. Before they make their appearance in Book V, however, there is much to prepare us and Socrates's companions for their arrival. The abstraction from the biological body is part of a continuing theme from the beginning of Book I. There the old Cephalus, in whose house the dialogue takes place, talks for a short while with Socrates. During the discussion women first appear; though Cephalus found them desirable once, his body now is weak and he no longer needs or responds to them. He describes his current condition with a quote from Sophocles who, when asked how at ninety he was faring with regard to the sexual passion, replied: "Most happily I escaped it, as if fleeing a raging and wild master" (329c). Cephalus thus signifies the death of sexual eros and the deadening of the bodily desires that had been so strong in his youth. Though the old man leaves the scene, he has bequeathed his abstraction from the physical body to the remaining group, who in turn must go through a whole evening of discourse without the dinner that was promised.

The training which is given to the warrior class of the just city reinforces this abstraction. The warrior class emerges because Glaucon has been dissatisfied with the true city, or the city of pigs as he calls it (372d). He wants relishes (among which are women who had not appeared in the earlier city). However, to protect these relishes and acquire more, a warrior class must be established, a class that itself must be purged of all the desires for delights. Their education is first presented as "gymnastics for the body and *mousike* for the soul" (376e). The former, though, is entirely forgotten except for a short passage buried in Book III in which the details of the gymnastic education are left to the well-trained mind (403d). Rather, *mousike* that dominates the warrior's education works to eliminate all concern with the body and to purge the young men of any strong physical desires for food, drink, or sex. The discussion of gymnastics is replaced with admonitions against all forms of excessive bodily passions. Even doctors who tend to the needs of the body are expelled from the city and the sick are left to die (405a–410a).

Prior to Book V, the women who do appear are the ones who excite men's erotic passions and are therefore in opposition to the process of abstraction from body that characterizes the founding of the just city. Cephalus focuses specifically on the sexual desire for women in his discussion of old age. When Glaucon gives his speech extolling the benefits of injustice, he refers to the queen of Lydia who is seduced by Gyges during his rise to power (360b).[4] In Glaucon's fevered city, women appear as courtesans right in the midst of an enumeration of delights including seasonings, perfumes, incense, and cakes (373a), as needing womanly dress or ornaments (373b), or as wet nurses (373c). In Book III, as the educational program for the warriors is developed, Syracusan tables (i.e., feasts), Sicilian relishes, and Corinthian maidens who serve as mistresses must be removed from the experiences of the youth (404cd). And it is noted later that members of the warrior class, having been deprived of all personal wealth, will be unable to make gifts to their mistresses (420a). Women, far from participating in the political structure in the early books,[5] are presented as the provokers of the sexual eros, which must be restrained among the guardians as well as among the founders of the just city. The one reference to the female as a member of this city before Book V has to do with "the [common] possession of women, marriages and the procreation of children" (423e), not with their participation in the affairs of the city, much less equal participation.

Thus, it is with much hesitation, as one who might "be an unwilling murderer of someone" (451a), that Socrates suddenly introduces the female as the equal of the male among all species, canine or human. In order to establish this equation Socrates must disregard his earlier portrait; he must de-sex the female, make her void of any special erotic attraction or function. In so doing he must disregard the principle that had guided his original search for justice, namely the principle of nature or *phusis* that dominated the founding of the first city and the subsequent definition of justice. Socrates's use of the concept of *phusis* is different from his Sophistic contemporaries who focused on the distinction between nature *(phusis)* and convention *(nomos)* and the inhibitions which the *nomoi* imposed on the pursuit of power and pleasure.[6] The Socratic definition of *phusis* has nothing to do with power or pleasure; it has to do with virtue *(arete)*. *Arete* is the excellence of a thing—a shoe or a man. *Arete,* in Plato, is no longer the exclusive property of the courageous warrior who fights nobly before the Trojan walls. Rather, one's excellence or potential for *arete* is defined by one's *phusis,* one's natural capabilities. A person's *phusis* is what that person does well or better than anyone else. The man naturally *(phusei)* fit to build houses is the man who builds the best houses most efficiently. If he builds them well according to his abilities he possesses *arete*. This interpretation of *phusis* and *arete* leads directly to a theory of specialization, to the performance by each person or thing of that for which he/she/it is most suited.

The definition of justice which Socrates discovers in Book IV is based on this ideal of specialization as each part of the polis (or the soul) performs that function for which it is most suited. The first city in Book II had originated through a process of specialization as each member performed the function for which he was suited by nature. "Each one of us grows *(phuetai)* not entirely similar to another, but differing in nature *(kata phusin),* each one fitted for a separate task" (370ab). As the city grows out of an agrarian community into a commercial society with expansion of trades and occupations, it does not turn into a city of convention such as we with our modern notions of a "return to nature" might imagine; as long as the specialization of function according to ability continues, this city is according to nature.

When Socrates begins to discuss the role of woman as potentially man's equal in his best city, he indicates the apparent contradiction that his earlier use of *phusis* based on specialization presents for his proposals. He puts the argument in the words of a fictitious opponent:

> Is it the case then that a woman does not differ very much from a man with regard to their nature *(phusis)?*

> How does she not differ?

> Then is it not fitting to assign a different task according to his/her nature? [453bc]

Socrates makes his apology by suggesting that men and women differ only as much as bald men differ from those with long hair, i.e., superficially and not with regard to their natures. Disregarding the sexual qualities of the female, he concentrates only on physical strength and notes that since women are weaker than men they will be given lighter tasks. However, while Socrates does give women this opportunity to participate in the protection of the city with man and recognizes only insignificant differences, he goes on to argue that there is no area except such ridiculous ones as weaving or cooking in which the male is not superior to the female (455cd). This is patently absurd, for Socrates, ignoring the sexual female, also ignores the peculiar biological qualities that women, and women alone, have. Clearly the female is superior to the male of any species in her ability to bear children; even those women least skillful in this task do it better than any man—except perhaps for Zeus. If one's *phusis* is defined by that which one does better than anyone else, then Socrates has disregarded the *phusis* of the female.

Socrates does acknowledge that "the female bears, while the male covers" (454de), but rather than consider the implications of this distinction he chooses to undermine it. Motherhood after birth is reduced to the bare minimum of nursing some child at appointed times. As Glaucon refers to it: "You describe an exceedingly easy child bearing for women guardians" (460d). This minimizing of the female's reproductive role is what makes women in Socrates's city not only weaker but ultimately also inferior to men. "There is no pursuit," he says to Glaucon, "concerning the governance of the city which belongs particularly to a woman" (455b). Her natural role in the preservation of the city through the procreation of the next generation is left unconsidered. By forcing her to participate in the activities of the male warriors and later philosopher rulers, Socrates removes from woman her individual *phusis*—that particular speciality in which she excels. Woman's sexual, bodily nature is forgotten and she becomes almost irrelevant in Socrates's best city.

Body or biological attributes apparently do not determine the *phusis* of the guardians; rather, it is the skill or *techne* which they have. "We said that the souls of a man and a woman who are skilled in medicine have the same nature" (454d). On the other hand, a doctor, male or female, has a nature different from a carpenter, male or female. This argument is surrounded by laughter (452a–d) and must be seen as comic in intent. One's ability to be proficient in any craft is dependent upon the use of one's body, with the notable exception of philosophy.[7] What craft one executes well cannot be dissociated from one's bodily abilities. As the first city grows in Book II, the artisans perform those tasks for which they are suited, but all of the tasks described require the full use of their bodies—housebuilding, weaving, sailing, farming, and so on. The men engaged in the lowly profession of trade (which cannot be called a craft) are those who are "weakest in body and useless for doing any other work" (371c). The female body as the bearer of children cannot be dissociated from her *phusis* by Socrates. Likewise, the body cannot be removed from the particular *techne* under discussion in Book V: warfare.

The importance of the body for warfare appears when the participation of women in the warrior class is discussed, particularly in terms of gymnastics. In the earlier books when the training of the warriors was under consideration and there was an attempt to abstract from body, gymnastics was left to the well-trained mind. Suddenly, in Book V in the sexually integrated group, the training of warriors focuses not on *mousike,* which one might expect would have greater appeal to the feminine, but on the exercise of the body. Once it has been purged of its pertinent biological characteristics and once its needs have been severely circumscribed, the body may be readmitted to the city. It is a body that is to be primed for war, not a body that responds to stimuli— whether food or sex. Women and men exercise in the palestra, naked next to each other; this causes neither laughter nor shame since both sexes are insensitive to the erotic qualities of their bodies and the desire for procreation.

After Socrates has purged the sexual desire so effectively in his equalizing of the male and female, he is confronted with the problem of reinstituting it in order to preserve his city through procreation. Women cannot bear children without attention to the biological aspects of their bodies and without yielding to the sexual eros. Socrates admits that men and women who are together all the time and in all circumstances

> will be drawn by an inner natural necessity to mixing with one another. Or do I seem to you to talk of needs?

> Not geometrical, he [Glaucon] said, but erotic needs, which may happen to be the sharpest of those for convincing and drawing the mass of common men. [458d]

The discussion in Book V prior to this point had been carried on as if there were only such "geometrical" needs, and indeed continues in this fashion; for Socrates disregards the bulk of the population and treats breeding among his warriors as if they were dogs or show birds. In fact, it is precisely an error in the mathematics of the breeding process that leads to the downfall of the best city (546b–d). The erotic necessities are to be circumscribed by what is most beneficial (for appearances' sake translated into what is most sacred, 458e). There is to be no mixing in a "disorderly manner" *(ataktos)* (458d). The image is that of a disorganized army; procreation is to be practiced with the same precision that warfare demands.

Socrates relies on a certain residual drive to surface only at precisely defined moments. These opportunities for intercourse may come as the result of a "sacred marriage" or as a prize for valor in war (460b). The sharing of a woman's bed as a reward for bravery does not mean that the warriors of Book V are driven during battle by a sexual eros. The laurel leaf was not of value in and of itself. The opportunity to sleep with a woman would represent such an honor and therefore be desirable for men who are driven on by spirit *(thumos);* the female prize, though, has social benefits in terms of reproducing the best warriors, which the laurel leaf does not. The sexual passion then reenters the city under the guise of the sacred and the honorable, but only to the extent that it serves the needs of the city.

The question must now arise as to why Socrates (or Plato) suddenly introduced women, de-sexed them, and put them on the same level as men. Why discuss them at all? Why not leave them as mistresses forsaken by the well-trained warrior class? Allan Bloom in his interpretive essay on the *Republic* argues first that men need women and that unless the women are also properly trained they will destroy the men whom the city has so carefully educated.[8] Second, he suggests that the male qualities developed in the education for battle must be tempered by female gentleness, that "humanity is a discreet mixture of masculinity and femininity."[9] Bloom then argues that feminine qualities cannot be forgotten as we are about to leave the warrior guardians, with their particularly male attributes, and encounter the philosopher guardians. The philosopher needs the gentleness of a woman, and must, like the woman of Socrates's city, strip himself bare of all conventions before he can function.[10] In this analysis, however, Bloom is overlooking the distortion which is perpetrated on the female in order to bring her into the political community and the significance that this distortion may have.

The sudden introduction of the de-sexed female must be studied within the context of Book V, the book in which the philosopher ruler makes his/her first appearance. However, we must note that the female is introduced into political life—which is historically, at least, alien to her—only through a perversion of her *phusis* or nature. In order to become political, she must sacrifice her role as the female of the species. When Aristophanes introduced women into the political arena in both the *Lysistrata* and the *Ecclesiazusae,* he did not remove from them their femininity or their sexuality. It is precisely their sexuality that is the motive cause in both plays, and it is their love of family life that gives the *Lysistrata* its central theme.[11] As far as we know, other literature of the time did not cast women into a political role. Rather, as Thucydides writes in Pericles's funeral oration, women were to bear children as a security to the state and, while doing this, to be unseen and unheard.[12] Socrates rejects this portrayal of women in Book V and goes even further to reject his own definition of nature. The female does not engage in politics in order to satisfy the female eros and *phusis* as Lysistrata and Praxagora do. Rather, she is destroyed as woman in order to participate. This is only preparatory to Socrates's perversion of philosophy. For just as woman is "de-natured," treated without regard for that in which she can excel, in order to be made part of the political world, so too is philosophy. To Socrates, try as he might to create the natural city where each individual performs according to his/her natural capabilities (whether it be the bearing of children or the making of shoes), politics can only be a perversion of what is natural;

*[margin handwritten note: if political life is going to be destructive to their nature, women shouldn't be in politics]*

for it turns some men and all women away not from the pleasure and power of the Sophists but from the pursuit of excellence.

The relationship of philosophy to politics parallels that of women to politics. Neither one naturally participates in politics, and in both cases the needs of politics distort the needs of the individual. While the female is brought into politics through a disregard for her body, the philosopher enters politics through a disregard for his soul. The absurdity of a naked old woman practicing gymnastics is matched by the absurdity of a philosopher ruling over a city. Socrates recognizes this as he dreads the tidal wave of laughter that threatens him just before he offers his famous proposals (473c). Glaucon's reaction is filled with warnings of the indignation that men "who are not foolish" will feel (474a). As the imagery of the cave is developed in Book VII, it becomes clear that it is not only the city that does not want philosophy but also the philosopher who does not want to be involved in the affairs of the city. The compulsion that fills this section of the dialogue is necessary because the philosopher does not by nature move to the world of politics. The philosopher hates the lie (485cd; 490bc), and yet as political leader he must lie (414c; 459c). Socrates in founding his just city is unjust to philosophers, whose souls are oriented away from the political world of opinion and toward the world of being.

In order to create the best city, Socrates must do the worst to philosophers; he must make them live worse lives, *cheiron zein* (519d). The injustice which Socrates does to the female at the beginning of Book V is a forewarning of the injustice that politics imposes on the philosopher himself. In other Platonic dialogues, women usually appear as an inferior form of human being (*Phaedo* 60a; *Timaeus* 90e). Socrates tells us in the *Republic* that as the political community may by its demands destroy even the lowest human natures (women), so too it may destroy the highest natures. For Socrates the human animal does not find fulfillment of his *phusis* through politics. Women and philosophers fit awkwardly into the political world, even the one which aims to be most just. Their *phuseis* are opposed to it, and it in turn makes unjust demands upon them.

## II. *Republic* VI: The Sexual Female

The equation between the female and the philosopher, which occurs in Book V of the *Republic,* is carried on to Book VI. Here, however,

Socrates is attempting to develop the characteristics of philosophy without the encumbrances that political life imposes. Consequently neither woman nor philosophy is perverted by her/its relationship to politics, and both regain their true *phuseis*. While the philosopher is allowed to pursue reality freed from the demands of the political community, the female regains her body, her reproductive capabilities, and her sexuality. In so doing she becomes a symbol of the vital pursuit of wisdom. Up through Book V, eros had been persistently eliminated from the discussion. Immediately after the introduction of the philosopher in Book V, words having to do with eros and desire begin to predominate. The philosopher is first compared to a lover of young boys, an erotic man who loves young men whether they have snub noses or long ones, and then to wine-lovers, to lovers of honor, and to lovers of food (474d–475c). With the emergence of the philosopher, the erotic and bodily passions are introduced into the purged city.

The eroticism of the philosopher is most fully developed in the sixth book, the book devoted to the discovery of the nature of the philosopher. It is here that the object of philosophy and the process of philosophy itself are described in feminine terms. The paedophile of the previous book is left behind; consummation there leads to no birth. As the male erotically desires the female, the true lover of learning is similarly portrayed at one point as desiring what is *(to on)*:

> He naturally struggles to obtain what is, and not tarrying by the many particulars which are thought to be, but he goes and is not dulled nor does he cease from his love until he has laid hold of the nature of each thing itself which is with the part of the soul that is suitable to seize hold of such a thing. It is suitable for that which is akin to it. Being near to it and joining together with what really is, having begotten mind and truth, he both knows and lives truly and is nourished and thus ceases from the pangs of labor, but not before. [490ab]

The language in this passage is explicitly sexual *(migeis, gennesas,* and *odinos)* and bears a close relationship to language and imagery found in the *Theaetetus*. In that dialogue Socrates frequently portrays himself as a midwife to philosophical ideas (e.g., 150b–151c; 157c; 161e; 210c). This analogy gives Socrates frequent cause to describe the philosophical process in terms of labor and birth, images which constantly call to mind the biological function of women (156a; 160e; 210b). Though most of the fetuses which Socrates brings forth turn out to be wind eggs, the relationship between the intellectual and bodily process of labor and birth ties Socrates and his activities to biological woman.

While the philosophic process is portrayed as resembling the sexual experience of woman from being desired to giving birth, philosophy itself in the *Republic* is also portrayed as a woman with the erotic qualities of the sexual female. At one point, philosophy is the deserted female, left unfulfilled by those who live neither appropriate nor true lives: "Others, unworthy, come to her, as one bereft of relatives, and defile her" (495c). Or philosophy is compared to the daughter of a lowly craftsman about to be married to the unworthy but recently wealthy employee of her father (495e). Socrates is concerned with the quality of the offspring of such a poor match: "What sort of things are such men likely to engender? Will they not be bastards and undistinguished?" (496a). They parallel the offspring of those men who are incapable of philosophy and yet attach themselves to her. "Whenever those who have been inappropriately educated come to her and consort with her not according to what is appropriate, what sort of thoughts and opinions shall we say they engender?" (496a)—again the language is of birth. Though the female may be deserted or married to someone who does not deserve her, she nevertheless preserves her feminine function and is defined explicitly by her biological attributes. Philosophy, too, is allowed to be itself and is not, at least in Book VI, forced into the service to the political community. Once this freedom is achieved, Socrates can begin the ascent to the good. Meanwhile, women submit to marriages arranged by their money-conscious fathers and bear children.

In Book VII the philosopher is once again perverted and forced to engage in politics. This brings on a new round of laughter (516e; 517d; 518ab), reminding us of the beginning of Book V. Then it was the naked women in the palaestras; now it is the philosopher returning to the world of the cave who is subjected to ridicule. The situation is the same; in each case the natural is perverted, and an injustice is done to the individual. Laughter arises at the sight of the absurd or fantastical—birds founding a city, women stopping a war, or a philosopher entering the world of politics. In Book VI there is little laughter;[13] *phusis* is permitted to fulfill itself, as both the philosopher and the female do that for which they are most suited. Eros has returned.

### III. Philosophy and the Female

Once the equation between the philosopher and the female has been suggested, the question arises as to why Socrates (Plato) introduces it and what he means to tell us about the philosophic pursuit through it. Bloom is again one of the few commentators to deal with this particular question. Considering the dramatic structure of the dialogue, he argues that the sexual metaphors will appeal particularly to Glaucon, the erotic young interlocutor,[14] though the sexual imagery that appeals to him is mostly concerned with pederasty (474de; 485c). Bloom argues further that the male, the *aner,* with his qualities of courage and strength, represents only half of humanity. Philosophy needs the feminine qualities like gentleness as well.[15] I believe that the significance of this analogy can be carried somewhat further.

Philosophers in the Platonic corpus and women in the Greek tradition are private individuals. They belong to the world of the *idios,* not to the community or the *koinon.* While women may stay in seclusion inside their homes, the philosopher must insulate himself not from the activity of the agora, but from the opinions of the city. He must remain independent of the demands that the city makes upon his intellect. To be a member of the city, a *polites,* one must sacrifice one's private knowledge and accept the views demanded by the city. This is something the philosopher cannot do. He must ask his questions without regard for the political consequences or the political needs of the community; women likewise perform their functions privately, irrespective of the political circumstances. Women bear children whether they live in Sparta, Thebes, or Troy. Their nature traditionally has removed them from politics. True philosophers pursue the good whether they live in Sparta or Thebes. But political man behaves quite differently wherever he may live. The female and the philosopher live apart from the political world. They both satisfy their erotic desires independently of the needs or demands of the city, though they both may need the security that the city offers.

The philosopher like Socrates may become dangerous, but more often, again like the woman, he is simply useless for the actual practice of politics. When Adeimantus specifically accuses the philosopher of being useless (487d), he recalls the words of Pericles who is made to say by Thucydides: "We alone think of one who does not participate in [public] affairs not as a quiet man, but as a useless one" (II.40.2). The Greek political community had no place for the *idios.* Thus, the tensions that surround the introduction of the female into political life are the same as those that surround the introduction of the philosopher. Both naturally belong to the world of the private. Yet the aim of Book V in which both enter political society is to make public all that previously had been private—from sexual intercourse to a hurt finger (462c).[16] In the process of becoming politicized the female and the philosopher are removed from their natural environments.

Pericles's oration is spoken for those who died in battle for the city. For Pericles the fulfillment of one's role as a member of the city is achieved through death for the city—the ultimate expression of the unity of the self and the political community. Participation in public affairs is defined in terms of war with other cities. It is precisely during war that the skills of women and philosophers are irrelevant. Yet it is war that is the theme particular to Book V.[17] War was a highly masculine affair in Greece. The word commending bravery in battle specifically denotes its masculine orientation *(andreia* from *aner)*. At no point, especially in fifth- and fourth-century Athens, could political activity be isolated from relations with other cities and the potential for war. Politics was inherently a masculine pursuit. Yet women guardians are obviously to be trained for war (452c; 453a; 457a). When Glaucon discusses their actual participation in a battle, qualifications to the original proposals for equality appear. After describing an army composed of "brothers, fathers, and sons," he adds the note: "And if the female part should join the campaign, stationed either in the line itself or behind in order to frighten off the enemies if ever there would be any necessity for aid, I know that with all these things they would be unbeatable" (471d). Glaucon still seems hesitant to accord women full equality in war. Even Socrates apparently undercuts his own arguments when he offers as a prize for valor in battle "more frequent opportunity to share the bed of women," as a means to increase the offspring of brave warriors (460b). The philosopher in battle does not appear in the *Republic,* but we do find him in Alcibiades's speech in the *Symposium.* Alcibiades reports Socrates's unshakeable countenance during battle, but he also makes the philosopher appear ridiculous. He uses a quote from Aristophanes to describe Socrates's stride during the retreat from Delium. The language of the comic poet underlines the absurdity of a philosopher engaging in war.

Though both the philosopher and women are cast uncomfortably into a political community that concentrates on war, there is a sudden shift in the discussion in Book V to the manner in which the best city will carry on war. With absolutely no warning, we are jolted away from the question of the possibility of the best city to a discussion which seems completely alien to the topic at hand.

> Is it not now left, I said, to go through whether it is possible among men as among the other animals, that there come into being such a community and in what way it is possible?
>
> You were the first to mention, he [Glaucon] said, what I intended to raise.
>
> About the affairs during war, I think it is obvious, I said, in what manner they will carry on war. [466de]

With this we are launched into several pages of how and whom the warriors shall fight. I would suggest that this sudden change in topic intrudes at this point to highlight the position of both women and philosophers as poor citizens in a city which needs to do battle against its enemies.[18]

The analogy presented in the *Politicus* between the art of statesmanship and the art of weaving (279b) creates some difficulty in the parallel opposition of both female and philosopher to the masculine art of politics. Weaving is a woman's craft that is practiced privately at home. Penelope, our most famous weaver, used the craft as an excuse to escape from involvement in the politics of Ithaca. Weaving is one of the two crafts, specifically mentioned in the *Republic,* where women may have a superiority (455c). In the *Politicus,* though, the analogy is developed of the statesman who, like the weaver, oversees the handling of the wool before uniting the wool and warp into a strong cloak. However, the most important task of weaving together the courageous and temperate souls is ultimately achieved through control over matrimony—the proper breeding of disparate types. The task becomes a sexual one, one having specifically to do with reproduction, the arena for female activity. Politics in the *Politicus* is isolated from the masculine pursuit of war (305a) and is more nearly akin to philosophy (299bc). The true statesman in the *Politicus* is the philosopher, only here he is not forced down into the world of politics, his *phusis* is not perverted. Instead of interfering with the nature of the philosopher, political communities in the *Politicus* are guided by depersonalized laws, a second-best but nevertheless practical solution. Thus, the feminine analogy may still be appropriate. In fact, we learn at the beginning of the dialogue that in this particular discussion it is possible for a private individual *(idiotes)* to be the true statesman (259ab). This would hardly be possible in the highly communal life of the rulers of the *Republic*.

The role of women as private beings cloistered in the home is related to their role in the bearing and raising of children. The female is generative; she gives birth and represents the beginning, but not necessarily the completion, of a project. It is this generative role that purposefully is ignored in the fifth book of the *Republic*. By forcing woman into politics, Socrates turns her away from the generation of life to a concern with death—politics in the *Republic* being identified with war and consequently with death as well. From the first step of Socrates down into the Piraeus, politics is discussed within a framework of death. It is death in the thoughts of Cephalus that introduces us to the discussion of justice, and it is death that concludes the dialogue. Gyges, who is to change from a private shepherd into a king, begins his transformation into a political man through contact with a corpse on whose finger he finds his magic ring (359d). The warriors of the just state must be trained specifically not to fear death lest they refuse to participate in the activities of the political community, which, as Pericles so powerfully expresses it, demand death. Thus, all the poets at the beginning of Book III must be purged of references to death. The cave imagery further supports the equation of politics with death. The image of the deep, dark cavern into which the philosophers are forced to return recalls Hades in the Greek myths. In the beginning of Book III the passages which must be excised from the poets are those that describe the world of Hades as a cave with fluttering shadows (386d–387a).[19] When women enter the world of politics in Book V they must forget their life-generating functions, for politics in this dialogue is not a life-generating process. To involve the female in politics, she must be reoriented toward death.

In the Socratic dialogues the practice of philosophy is likewise generative and characterized not as the attainment of knowledge but as the pursuit of knowledge. In the *Theaetetus,* Socrates portrays himself as sterile, incapable of giving birth to any idea himself (150cd), but skilled at assisting in the birth of ideas. In the development of the *Theaetetus* no successful birth actually occurs, but in the process of trying to discover what knowledge is, the generative process is frequently described in terms of birth, and this tells us more about the complexities of the notion of knowledge than any specific definition might. While the body of the dialogue is devoted to an inquiry that replicates this process of birth, the *Theaetetus* is introduced with a brief conversation between Eucleides and Terpsion in which death and politics are once again united. Eucleides reports that he has just been with Theaetetus who was being carried away from battle, "living, but barely" (142b). The demands of politics force Theaetetus into battle for Athens and his involvement there leads to his death. It is the masculine activities of war that lead to his death; the feminine activities in which he engaged earlier with Socrates, and which are recorded in Eucleides's book, are related to life, birth, and generation. The short introduction to the *Theaetetus,* which may at first appear almost irrelevant to the subsequent dialogue, actually presents again the important contrast between the masculine/political world of death and the feminine/philosophical world of life.

The presentation of philosophy not as the completion but as the pursuit of knowledge is developed most vividly in the myth of the birth of Eros told by Diotima in the *Symposium.* She intends to equate eros and philosophy: both are described as the pursuit of the good (204b). It is the striving of both eros and philosophy that is important, not the final attainment. Once the good is attained, philosophy and eros cease. "No one of the gods philosophizes nor desires to be wise—for he is— and if anyone else is wise, he does not philosophize" (204a). Hans Kelson in his psychoanalytical study of Plato's sexual orientation finds in the story of the birth of Eros evidence of the hostility which Plato felt toward women. Poros, or Plenty, is the father of Eros, Penia or Need the mother. "The sex act," Kelso argues, "occurs only against the will of the man, everything good in its result comes from the father, everything bad from the mother."[20] While this is true in conventional terms, Eros would not be the philosopher without Penia as his mother. It is the mother who bequeaths to Eros those characteristics that make him so similar to Socrates: his squalor, his bare feet, his lack of bed, his hanging around gates and doors, and the like (203d). He is like his father in his manliness *(andreios)* and his eagerness and even in his "philosophizing throughout his life" (203d). But without the feminine qualities of incompletion and generation, Eros would not strive for the good or parallel the philosopher. In all the speeches prior to Socrates's in the *Symposium* (except for a moment in Phaedrus's speech, 179bc) heterosexual love is either forgotten or else mockingly scorned. Though later in Diotima's presentation, love of a female and the generation of a child puts one on the lower rungs of the ladder of love, Eros is born from such a heterosexual relationship—not a necessity among the gods—and it is only through those qualities inherited from Penia, from the necessity to create, that Eros and philosophy are united in their pursuit of the good.

If, then, we see philosophy as united with the female in its generative powers and in its privatism, a failure or refusal to participate in the public world of politics and war—the paradoxes suggested by the notion of a philosopher-ruler—becomes distressing. In the same way that masculinity is the opposite of femininity, so too is (masculine) politics the opposite of (feminine) philosophy—just as going up out of the cave is the opposite of going down into the cave. However, in both cases the opposites are in need of each other. Male needs female in order to preserve the species, or, in more particular terms, to give the city sons; female needs male in order to fulfill her nature as the bearer of children. The philosopher, as both the *Apology* and *Crito* so vividly demonstrate, needs the city, the organized political unit, for without the city the philosopher would have no place to practice. Though the relationship is more tenuous, the city needs the philosopher as well. In the *Apology*, Socrates likens the city to a noble horse, which "because of its size is sluggish and in need of being stirred on by a certain gadfly, so that, it seems to me, God has given me to the city, who sitting down everywhere and for the whole day does not cease stirring you up and persuading you and chiding you about everything" (30e).

The need which each opposite has for the other, though, emphasizes that they must not be equalized. The female with her particular characteristics must not be turned into a male. The philosopher similarly cannot be made into a politician. The attempt to do both of these things in Book V of the *Republic* leads to much laughter among the listeners and talkers, but more seriously it shows an attempt to destroy the natural or *phusis* in both categories. That Socrates must so pervert the natural in order to create the best political system must raise doubts about its value. The appearance of women in the *Republic* must not be seen as an instance of "anti-Platon chez Platon,"[21] nor as a remnant of a "real" Socrates who was close to being a feminist,[22] but rather as a means of casting an important and philosophically significant shadow over the whole enterprise of trying to create the perfect city. Perhaps the *Republic* tells us that politics is fundamentally imperfectable and must always be plagued by the conflicts between the public and the private, between opinion and wisdom, between warfare and weaving.

## Notes

I am greatly indebted to the thoughtful insights offered by Martha Meier Dean in her paper "On Women in the *Republic.*"

1. E.g., James Adam, *The Republic of Plato,* with critical notes, commentary, and appendices (Cambridge: At the University Press, 1902), Vol. 1, p. 280; Ernest Barker, *Greek Political Theory* (London and New York: University Paperbacks, 1960), p. 254; Benjamin Jowett, *The Dialogues of Plato,* trans. with analyses and intros. (New York: Scribner, 1871), Vol. II, pp. 129–130; H. D. Rankin, *Plato and the Individual* (London: Methuen, 1964), pp. 92–93; Dorothea Wender, "Plato: Misogynist, Paedophile, and Feminist," *Arethusa,* VI, 1 (Spring 1973), 76.

2. Standard Stephanus pagination will be used for all citations from the *Republic* and other Platonic dialogues.

3. In the first two instances Socrates uses the word *aner,* a specifically masculine word, to refer to the members of the auxiliary and guardians class. In 467c he refers only to fathers.

4. In Herodotus's story the queen does not have a passive role nor does she excite erotic passions; rather, upon secretly being seen naked by Gyges at the request of her husband, she instigates the overthrow and murder of the king, with threats to Gyges if he should not comply (I. 10–11).

5. Other references to women in Books I–IV show women to be weak, weepy, and unworthy of imitation (387e; 395de; 396a; 398e; and 431c).

6. See Antiphon, "On Truth," in Barker, *Greek Political Theory,* pp. 95-98; Callicles in Plato's *Gorgias;* and the Melian Dialogue in Thucydides, V., 85–112.

7. See Cephalus, 328d, and especially Theages, 496bc, whose care of a sickly body kept him from politics. Leo Strauss argues that this abstraction is necessary in order to "understand the city as an association of artisans or in order to effect as complete a coincidence as possible between the city and the arts" (*The City and Man* [Chicago: Rand McNally, 1964], p. 95).

8. Allan Bloom, *The Republic of Plato,* trans. with notes and an interpretive essay (New York and London: Basic Books, 1968), p. 383.

9. Ibid., p. 384.

10. Ibid., and p. 458, n. 11.

11. See Cedric H. Whitman, *Aristophanes and the Comic Hero* (Cambridge, Mass.: Harvard University Press for Oberlin College, 1964), pp. 205–211.

12. Thucydides, *History,* II. 45.2; see also Xenophon's *Oeconomicus,* VII, where the wife is active but exclusively inside the home, directing domestics, supervising weaving, and managing what is brought in from without.

13. References to laughter are infrequent in Book VI and appear in a concentrated form only in section 504d to 509c (four times) when Socrates is being forced to discuss that which he should not—the good.

14. Bloom, *The Republic of Plato,* p. 461, n. 1.

15. Ibid., p. 384.

16. Ibid., p. 380.

17. From the moment that the inhabitants of the fevered city "cut off land from their neighbors" (373d), the focus of the *Republic* is on war. Neighbors

are assumed to be present, and the good city must be concerned with self-protection (422a–d). In contrast, in the *Laws,* where there is the assumption of relative isolation from all other political communities, the Legislators can concentrate on the inculcation of individual virtue.

18. Benjamin Jowett and Lewis Campbell *(Plato's Republic: The Greek Text* [Oxford: At the Clarendon Press, 1894]. Vol. II Notes, p. 24) offer this explanation of the sudden change in topic: "The real motive of the digression is an artistic one. The great *peripeteia,* the on-rushing of the 'third wave,' is made more impressive by being delayed." This is hardly satisfactory.

19. The parallel between these two sections is further emphasized by the repetition of the quote of Achilles from the *Odyssey* (386c and 516d).

20. Hans Kelsen, "Platonic Love," *American Imago,* Vol. 3, Nos. 1 and 2 (April 1942), 15.

21. Wender, "Plato . . . ," p. 85.

22. A. E. Taylor, *Plato: The Man and His Work* (Cleveland and New York: World Publishing, Meridan Books, 1956), p. 278.

# 7

# Was Plato a Feminist?

*Gregory Vlastos*

Was Plato a Feminist? Hot scholarly controversy has swirled around this question. Plato has been hailed as Ur-feminist by some, denounced as anti-feminist by others. When we view such collisions between honest readers of the same texts we may suspect that not all of three desiderata have been fully met: clarity of definition; awareness of complexity; dispassionateness of judgment.

How should we define the term? For "feminism" the *OED* lists "advocacy of the claims and the rights of women", dating the entry to 1895. This is too loose. To tighten it up I borrow wording from the Amendment to the United States Constitution proposed earlier in the present decade (failing to pass, though strongly supported by feminists and favoured by a majority of the American electorate): "Equality of rights under the law shall not be denied or abridged by the U.S. or by any State on account of sex." Dropping everything unessential for my purpose I get a shorter formula whose scope is wide enough to cover all personal rights that may be claimed for women—not just the legal ones envisaged by the Amendment, but social, economic, and moral rights as well: "Equality in the rights of persons shall not be denied or abridged on account of sex."

Does this give a defensible definition of "feminism"? I believe so. But I shall waste no time defending it. The focus of my interest is Plato, not feminism. It suffices for my purpose, making the question under debate entirely clear: Plato will qualify as a "feminist" if his ideas, sentiments, and proposals for social policy are in line with this norm.

Well, are they? When the question is put in that way any informed reader of the *Republic* and the *Laws* should be able to see that there is no simple answer. I would argue that it takes no less than four distinct propositions to formulate one that takes account of everything he says: 1. In the ideally best society outlined in books IV to VII of the *Republic* the position of the women in its ruling élite, the so-called "Guardians", is unambiguously feminist. 2. In that same society the position of the great majority of its free women, composing its industrial and agricultural class, is unambiguously anti-feminist. 3. In the alternative, second-best, society laid out in the *Laws,* the position of free women is a hybrid, feminist in some respects, anti-feminist in others. 4. In his personal attitude to the women in his own contemporary Athens Plato is virulently anti-feminist.

That Plato can run the gamut of these extremes will raise hackles of incredulity. It would take a whole book, a fat one, to allay them completely. All I can do here is to show that the initial impression of inconsistency between them is false. To do this I shall have to focus sharply on the first, short-shrifting the other three. For this is the eye of the controversial storm. Plato's feminism has been denied even here. Claiming that Plato's affirmation of feminism within the ruling class of the *Republic* is the strongest ever made by anyone in the classical period, I have no choice but to defend that claim in detail, letting the other three come in for their due as I proceed.

I begin by listing rights systematically denied to women in Plato's Athens which we have reason to believe would not be denied or abridged within the Guardian class of his *Republic:*

1. Right to Education. In Athens schools, gymnasia and palaestrae were a male monopoly. In Plato's *Republic* access to them by members of the Guardian class would be the same for women as for men in all respects, down to that last detail which has drawn so many prurient smirks: exercising in the nude with men. As we know from Herodotus and Thucydides, the Greeks thought total nudity in athletics a salient feature of their Hellenic culture. Plato would not dream of rescinding it for males. To deny it to females would have been discriminatory.

2. Right to Vocational Opportunity. No secular gainful employment was open to all women in Athens, except prostitution of varying degrees of elegance or squalor. Within the lowest social strata there were other options outside the home: working-class women could be midwives, wet nurses, vegetable sellers, chaplet makers, and so forth. Aristotle apologizes for this exception to the rule, explaining it as a product

of dire economic necessity: "How could you stop the women of the indigent from going outside the house?" (*Politics* 1300a6). In Plato's *Republic* career for highest talent is as open to women as to men. Both sexes qualify on equal terms for admission to Guardianship and therewith to all those professional occupations bundled up in that nominally single job: military to begin with and, thereafter, all political offices—executive, legislative, and judicial—and all of the assorted tasks that would come along with these: economic planning, population management, critique and censorship of literature and the arts, direction of schools and sports, supervision of the military and religious establishment—all these along with research and teaching in the sciences and philosophy.

3. Right to Unimpeded Social Intercourse. Mingling with free men other than close relatives is denied in principle to all Athenian women except priestesses, hetaerae, prostitutes, and tradeswomen. Such segregation is wiped out in Plato's Guardian class, where men and women "live in the same house, eat in common dining halls" (458C), and exercise in the same gymnasia.

4. Legal Capacity. In Athens only men have it. Women are wards of their nearest male relative, their *kurios*. They cannot sue or be sued, and even their right to give testimony in court is marginal. Among Plato's Guardians such differences could not exist. Whatever legal capacity male Guardians have, female ones have also.

5. Right to Sexual Choice. In Athens women have little say as to whom or when they will marry. The marriage contract is negotiated between their nearest male relative and the bridegroom. To what extent, if any, this gentleman was required to take the wishes of his female ward into account is unclear. Heterosexual intercourse outside of marriage is forbidden to women with the utmost severity. The ferocity of the interdict may be gauged from this: an Athenian virgin in breach of the rule may be sold into slavery by her *kurios*. This is the only case in which the law recognizes penal enslavement for an Athenian. In the case of a married woman caught in adultery "anyone whatsoever may do to her at will anything short of death". On men there was no counterpart constraint. They could have any sexual relations they pleased with women other than Athenian virgins or spouses without incurring any legal disability, or even any moral censure so long as they did not

do it for money and did not overdo it. Among Plato's Guardians the interdict on sexual intercourse outside of the eugenic unions during the child-bearing age is the same for men as it is for women. The liberty after that age is also the same for both. The double standard of sexual morality is wiped out.

6. Right to Own and Dispose of Property. Under Athenian law only men have it. Among Plato's Guardians private property is denied equally to men and to women, public support is assured equally to both.

7. Political Rights. None for women in Athens. The same for women as for men among Plato's Guardians.

Given this array of equalities of rights for women Guardians in Book V of the *Republic,* can it be doubted that Plato's programme for them is rigorously feminist in the sense defined?

To appraise its rigour we should compare it not only with Athenian practice, but also with Athenian fantasy in Aristophanes' *Ecclesiazousae.* The two dreams of gender equality have often been compared and the question of who cribbed what from whom has been debated. But I have yet to see it noticed that the philosopher's argument is bolder than the poet's whimsy. When Praxagora's conspiratorial women capture the state and turn their wishes into law, it never occurs to them to break up the segregated public rituals and private work-roles which had always been the lot of women. When a state banquet is laid on only the men sit down to it: the ladies do not invite themselves to dine with the gentlemen. When Blepyros, on being informed that all of his work will now be done by slaves, asks where his clothes will be coming from, Praxagora replies, "When you wear out the ones you have, we will weave you new ones" (651–4): the women are still behind the loom where they have been since Homer.

The most radical innovation in Plato's vision of a new society is not the extension of legal and political rights to women. That had been thought of already, though it had taken the comic genius of Aristophanes to think of it. Nor is it the liquidation of the nuclear family; for this there had been earlier models in Herodotus's album of anthropological oddities. It is the reasoned rejection of the age-old dogma, never previously questioned in Greek prose or verse, that difference of sex must determine difference of work-allocation.

Is there any reasonable ground on which the feminist intent, so thoroughgoing on the face of it, of Plato's programme for the ruling class of his utopia might still be doubted? Sarah Pomeroy has argued that there is, finding it in that curious language in which Plato speaks of the breeding unions: he refers to the women and the children as belonging in common to the men, with never a balancing allusion to the fact that the men, as also, of course, the children, belong in common to the women. Here are the suspect expressions: "community *(koinonia)* of children and wives for the Guardians" (450C); "possession *(ktesis)* and use *(chreia)* of children and of wives" (451C). From this asymmetry of references to who-belongs-to-whom Pomeroy infers that the female Guardians are to be the property of the male ones. The inference is unwarranted. The conclusion is not entailed by the evidence, and it is inconsistent with the following data: in any given marriage-group every woman belongs to all the men in the peculiar, but precise, sense that, so far as she knows and so far as they know, the eugenic "lottery" might make any one of them the father of her child. *Mutatis mutandis* every man belongs to every woman in his group in exactly the same sense. And there is no other relevant sense of "belonging". So the relation cannot be ownership. It would make no sense to say that $x$ is $y$'s property when $y$ is also $x$'s property.

Why then should Plato have used that kind of language? One could reply that this is the way group-marriages are talked about: they are always viewed from the man's point of view. Thus Herodotus writes that the Agathyrsoi "have in common intercourse with the women" (4.104) and that the Namasonians "believe in having many wives and in having intercourse with them in common" (4.172.2). Aristophanes makes even Praxagora, the liberator, talk in the same arsenocentric way. Though the licensed promiscuity is perfectly symmetrical, she speaks of it as "making the young women common bedmates for the men to produce children for any man who wants it" (614). Should we be surprised that Plato should have used similar language? Verbal habits could outlast the prejudices which created them. But can we be sure that Plato has outgrown the prejudices? Some of them he must have, else he could not have written book V of the *Republic*. But there are others he has not. The evidence has been surveyed brilliantly by Dorothea Wender. Here is part of it: that Plato's estimate of the common run of female intelligence is very low slips out even within book V of the *Republic*. Remarking that people who desecrate enemy corpses must be acting on the stupid belief that your enemy's body is your real enemy, he says that to give credence to this notion would be "the mark of a womanish and small intellect" (469D). To distinguish the higher from the lower appetites he says earlier on (431B–C) that the former are those "you would find among the few, those with the best nature and the best education", while their opposites "one would find chiefly in children and in women and in slaves and among so-called freemen, in the base multitude". So too in his critique of music and of poetry. The great complaint here is that in their present form these arts weaken the controls on strong emotion which decent persons ought to keep and women typically don't: "We pride ourselves on bearing up quietly in affliction, for this is the part of a man, while the other is the part of a woman" (605D–E). He refers to scenes in Homer and tragedy where heroes and other great men abandon themselves to outbursts of grief whose pathos, softies that we are at heart, we enjoy sharing vicariously, though we would feel disgraced if we had so behaved ourselves.

"The element common to all that was said of women by the Greeks", writes Kenneth Dover, "is the woman's inability to resist fear, desire, or impulse. . . . A woman, in fact, was thought to have a 'butterfly mind', equally incapable of intelligent, far-sighted, deliberation and of foregoing the emotional reaction of the moment in pursuit of distant and impersonal aims." We may note that he is not saying that this is how individual women are always portrayed. He knows well this is not so. He says that this is how they are generalized about on the stage and in oratory, and not only by men: women too are made to say such things about themselves. From women's lips we hear in Euripides and Aristophanes that their sex is weak, weepy, impulsive, irresolute, perfidious, garrulous, gluttonous, bibulous, lascivious. What I have just quoted from Plato fits this stereotype.

And now one last item to the same effect from the venomous caricature of Athenian democracy in book VIII of the *Republic*. Plato pictures its mania for liberty as condoning the collapse of all deference due to authority: citizens no longer obey the magistrates; nor do sons their parents, nor pupils their teachers, nor slaves their owners and "even the horses and donkeys have the habit of promenading on the street with all the rights and privileges of freemen". Just before the promenading quadrupeds at the climax of the satire (563B), comes the following: "I nearly forgot to mention how great *isonomia* and liberty has entered the mutual relations of men and women." *Isonomia* is a very strong word. It stands not just for equality before the law, but for equality by means of law—for substantively equal civic rights established and maintained by law. Now if progress towards sexual equality were being currently made in Athens, the last person in the world we might expect to damn his city for it would be the author of book V of the *Republic.* What then should we make of his conduct in the present passage? Must we reckon it a great man's lapse into peevishness, his hatred of democracy blinding him at this point, making him forget the feminist line he had taken just three books earlier in the *Republic?* We can make better sense of it if we connect it with the image of Athenian womanhood he must have carried in his head, judging from those chance remarks in which "womanish" stands for persons with diminutive intellects, obsessive appetites, and ungovernable emotions. If this is how Plato thought of the common run of women, he might well believe that in the present state of society continued subjection would be better for them than any degree of emancipation. Keeping them down, under their nearest male relative's thumb, he could hardly think an ideal solution, considering how benighted most of those males were on his own reckoning. But it might still strike him as the lesser of two evils: *isonomia* for creatures who cannot reason and keep their baser impulses under control would be worse.

This is the streak in Plato's thinking I had in view when putting forward the last of the four theses above. Whatever improvements had occurred within his lifetime must have been so minuscule as to leave no discernible record in Athens's legal history and provide no known relief from those massive inequalities I have detailed. That Plato should have seized on those minute changes, magnifying them in hostile fantasy, blowing them up into *isonomia,* should suffice to show that on the emancipation of women within the framework of his own society Plato's position would be not only conservative but reactionary.

But could he retain this attitude side by side with the feminism of book V? On the face of it, it looks as though only schizophrenia could have enabled him to do this. I want to argue that this appearance is false. Prisoner of the sexist stereotype though Plato was in his reactions to the contemporary scene, he could still take, without formal inconsistency, a radically opposite view of the place women were to have in the highest stratum of his ideal society. He could do so because the "womanish" traits he denigrates are those of the great mass of women, not of those brilliant exceptions from whom the Guardians would be recruited; and, moreover, they are the traits common to women *now,* under conditions now prevailing which do not foster the development of energetic minds and resolute characters. In the most damning of the disparaging remarks cited it is clear that he is speaking of women as they are under present, non-ideal, conditions: those motley appetites predominant in women, along with children, slaves, and men of the vulgar mass, are those, he says, "which one would find" (431C) in these creatures. What one "would find" is what is already there. And he is not saying that it is there as the permanently fixed, invariant, character of the female of the species, its nature: there is no reference to women's *phusis* in this passage or any of the others I have cited from the *Republic,* as there would have been if his point had been that those bad "womanish" traits were inherent in femaleness as such. In the absence of any such indications the right way to read those passages is as reflections on what Plato thinks women are now, formed and shaped, deformed and misshaped, by the society which has reared them.

We should recall here his vivid sense of the power of a corrupt society to pervert the heart and conversely of the power of education to improve moral character. Putting into that context those woman-denigrating remarks, we can understand them as voicing what Plato thinks most Athenian women grow up to be in their present habitat, the domestic ghetto, which stunts them intellectually and warps them morally, robbing them of what they might have been had they enjoyed that marvellous *paideia* which both sexes are to have in the ideal *polis.*

Moreover the butts of those nasty remarks differ in still another way from the women for whom Plato reserves the feminist programme of book V. They are females of the common run, while those who will be Guardians are as exceptional within their own sex as the male Guardians are to be in theirs: in each case Plato is counting on paragons of intellect and character. And if you ask: why should he expect the female half of the population to produce such superlative specimens? the answer is: why not, when he expects this of its male half? If there are to be stars in the population why should they be only male? Why should Plato have assumed that being female would decrease one's chances of turning out to be a super-person instead of a mass-person?

√ The Greek poetic vision of humanity would give no quarter to that prejudice. Homer and tragedy present a gallery of distinguished women who rise as high above ordinary females as do its heroic males above the mass of men. Consider Penelope. In cunning, in far-sighted purpose, in composure under nagging harassment, in unrelenting steadfastness of resolve, she dwarfs the people, male or female, who

crowd her world. Compared to her the suitors are pygmies and Telema-
chus a likeable mediocrity. Only the great Odysseus is her match. In
tragedy we have Clytemnestra, the counterpart in Aeschylus's master-
piece of Lady Macbeth in Shakespeare's. That both are evil is beside
the point, which is that each is as far as human flesh and blood could
be from Dover's "butterfly mind". Each has the qualities which, differently used, could have produced heroic goodness. The same is true of
Medea. And if we are looking for high stature in a woman who stays
completely within the conventional social role, instead of breaking out
of it, like Antigone, in her defiance of an unjust decree, consider Alcestis in Euripides. Of perfect outward self-possession while suffering
inner agony there is no better example in Greek literature than Alcestis
as she moves towards her death. Dressed and adorned as for a festive
occasion, she makes the round of the altars in the palace "without a
tear, without a groan, without a change of colour on her lovely face"
(173). So long as she remains on public view even skin-colour is under
control. ⋏

But there is no need to give the poets sole, or even major, credit for
freeing Plato from the prejudice that an intellectual and moral élite
could only be recruited from male stock. We know of two other liberating influences: the theory of moral virtue he learned from Socrates and
the metaphysical theory he invented himself.

One could scarcely over-stress the shattering effect in Plato's mind
of Socrates' rejection of the age-old axiom that excellence of character
was class-bound and gender-bound. The Socratic doctrine that virtue
is the same in women as in men may seem a commonplace to us. But
it flouts the certainties of his people and it outrages Aristotle, who
takes their parochial intuitions for universal moral truths. Nothing
shows up so well the novelty of the Socratic view as do Aristotle's remarks in book III of the *Politics* (1277b20–23). To prove that virtue *is*
different in women Aristotle argues that if a man were no braver than
a brave woman he would be a coward, and if a woman were as talkative
as a decent *(kosmios)* man, she would be a chatterbox; female excellence, he assumes, could be no better than male mediocrity. If Plato
had shared that premise he could not have composed book V of the
*Republic,* even if he had written everything else in that work. He did
not share it because he derived from Socrates the conviction that
human excellence, intellectual and moral, is unisex. So when he designed a state where that kind of excellence would be the passport to

dictatorial authority, he had to make the tenure of political power also unisex.

To his Socratic heritage Plato adds his own metaphysical theory without which the absolute powers entrusted to his philosopher-kings would be incomprehensible. Assured of access to the world of Forms, they will come to know the Form of the Good and be themselves transformed by that knowledge. Their initiation into that eternal world Plato calls a "turn-about of the soul from a day that is like night to the true day" (521C). The change is so profound that not only the mind, but the whole psyche, down to the libido, is transformed. It is a translation into a world of the mind whose magnificence beggars the prizes of the world of sense. *Sub specie aeternitatis* sensual attractions pale: Plato's imagery makes them fugitive, flat, unsubstantial—shadows on a wall. This in the last analysis is what he expects will keep his philosophers from misusing their vast unchecked authority. Their power will not corrupt them because to denizens of eternity the bribes and lures of power are trash.

Now obviously there is nothing about maleness that fits one to experience this rebirth. What one needs is, first of all, the capacity to go through its preparatory *paideia* in one's teens—a capacity Plato must think unrestricted by sex since he prescribes that *paideia* for both sexes—and thereafter the intellectual talent and the moral fibre to survive the gruelling fifteen-year course of graduate studies in mathematics and dialectic. There is a cut-off point here that will separate the men and women who are to rule from those they are to rule. Plato has no way of specifying that point. But it is clear that he is thinking of a threshold that can be crossed by persons who, though vastly superior to the great mass, may still differ considerably in ability among themselves. He believes that when the male population, taken as a whole, is compared with the female population, taken as a whole, the incidence of ability is on the average higher among males than among females. Does he then believe that in the small subgroup which passes the tests for admission to the higher studies the same differential obtains? He may, though he nowhere says so. If so, he would believe that within the Guardian class men are on the average abler than women in each of the tasks to be performed. It would then follow that on the average there would be more men than women in the higher offices. It would not follow that there would be no women in the highest ones.

That women are expected to share in the topmost offices becomes explicitly clear at the close of book VII. Here Socrates speaks of those "who have survived the tests and have excelled in all things in action and in knowledge", have beheld the Form of the Good, taken their part in governing, and at their death received quasi-divine honours. Glaucon is moved to exclaim: "Like a statuary, you have made your men-rulers matchless in beauty." Socrates retorts: "Yes, the women-rulers too, Glaucon, for you must not suppose that my description applies to men any more than it does to all the women who arise among them with the requisite natural endowment."

If the foregoing argument has been sound, the feminist programme for the ruling élite in book V of the *Republic* becomes perfectly understandable as a consistent application of Plato's theory of social justice. According to that theory the rights and duties justly allocated to citizens of the *polis* would be all and only those which would enable each of them to make the greatest personal contribution to the happiness and excellence of the whole *polis,* their own included. This is the criterion by which the abolition of private property for the Guardians is justified: Guardians must own no property because they would be "best craftsmen at their own work" (421C) without rather than with private property. The same criterion would dictate full equality of rights within the Guardian class in all of the categories I detailed at the start. Nothing less will explain the rationality of Plato's extraordinary programme, so unprecedented in Greek experience, philosophy, or even fantasy. In particular, it cannot be explained as a mere by-product of the decision earlier on in the *Republic* to deprive Guardians of private property, thereby abolishing in their case the traditional pattern of Greek marriage whose base was private property. The claim that this is the correct explanation has been made repeatedly in the scholarly literature. The conclusive objection is that Plato could have abolished the private family along with private property in the Guardian class, could have followed to the letter the formula "common possession of goods and wives", *without* granting equality of status to those wives. He could have made them collective consorts, nurses for the children, factotums for the men, but not Guardians, rulers of the state, sharing supreme political authority and civil dignity.

That the theory of social justice propounded in the *Republic* is the decisive reason for the feminism of book V gets added support from what happens when Plato turns away from that theory in his last work, the *Laws*. That move marks a retreat along a broad front from his stand in the *Republic*. The retreat is not a rout. The equal right to education and to unimpeded social intercourse women retain in the *Laws,* and here all citizen women will have it, regardless of class. But they lose equality in vocational opportunity, in legal capacity, in the right to own property, and in choice of marriage partner. I would argue that both changes—in the theory of social justice and in the conception of the status of women—are due to the more conservative philosophical and political outlook which comes over Plato with increasing age. So if we are looking for feminism in Plato there is only one place where we do not need to invent it: in the legislation for the Guardians in the *Republic*. Among all of Plato's writings and among all the writings which have survived from the classical age of Greece, that work alone projects a vision of society in whose dominant segment the equal rights of human beings are not denied or abridged on account of sex.

This innovation owed nothing to a belief in what we have now come to call "human rights"—rights which belong to persons as their human birthright, without regard to their membership in any ethnic, political, economic, or religious grouping, rights pertaining to each of them individually as human beings for no reason other than their humanity. It should go without saying that Plato had no such belief. His ideal society has no place for the freedoms enumerated in the Bill of Rights: freedom of religion, of speech, of assembly, of the press. It never occurs to him that without these any attempt to apply his pattern for that society in the real world would result in the opposite of his dream of it—corruption in the rulers, oppression of the ruled. Who, man or women, should want equality on those terms? So to think of Plato as an advocate of "Women's Liberation" would be perverse. Liberation Plato advocates for no one, man or woman. Excellence, not liberty, is his goal, and he rejects liberty as the enemy of excellence. Still less could we think of him as a champion of "Affirmative Action". Nowhere in the presentation of his programme does one catch a gleam of a desire to right wrongs sexist oppression had done to women in the past. Of compassion there seems to be all too little in Plato even for men, so how could there be for women, given those sour views of them he voices in the *Republic?*

I would not call him a misogynist on that account. Certainly those derogatory remarks of his would have warmed the heart of a real woman-hater. But they hardly warrant classifying him as such himself. If they did, then by the same token we would have to classify as woman-haters the women in Euripides and Aristophanes who say equally bitter things about their sex. And while it is not unknown for members of an oppressed group to internalize masochistically the sentiments of their oppressor, it would still be misleading to say that those women hate their sex. Anyhow, "hatred" would just misdescribe the feelings Plato harbours for the women in his world: a certain dislike perhaps, condescension tinged with disdain, though more striking is the fact that he so largely ignores them in his reflections on the state, in his analyses of moral concepts and, what may be more significant, in his references to human beauty. (In the great erotic passages in the *Symposium* (210–212) and the *Phaedrus* (245–257) human beauty is desired by men desiring boys; to females desired for their beauty by men or desiring it in one another and in men there is no allusion.) When he does encounter them on the human landscape he seems to view them with an abstract gaze, as he would stare at members of a curious species, distantly related to his own. (In all other passages where Plato's Socrates expresses or simulates sexual longing the object is male; only in Xenophon (*Mem.* 3.11.3) do we ever see Socrates sexually excited at the sight of a beautiful female.) This is perhaps all that could be expected of a one-track paedophile deficient in that instinctual attraction which women would have had for him if he had been one of those regular Athenians for whom Aristophanes cracked his bisexual jokes.

But whatever may be the right account of his personal feeling for living women, we can be sure it was not sentiment that moved him to legislate for the ruling class of his utopia rights for women equal to those of men. If he had followed sentiment he would have gone the other way. His achievement is all the more remarkable on that account. In a triumph of imaginative impartiality he separated the character his inherited prejudices imputed to the mass of women in his own society from the character which, he reasoned, a few exceptional women could develop under ideal conditions of equal nurture, awarding to them what his own theory of social justice required: status commensurate with the greatest contribution each of them could make personally to their own society and *therefore* equal in all respects to that of men. Few philosophers have achieved such transcendence of personal inclination in response to the dictates of impersonal moral theory.

## Note

The most recent bibliography, compiled by Sister Elena Blair of Xavier University, lists over forty contributions to the debate concerning Plato's attitude towards women. For sample views *pro* and *con* see Dorothea Wender, "Plato: Misogynist, Paedophile and Feminist", *Arethusa* 6 (1973), 75–80; Julia Annas, "Plato's *Republic* and Feminism", *Philosophy* 51 (1976), 307–21. For the position of Athenian women as reflected in myth, literature, and law see J. P. Gould, "Law, Custom and Myth: Aspects of the social position of women in classical Athens", *Journal of Hellenic Studies* 100 (1980); Mary Lefkowitz, *Women in Greek Myth* (1986); A. R. W. Harrison, *The Law of Athens, Volume One: The family and property* (1968).

# 8

# The Naked Old Women
# in the Palaestra

*C. D. C. Reeve*

*Dicaerarchus, a pupil of Aristotle and a contemporary of Theophrastus, tells us that there were two women among Plato's students in the Academy. He adds the intriguing detail that one of them wore men's clothes. The names of these two women were Axiothea of Phlius and Lasthenia of Mantinea. The following is a dialogue between Lasthenia and Plato about the treatment of women in the Kallipolis, the ideal city described in the* Republic.

LASTHENIA: I wonder, Plato, whether or not we might discuss Book 5 of the *Republic*. I've read it a number of times now and there are still some points I'm not clear about.

PLATO: I'd be glad to discuss Socrates' views with you.

LASTHENIA: Good. Then I'll begin by reviewing a few of them. When Socrates returns to the topic of the way of life appropriate to the guardians in Book 5, he raises the question of how female guardians should be trained and educated. Should they reduce the amount of work required of the males by sharing their duties, he asks, or be kept "at home as incapable of doing this since they must bear and rear the puppies?" (451d6–8). In other words, he wants to know whether these women should be active participants in the traditionally male world of honor, politics, and philosophy or be kept in seclusion because of their role in reproduction. Socrates' imaginary opponent argues that since

129

males and females have different reproductive roles, they must also have different social roles, or do different jobs as well. For that's what Socrates' own *principle of specialization* seems to require. It's the principle that says that each person in the Kallipolis should stick exclusively to the one job for which his or her natural abilities are highest. You remember, Plato, that Socrates makes a lot of that principle in Book 2, and then uses it to define justice in Book 4.

PLATO: I do.

LASTHENIA: Then you'll also remember that Socrates sees through the argument from reproduction, pointing out that it isn't clear that someone's role in reproduction has anything to do with his aptitude for a craft:

> If the male sex is seen to be different from the female with regard to a particular craft or way of life, we'll say that the relevant one must be assigned to it. But if it's apparent that they differ only in this respect, that the females bear children while the males beget them, we'll say that there has been no kind of proof that women are different from men with respect to what we're talking about, and we'll continue to believe that our guardians and their wives must have the same way of life. (454d7–e4)

Thus to make out his objection the opponent must show that men and women have natural aptitudes for totally different crafts. And Socrates doesn't think that he will be able to do this. Why? Because on his view, though men are in general better than women at most things, natural aptitudes "are scattered in the same way among both sexes" (455d2–e2). Consequently, the general superiority of men to women provides no basis for assigning women as a sex to one lot of tasks, and men as a sex to another. Individual women are either money-lovers or honor-lovers or philosophers, just like individual men. Hence women in the Kallipolis won't be confined to the home, but will be trained in a craft—whether it is producing or guarding or ruling (456a4–5, 540c5–7), for which their natural aptitude is highest—even if this means that people will have to get used to the sight of old women exercising naked in the palaestra alongside the men (452a7–e3). For, as Socrates remarks—and I've always thought it one of his better sayings—"it's foolish . . . to take seriously any standard of what is fine and beautiful other than the good" (452e1–2).

All right. I understand that much. But what I don't understand is whether these proposals are intended to apply to *all* women in the Kallipolis or only to the *guardian* women. I don't think the text is very clear on this, Plato. So maybe you could tell me what you think Socrates had in mind?

PLATO: Because the discussion of women is part of the account of the way of life of the guardians, and because female producers are never explicitly discussed, it's easy to get the impression, I agree, that Socrates' revolutionary proposals apply only to guardian women, and that female producers are intended to lead lives modeled on those of their working class Athenian counterparts. But some stray remarks that Socrates makes, which have clear application to female producers, suggest that the life he envisages for them is very different from that. In Book 4, for example, Socrates remarks that the greatest cause of good to the Kallipolis is the presence "in children and in *women,* in slaves and in freemen, in producers, rulers, and ruled" of the principle that "each one should do his own work and not be meddlesome" (433d1–5). The clear implication is that female producers, being just as subject to the principle of specialization as any other member of the Kallipolis, will be trained in the one craft for which they are naturally best suited. Since Socrates implies that there are women with a natural aptitude for carpentry (454d5–9), explicitly mentions female physicians, and claims that natural aptitudes for each craft are to be found in both sexes (455d6–e7), it is difficult to avoid the conclusion that he intends female producers to be apprenticed in an appropriate craft in precisely the same way as the males. For carpenters, physicians, and craftspeople are all producers in the Kallipolis, not guardians. It could be too—though again he is not explicit on the matter—that Socrates thinks that *nursing* is a craft to which the principle of specialization applies, so that it will be in the hands of those men and women that have a high natural aptitude for child-care. None the less, I grant you that Socrates is somewhat vague about the producers, whether male or female, and that he has simply left us somewhat in the dark on the important question of who will do the housework and rear the children, if, indeed, both parents are employed full-time in other crafts. Perhaps, he should have provided day-care centers for older children in addition to the rearing pens he provides for infants.

LASTHENIA: Thank you for reminding me about those important passages, Plato. I don't think Axiothea and I paid sufficient attention to them when we were talking about this matter earlier.

PLATO: They're easy to overlook, no doubt, and you are not alone in failing to bear them in mind. Others have made the same mistake, claiming it as an obvious fact that Socrates is only a "feminist" where guardian women are concerned.

LASTHENIA: I'm glad you brought up the issue of feminism, Plato, because that's the next topic I want to ask you about. Do you think that Socrates really is a feminist of any sort? Does he advocate the claims and rights of women?

PLATO: If a feminist is someone who advocates the claims and rights of women, Lasthenia, is a "masculinist" someone who advocates the claims and rights of men?

LASTHENIA: I suppose so.

PLATO: In that case Socrates is both a masculinist and a feminist, since it seems to me that in the *Republic,* he advocates the claims and rights of people generally, whether they're male or female. I would have thought, however, that a better definition of a feminist is someone who *especially* advocates the claims and rights of women or who *exclusively* advocates the claims and rights of women. And by that definition of course, Socrates was definitely not a feminist (or a masculinist either, for that matter), and nor would anyone else be who cared about justice? Don't you agree?

LASTHENIA: Well, I see your point anyway. You mean that it would be unjust to think that the claims and rights of women have more weight than those of people generally?

PLATO: Something like that.

LASTHENIA: You don't dispute though, do you, that it may be more important to devote more energy to the claims and rights of those who are most oppressed?

PLATO: No indeed. It's just that some feminists seem to think that men ought to be abolished from the world as a scourge and a plague, whereas Socrates' view is that bad people (whether male or female) are to be removed and good ones (whether male or female) kept. In this respect he is to be contrasted with men like Hesiod who represent women as the source of all evil by retelling the myth of Pandora, but he is also to be contrasted with women who believe equally obnoxious myths about men.

LASTHENIA: That's an important point, I admit, but don't you think though that for all his revolutionary views about women, Socrates often says things to suggest that he's a traditional male chauvinist at heart?

PLATO: What do you mean?

LASTHENIA: Consider the following passages and you'll see:

> Now one finds all kinds of diverse desires, pleasures, and pains mostly in children, *women,* household slaves, and in those of the inferior majority who are so-called free. (431b9–c3)

Notice how Socrates here groups women together with slaves, children, and the inferior majority. That doesn't sound very liberated. Indeed, it's the sort of thing that men say about women in the agora or the gymnasium. Here's a second example:

> Don't you think it's slavish and money-loving to strip a corpse? For isn't it small-minded and *womanish* to regard the body as your enemy, when the enemy himself has flitted away leaving behind only the instrument with which he fought? Or do you think such behavior any different from that of dogs who get angry with the stone that hits them and leave the thrower alone? (469d6–e2)

I need hardly comment on that. Just think what Axiothea and I feel when we hear him saying something like that. It's bad enough when ordinary men say such things, but when one's heroes and teachers say them it's heartbreaking.

PLATO: I have to tell you, Lasthenia, that I'm not persuaded by the evidence you cite. After all, Socrates is talking about women as they were in Athens in his time and as they still are today, women who have been oppressed by men and kept in seclusion. He would hardly say the same things about women in the Kallipolis, or about liberally educated women like you and Axiothea. Or do you think he would?

LASTHENIA: I suppose not.

PLATO: Then what he disparages in these remarks isn't women in general, or women as such, but women who've been turned into silly creatures by an even sillier society.

LASTHENIA: That response seems to work quite well for the examples I've cited so far, but will it also work for this one, I wonder. It's from Book 5: "Do you know of anything practiced by human beings *in which the male sex isn't superior to the female in all these ways?*" (455c4–6). Here Socrates is surely talking about women as such, and what he's saying about them is that the female sex is inferior to the male in all the arts, crafts, and sciences. And it seems to me that in making this claim he is illegitimately extrapolating from facts about *oppressed* women (for that's the only kind there have ever been) to conclusions about women in general, including women who have been given the same opportunities as men.

PLATO: Well, I think I'm going to have to concede that. Socrates does seem to have forgotten that the basis for his claim is tainted, and that in the Kallipolis, or any other just and non-oppressive society, the female sex might turn out to be far superior to the male at everything.

LASTHENIA: Since you've started to make some concessions, Plato, let me now bring up an even more damning piece of evidence. It's from Book 8:

> The uttermost freedom for the majority is reached in a democratic city, I said, when bought slaves, both male and female, are no less free than those who bought them. *And I almost forgot to mention the extent of the legal equality of men and women and of the freedom in the relations between them.* (563b4–9)

Doesn't Socrates clearly imply here that legal equality between men and women is a bad thing? And doesn't that suggest that he doesn't plan to incorporate such equality into his Kallipolis?

PLATO: I agree that the text seems to imply and suggest the things you say. But implications and suggestions aren't explicit statements, are they? And we have Socrates' explicit statements in Book 5 that men and women with equal natural abilities will be treated in exactly the same way. In any case, it seems obvious to me that what Socrates is criticizing is the fact that men and women with unequal natural abilities are treated as equal in Athens. I see no reason at all to leap to the more extravagant reading that you yourself have adopted.

LASTHENIA: Well now it's my turn to be concessive. For I do see, now that you've pointed it out, that the text will bear the interpretation you've given it, and that so interpreted it is consistent with the explicit doctrine of Book 5. I concede, therefore, that you may be right about it, and that I was hasty.

PLATO: Friends are important, Lasthenia, but the truth is more important. Socrates was a great friend and I would defend him to the hilt, but you know as well as I do that he would always have wanted us to follow the argument where it led, even if it meant refuting our friends.

LASTHENIA: I sense that you think our discussion has come to an end, Plato, but I have saved the very best argument till last.

PLATO: Let's hear it then.

LASTHENIA: If women and men were treated equally in the Kallipolis, wouldn't the things that women value have to be given as much initial weight as the things that men do?

PLATO: I suppose so.

LASTHENIA: Good. Now men place a very high value on warfare and philosophy, don't they?

PLATO: They do.

LASTHENIA: Whereas women don't traditionally value these things at all?

PLATO: That's right.

LASTHENIA: Instead, they traditionally value weaving, cooking, bringing up children, and the emotional closeness and intimacy that married life makes possible.

PLATO: That's true.

LASTHENIA: Good. Then if men and women were treated equally in the Kallipolis, these two lots of things, philosophy and warfare, on the one hand, and domestic things (as I'll call them for short), on the other, would have to be assigned equal weight, at least initially. And surely they aren't. Rather, Socrates just assumes that philosophy and warfare are valuable, and that anyone, male or female, will want to engage in them if he can, while domestic things are valueless and to be abandoned altogether. Hence he puts the rearing of children (anyway, guardian children) into the hands of "nurses," and deprives the guardians of intimacy and domesticity altogether. The result, it seems to me, is that Socrates has not treated women justly at all, and has not advocated their claims and rights in the way that he does those of men. What he has done instead is, first, to make an entirely "masculinized" world and then give women the freedom to be "men" in it. This isn't equal treatment. And you can see this clearly if you imagine the kind of Kallipolis that *I* might have designed, one in which men were given the freedom to weave, cook, and bring up children, but found that philosophy and fighting had been abandoned altogether, or put exclusively into the hands of others. What man, looking at such a society, would think that his sex was treated with equal justice there? The hegemony of males in the Kallipolis is more subtle and insidious than it first seems. Indeed, it has so infected the imagination of Socrates that the Kallipolis he projects is tainted with it in a way that even he doesn't seem to notice. The result is that his ideal society, while it strives to treat men and women equally, actually subordinates women to men more effectively than ever, by extirpating women's values from it almost entirely. What it gives us is not a world in which men and women are treated equally, but a world in which *women* don't exist, a world which is really a world of men with penises and men without them. Closer to home, you might notice that Axiothea has begun to wear male clothing here in the Academy, so that she can almost pass for a man. What this shows, I think, is what a "masculinized" place the Academy is, for all that you are open-minded enough to admit women students to it.

PLATO: That's a powerful criticism, Lasthenia, and one that I've not heard before. It makes me glad to have you here in the Academy, because it's not obvious to me that any man, not even one as bright as

Aristotle, would have come up with it. It's so good in fact, and raises so many doubts in my mind about my own thought and imagination, and how *they* may have been colored by the insidious sexism you mention, that I'm almost afraid to criticize it for fear of seeming to be just another male oppressor of women. So let me ask you: Are you willing to let the argument decide between us? Or will I lose your respect and become your enemy if I argue with you?

LASTHENIA: A few days ago, I said to Axiothea that argument and dialectic, what we do here in the Academy under the name of philosophy, is just aggression and competition with words instead of swords. One of the male teachers—Speusippus, I think it was—overheard me and he said "the rational part of the soul has no gender." It was clear that he meant that reason—and hence philosophy, argument, and dialectic—is neither male nor female. I didn't know quite what to say to that, but afterwards Axiothea put the issue to me somewhat differently. She said that it would be foolish for women to treat anything that might do them some good as "masculinized" and unusable. Women should be opportunists, not purists, willing to use pretty well anything to liberate themselves. I think she's right about that, and that women weaken themselves when they argue that nothing that males have made is pure enough for them to use. We should take the good, no matter who has made it, and get rid of the bad, even if it's something that women have long held dear—like marriage, for example. So I suppose that I'm willing to hear what you have to say. But if I think the conclusion will help oppress women or make them accept oppression, then I won't agree to it, because I'll assume that no truly objective and unbiased philosophical argument could support a conclusion like that.

PLATO: Axiothea's advice was good, I think, and your own provisos are no doubt wise. Here then is what I have to say in response. It's a fable I once heard from Diotima, a wise woman from your own city of Mantinea. She said that when the gods were making the world, they gave good things to all the animals, and to all the animals they also gave things that seemed to be good but weren't. Among the things they gave to human beings were the things you mentioned earlier: philosophy, warfare, weaving, cooking, the capacity to form deep emotional ties, and to rear offspring successfully. They put these things into human beings in a more or less random fashion. But because of the luck of the draw men mostly got philosophy and warfare and women mostly got what you called the domestic things. As time went by, and habit and tradition did their work, each sex came to think that the things that it had been given were the real goods, while the things the other sex had been given were only apparent goods. That was what Diotima told me, and what she meant surely is that we cannot settle which of these things are really good just by appealing to what their possessors think. For each sex thinks that what it got is alone really good, and they can't both be right about that.

LASTHENIA: I think I see what you mean. You're saying that if the things that males traditionally value, such as warfare and philosophy, are the really good things, while the things that women traditionally value are only apparently good, then Socrates will not have been unjust to women in doing what I described as "masculinizing" the Kallipolis, since women will be deprived of only apparent goods, while being given real goods in their place. It was very clever of Diotima to have noticed that response to my argument—and I thought that *I* was the first woman philosopher from Mantinea! But is it really a compelling response? Is it really plausible to believe that all women are wrong in finding value in their traditional activities and pursuits, and that all males are right in finding value in their traditional activities and pursuits?

PLATO: I can best answer you with another of Diotima's stories. In this story the gods gave everyone, male and female, all the goods and apparent goods. But this time all of them agreed that the domestic things were the really valuable ones. Because it happened that the males were physically stronger than the female, however, they tried to take these things for themselves, leaving warfare and philosophy to the females. But because the men couldn't bear or suckle children, they had to allow the women some part of the domestic things as well. So they allowed them to have the children for the first five years. The women fed the male children's heads with tales of military valor and the joys of philosophy and portrayed their fathers as effeminate sissies. In due course, when habit and tradition had done their work, the males were all devoted to warfare and philosophy and the females had got hold of all the really good things for themselves.

LASTHENIA: Again I see Diotima's point. She's saying that people's opinions about what is valuable cannot by themselves settle the question of what is truly valuable. And that's true whether the people in question are males or female. But if she's right, if we can't appeal directly to the testimony of people about what is and isn't valuable, how are we to settle whether in "masculinizing" the Kallipolis, Socrates has been unjust to women or has, on the other hand, given them true goods in place of apparent goods?

PLATO: It seems to me that that's really what the *Republic* is about.

LASTHENIA: Of course it is. In the heat of the argument, I'd almost forgotten, that the *Republic* isn't primarily about women, but about how we might acquire stable and objective knowledge of values. But, Plato, we don't now have that knowledge and maybe we'll never have it. So what are we to do in the meantime?

PLATO: In the meantime we are to recognize that we don't have the kind of knowledge of values that would justify us in being dogmatic about them, and that we must strain every nerve to acquire it. For when you think about it, it just isn't obvious, is it, that either warfare or domestic life is really good?

LASTHENIA: What about philosophy, Plato, is the same true of it? Might philosophy turn out to be something that we have to give up?

PLATO: That's a hard question to answer in the abstract, Lasthenia. But it was philosophy that enabled Socrates to see through so many bad arguments that men have used to justify their oppression of women. It was philosophy, too, that enabled him to overcome his culture's prejudices as far as he did. Maybe he didn't see everything that we think he ought to have, maybe he made some mistakes, but isn't it your own knowledge of philosophy, isn't it your own training here in the Academy, that has enabled you to diagnose his errors and do better?

LASTHENIA: I worry still, though, that philosophy is so agonal and competitive, so much like fighting, so—if you'll forgive me—*male.*

PLATO: Philosophy wears men's clothes, Lasthenia, because it has been the prerogative of males.

LASTHENIA: But underneath the clothes it's neither male nor female, is that what you're saying?

PLATO: Speusippus said that reason has no gender. I think the same might be said of philosophy.

LASTHENIA: I wonder whether you'd still think that, Plato, if you had to wear *women's* clothes in order to feel comfortable practicing it.[1]

Plato was called away before he could respond, but a few days later, I reported our conversation to Axiothea. She was impressed with Plato's closing arguments, but thought that my major objections were too abstract, too "philosophical." Her own, she said, were more down-to-earth. I'll let her speak for herself.

"Socrates says that the best women will be assigned as sex partners to the best men through a rigged lottery (458c–460b). But what would happen, do you think, if one of these women didn't want to have sex with the partner she was assigned? What, indeed, would happen to women like us, who don't want to bear children at all. Or to a woman like me, who doesn't even want to have sex with men? That's one problem that Socrates doesn't address.

"Another, yet more pressing difficulty is this. The best women in the Kallipolis will very often be pregnant—far more often than their less able sisters. Since frequent pregnancy is debilitating and often life-threatening, this means that their chances of becoming philosopher-kings at the age of fifty-five are likely to be quite low. In any case, they are likely to be substantially lower than those of a comparable male guardian. It follows that women, just because they bear children and men don't, are less well off in the Kallipolis than men with the same natural abilities.

"Now, I don't claim that there are no answers to these difficulties, but I think that the fact that Socrates doesn't even notice them shows that he has not thought carefully enough about the women of the Kallipolis, and the lives they will lead there."

In the months that followed, I reflected on Axiothea's comments. I found myself wondering whether anything could be done to prevent the biological differences between men and women from resulting in social differences that were prejudicial to women. I thought about how sex and reproduction might be separated, about genderless societies, about same-sex couples, about how the burdens (and joys) of child bearing and rearing might be better shared between men and women.

Soon, I hope to write a *Republic* of my own.

## Note

1. This dialogue was first presented as a Freshman Humanities Lecture at Reed College. It was printed by Hackett Publishing Company (Indianapolis) as part of its Fall 1992 Complete Catalogue, and reprinted in the *The Fortnightly Review* (Sri Lanka, 1994) and in Japanese in *Aichi* (Kobe, 1995). The epilogue which follows is based on discussion with my own women students.

# 9

# Understanding and the Good: Sun, Line, and Cave

## *Julia Annas*

The person with knowledge . . . is the person who thinks things through where others remain unreflective, and who realizes that there are objects of knowledge that are not to be found in experience, the Forms. From Plato's discussion of knowledge, and from the passages of argument that serve to introduce Forms, it does not follow that knowledge is *only* of Forms; and because Plato links knowledge with understanding rather than with certainty he has no obvious reason to demand a wholesale critical rejection of our previously held beliefs. Indeed, given his account of justice he has reason not to introduce a concept of knowledge that requires such wholesale rejection. In Books 6 and 7, however, Plato gives a long and detailed account of the requirements of knowledge, in the form of the three figures of Sun, Line, and Cave and a description of the further education needed to train the Guardians who are to achieve the highest kinds of knowledge. And we find that the upshot of these famous passages is a much more revisionary account of knowledge (and, with it, of justice) than has emerged so far.

Knowledge, for Plato, requires understanding; but what does understanding require? Two things emerge from Plato's discussion. One is that understanding is *systematic* because it involves explanation. The person with mere 'true belief' is in possession of various truths, and so has what we are prepared to call knowledge of various matters of fact. But these truths are isolated, or hang together for arbitrary reasons; knowledge, by contrast, forms an explanatory whole. The user of bridles is in a better state than the maker because, although the maker may have a perfectly good grasp of certain facts about bridles, he has no unified grasp of the function and use of bridles such as enables the expert to say why the various requirements for a good bridle are as they are. Understanding is connected with explanation, with being able to say why things are the way they are; and to be able to explain things is to be able to relate them systematically and show what is basic and what dependent, and how they are interrelated. Modern theories of explanation often claim that to explain a particular occurrence—to be able to say *why* it happened rather than just *that* it happened—we must show that it falls under a law relating kinds of occurrence. Plato does not talk of laws or generalizations, since his model is not any kind of science, but he shares the general idea that a particular claim may be true, but is not explanatory in isolation. For it to be a case of knowledge—something we understand, as opposed to mere belief—something that is held to be true in isolation—it must be shown to fit comprehensibly into an explanatory system of truths. His model for such an explanatory system is mathematics.

The other requirement for understanding is that it must crucially involve reference to goodness. This claim is more startling than the other, and not just because of its abstractness. If our paradigm of systematic explanation is scientific or mathematical, reference to goodness seems out of place. We tend to think of goodness as something that defies systematic explanation; statements about goodness are often interpreted as being arbitrary expressions of personal taste, rather than objective claims about something that can be systematically explained. Plato, however, is far from thinking that goodness is subjective, or marginal, something that cannot be part of an organized explanation. Indeed, he makes it fundamental to all real explanation, and hence all understanding.

At 505a Socrates says that the greatest of the philosopher-rulers' studies is the Form of Good, from which just actions and the like derive their usefulness and beneficial qualities. But, while all agree on the importance of knowing the nature of the good, and in this matter alone are not satisfied with appearance, wanting what is really good, there is little agreement over what the good is—though suggestions that it is knowledge or pleasure are obviously not adequate (505a–506b). Socrates himself says that he does not know what the Good is, and has only feeble beliefs (506b–e), but consents to point out its nature by an analogy. He gives, in fact, three: Sun, Line, and Cave, all of which explicate the place of the Good in the just person's knowledge, and the form that knowledge takes.

Before going on to the Sun, it is worth noticing some points of interest in Socrates' procedure. Firstly, a Form is again brought in from outside the discussion as something the interlocutor has 'often' heard about. Socrates does not argue for it, and he refuses to discuss it except indirectly. Plato is helping himself to the claim that the Good, the object of all human strivings, is the Form of Good. We can see by now why he finds this obvious (though recognizing that others do not). Everyone, he says, wants what is really good; their behaviour is not otherwise explicable (505d–e). But then the Good that all seek must be what is really and unqualifiedly good; and what is unqualifiedly good and never evil is just what Plato calls a Form, the only unqualified bearer of the predicate 'good'.

All the same, we, if not Plato, should pause. For Forms are crucially *distinct* from particular things to which the same predicate applies. The Form of Good is not in the world of our experience, since it is not the same as anything we call good. But is it not then odd, that when people seek what is good they are looking for something which is *ex hypothesi* different from anything to be found in people and actions? Aristotle criticizes Plato sharply, clearly with his passage in mind, at *Nicomachean Ethics* I, 6: it is absurd, he says, for the object of people's strivings to be something unattainable in the world of particular actions, a Form separate from particular good things. This is a serious problem, because the Good is what is studied by those who are to rule: if they learn about something that is never to be found in experience, how can their knowledge of it be the *practical* wisdom they are to have? Right at the very beginning of Plato's discussion of the Good and its role for knowledge we find him making an assumption about the nature of the Good that seems to turn it into an object of detached, rather than practical, knowledge.

But even if we waive the special problems arising from Plato's Good being a separated Form, is it legitimate in any case to talk of *the* Good? Aristotle makes this criticism too in the same chapter. There is, he says, nothing which is just good, good without qualification, as *the* Good would have to be. 'Good' is a term that has no such absolute, unqualified employment. Its use is always relative to some set of criteria. What makes for a good man is essentially different from what makes for a good action. Aristotle distinguishes senses or uses of 'good' according to what it is that is said to be good. (Modern discussions concentrate more on the fact that what is good from one point of view may not be good from another.) Plato produces no arguments against this position, one which is often simply taken for granted in modern discussions. For him to have done so would have been tantamount to arguing for the existence of the Form of Good, which is something he chooses not to do. So right at the start of the discussion Plato parts company with someone who believes that for something to be good is always for it to be good *for X,* or *from Y's point of view,* or *a good Z.* He clearly thinks that an ethical discussion cannot get off the ground with someone who rejects the starting premise that besides particular goods that are relative to various interests and criteria, there is also *the* Good, which is, objectively, just good, not good relative to anything. As with Forms generally, Plato offers no direct argument. Presumably we are to become convinced of the truth of his claim more indirectly, by the whole long passage which follows.

The first figure, the Sun, begins from the distinction between Forms and 'the many', Forms being objects of thought as opposed to the many things and actions that are instances of Forms, which we know through experience. Sight is the most prominent of the senses that inform us about the world of experience, and it is also distinguished from the other senses by the fact that it needs a medium—light. Light is provided by the sun, which thus makes sight possible, since we can only see things clearly to the extent that they are illuminated for us by the sun.

The sun, supreme in the visible realm, corresponds to the Good, supreme in the realm of thought. It enables the objects of knowledge to be known by the mind, as the objects of sight are seen by the eye. Further, just as the sun causes things not only to be seen but to grow and come into being, so the Good gives the objects of knowledge not just their knowability but their reality, though it is itself 'beyond reality' (or 'beyond being').

'Plato's Good', which he refuses to clarify here, became a byword for obscurity. How can the Good make things known, still less make them be what they are, in a way comparable to the workings of the sun? Plato is putting forward two thoughts, though he leaves them deliberately schematic. Presumably he believes that they are true, but has no idea how to argue for them, and perhaps thinks that they are not the kind of truth that can be argued for, but must be accepted in the light of other considerations and arguments taken as a whole. The first thought, that the Good makes things known, is what we might perhaps express by saying that goodness is fundamental in any explanation. This is a perfectly comprehensible idea, though one that the majority of modern philosophers would reject. Many philosophers draw a sharp distinction between matters of fact and matters of value, and hold that, since a thing's goodness is a matter of value, it cannot enter into the same kind of explanation as matters of fact about it. But Plato holds not only that facts and values are not radically different kinds of thing, known in different ways, but that values are fundamental to explaining facts. He willingly commits himself to the claim that values can be *better* known than facts, that they are *more* fundamental to our understanding. Many modern philosophers would find such an idea extraordinary; but it is not clear at this level of generality where the truth lies. We can understand Plato's very programmatic claims only when we see the use he puts them to, in all three of the figures and not just one.

The second thought is that the Good makes things not just knowable, but actually makes them what they are. This, and the enigmatic claim that the Good is itself 'beyond being', have led to many complex metaphysical interpretations, particularly by the Neo-Platonists. But it is possible to take the thought fairly simply, as being just the correlate of the claim about knowledge. If goodness is fundamental for our understanding of the nature of things, then it must be fundamental in the nature of things, else our understanding would not reflect the world as it is. For Plato, not only is there no gap between our knowledge of facts and our knowledge of values, there is no difference of ultimate nature between facts and values in the world. And if goodness is basic for our understanding of things, then in the world goodness and other values are not peculiar or derivative entities; they are just as real as other things, indeed in some obscure way *more* real. Without going into the metaphysics of this claim, which he leaves hanging, we can see that Plato commits himself to the very general claim that goodness is supreme in the order of things, and hence basic to any attempt to make the world intelligible. We must be careful not to confuse these beliefs about the sovereignty of good with shallow optimism about Providence and all being for the best. Plato's enthusiasm for what is absolutely good, the separated form, coexists with extreme pessimism about the amount of goodness to be found in the actual world.

One thing clear about the Sun figure is that it is an analogy: *as* the sun is in the visible realm, *so* the Good is in the intelligible realm. The distinction between visible and intelligible is now further explicated by the figure of the Line (509d). The difference is illustrated by the ratio of an unequally divided line, its parts divided in the same ratio. The result is:

where BD : DC and CE : EA as BC: CA. (Plato does not himself remark that this results in DC and CE being equal.) These sections represent levels of clarity. BD contains 'images' *(eikones)* of which examples are shadows and reflections of objects. These are later (511d–e) said to have as the corresponding mental state *eikasia*. I leave this untranslated because it is very disputed what the correct translation should be.

DC contains the originals of these images; examples are living things and natural or manufactured objects. The corresponding mental state is *pistis* or 'belief' (the word suggests confident belief).

CE and EA are harder. Plato is referring very elliptically to issues that are later made clearer in Book 7. In CE the mind uses the contents of DC in turn as images and thus is forced to seek on the basis of hypotheses—for example, students of mathematics reason on the basis of certain mathematical assumptions or hypotheses, and are forced to use visible illustrations, although they are reasoning about intelligible objects, not the contents of DC. This is *dianoia* or 'thinking'.

In EA the mind proceeds entirely by means of Forms, reasoning not from hypotheses but rather *to* an unhypothetical first principle. This is *noēsis* or 'intellect'.

Since BD : DC as CE : EA the contents of BD should stand to those of DC as those of CE stand to those of EA. The contents of BD are images or reflections of those of DC; but with CE and EA Plato does not say this straightforwardly, but presents the difference between the sections as being one of method.

Is the line an analogy, like the Sun? In that case, the lower part is merely illustrating facts about belief and its objects which illuminate knowledge and its objects in the upper part. Some features of the Line suggest that this is indeed the case.

Firstly, the Line is introduced as classifying the intelligible and *visible* world, carrying on from the Sun; and the language of vision is sustained throughout. But this is weak, for at 510a (and 534a in a passage that refers back to this one) the lower part is said to represent the whole world of *belief,* not just of vision.

Secondly, the equality of DC and CE suggests that Plato is not interested in having each section of the Line illustrate an increase in clarity over the one before; his interest lies rather in the ratio BC : CA and the light cast on CA by BC and the internal structure of each, not in the whole line that results.

Thirdly, the lowest stage of the Line, *eikasia,* is not a significant state in its own right. How much time do we spend looking at images and reflections, and how interesting is this? It has a point only as illustrating the relation of imaging holding between the contents of BD and DC (which in turn illuminate the upper part of the line).

So it does look as though the relation between BD and DC is an easy one (literal imaging) to aid us in understanding the very obscure relation between CE and EA. And so we have the visible illustrating the intelligible, just as in the Sun figure, the only new feature being the use of the contrast between image and original to express the relation between the visible and intelligible realms (as well as the relation within the visible realm which illuminates that within the intelligible).

However, as often happens with Plato, his eagerness to use analogy and images to illustrate a point leads him into intellectual unclarity. For there are also convincing signs that the Line is not just an extended analogy, but is also meant to be in its own right an ambitious classification of the different states a person may be in with regard to knowledge, from the lowest to the highest.

Firstly, we do have one line, not two, whereas in the Sun the two terms of the analogy were quite distinct. And the stages of the continuous line are said to correspond to degrees of clarity (509d, 511d–e), suggesting that the Line is not merely a device to let the bottom part provide an analogy for the top part.

Secondly, the passage stresses something which is odd if all that is going on is an analogy of visible and intelligible realms. Mathematicians, we are told, use the contents of DC as images, though the DC inhabitants are originals of the images in BD. This point is made three times (510b, 510e, 511a) in a very brief passage, and it precisely links the perceptible and intelligible worlds that have to be held in contrast if the Line is only an analogy.

Thirdly, the passage at the end of the Line (511d) has Socrates listing four mental states which differ in clarity as do the objects to which they correspond; the mental states are said to be clear in so far as their objects partake of truth or reality. This seems to be an explicit attempt to present the Line as a classification of cognitive states and their objects, not just a limited analogy.

So the Line, uncomfortably, both distinguishes the visible and intelligible realms to compare them, and also puts them on a continuous scale of epistemological achievement. Undoubtedly one function of the Line is to grade our cognitive states according to their distance from full knowledge with understanding. We learn from the Line various important points about knowledge. One is that the prominence of the image/original relation shows that Plato puts a premium on knowing a thing directly, rather than indirectly via reflections or images. Another is that in the crucial stage of moving from objects adequately apprehended by experience to Forms, an important role is played by mathematics. Another is that mathematics is nevertheless inadequate, for two reasons: it relies on visible illustrations, and it depends on hypotheses, whereas the true 'intellect' of the philosopher is free from these defects and operates only with reference to Forms (511b–c). We already know why mathematics is specially useful; it more than other subjects forces one to think out problems rather than being satisfied with what we can see; and this is the beginning of wisdom. But what these defects of mathematics are, and whether they are linked, and how philosophical reasoning avoids them, are matters not clarified until Book 7.

There are some oddities with the Line's classification of cognitive states and their objects. For one thing, the lowest stage, *eikasia,* seems not to correspond to anything significant in our lives, and appears to be there only for the sake of the analogy to be made between visible and intelligible worlds. Everyday beliefs mostly fall under 'belief', and the important stage is the one where the person is forced (by mathematical reasoning or whatever) to think things through and realize that there are Forms as well as particulars. Another, related point is that 'thinking' *(dianoia),* the all-important stage of forcing oneself to think things out, is confined to mathematical thinking. This seems too restrictive. In the Book 7 passage at 523–5 mathematical concepts are only some among those that make the mind work out what experience does not satisfactorily settle. Further, where in the Line is the Good, so stressed in the figure of the Sun? Reading the Line after the Sun we are naturally led to think that the Good is identical with the 'unhypothetical first principle' grasped by the person with *noēsis* or 'intellect'. But it does not fit into the scheme of the Line very happily. It cannot be just one of the contents of EA; but if not, where can it go? Worst of all, however, the Line's uncertainty of purpose makes it unclear how the cognitive states are being classified—by their objects or by their methods. In the lower part it seems clearly to be by object—one moves from *eikasia* to 'belief' by looking at trees rather than at reflections of trees. Does the same, though, hold in the upper part?

Pressing this question creates unexpectedly annoying difficulties; no answer seems quite right. Unless we are content to say that the contrast between BD and DC is of a quite different kind from that between CE and EA (which would be an admission that Plato's analogy is inept) we have to choose one of two unsatisfactory alternatives.

(1) The analogy does carry over; the logic of the passage demands different objects for the mind in CE and in EA. But since EA contains Forms, what does CE contain? Now we know from Aristotle that Plato at some point held that mathematics studies not Forms but 'intermediate' objects, which are different from the objects of sense-experience but distinct also from Forms, since they are 'many but eternal'. A little reflection shows the plausibility of this: mathematicians talk about *circles* and *lines,* not about the physical diagrams that illustrate them, nor about the unique Form of Circle and Form of Line. But while this idea makes most sense of the passage and its reference to mathematics, nothing in the *Republic* has prepared us for it. And it conflicts directly with what is said in the passage at 510d, that mathematicians talk about the 'the square itself' and 'the diagonal itself' (surely Forms) as well as the stress throughout the central books on mathematics as the best introduction to the kind of thinking that recognizes Forms.

(2) But if 'thinking', especially mathematical thinking, leads us on to Forms, then the contrast between it and 'intellect' or purely philosophical thought must be a difference of method as regards the same object. Such a difference is not hard to find, especially in the light of Book 7: 'thinking' studies Forms in isolation, for the purpose of special subjects like mathematics, whereas 'intellect' studies them for their own sake, and in systematic connection, as being dependent on the Form of Good for their nature and intelligibility. However, if this is the case, then the scheme of the Line breaks down—the structure of the bottom part has no real analogy in the top part—and Plato is misleading when he concludes the passage by listing four states (each with its own subject) that are stages of progressive cognitive improvement.

The insolubility of this problem is a good illustration of the difficulties that Plato runs into by using images to make a philosophical point. The imagery is apt to get overloaded, as happens with the Line, because Plato is trying to do two things at once with it. And the detail of the imagery tempts us to ask questions that cannot be satisfactorily answered within the terms of the imagery; if we treat it with philosophical seriousness the image turns out incoherent. As Iris Murdoch says (*The Fire and the Sun,* p. 68), 'The Theory of Forms, when read in conjunction with the explanatory tropes of the Line and the Cave . . . can certainly produce some blazingly strong imagery in the mind which may well in the long run obstruct understanding.' Plato might well agree; he certainly warns us that he is providing *only* images.

The Cave is Plato's most famous image, dominating many people's interpretation of what Plato's most important ideas are. This is a pity, because, as with the Line, severe problems arise over interpreting the imagery philosophically, and there are persistent disagreements.

Imagine, says Socrates, prisoners in an underground cave with a fire behind them, bound so they can only see the shadows on the wall in front of them, cast by puppets manipulated on a wall behind them. They think that this is all there is to see; if released from their bonds and forced to turn round to the fire and the puppets they become bewildered and are happier left in their original state. They are even angry with anyone who tries to tell them how pitiful their position is. Only a few can bear to realize that the shadows are only shadows cast by the puppets; and they begin the journey of liberation that leads past the fire and right out of the cave to the real world. At first they are dazzled here, and can bear to see real objects only in reflections and indirectly, but then they look at them directly in the light of the sun, and can even look at the sun itself.

The prisoners are 'like us', says Socrates (515a). The Cave is, then, not just the degraded state of a bad society. It is the human condition. Even in the ideally just society, we all start in the Cave. We don't all end there, though; at least in the ideally just society some, who are the Guardians, journey upwards to achieve knowledge and wisdom.

The Cave is Plato's most optimistic and beautiful picture of the power of philosophy to free and enlighten. Abstract thinking, which leads to philosophical insight, is boldly portrayed as something liberating. The person who starts to think is shown as someone who breaks the bonds of conformity to ordinary experience and received opinion, and the progress of enlightenment is portrayed as a journey from darkness into light. Unlike the passive majority, people who start to use their minds are doing something for themselves; after the first (admittedly mysterious) release from bonds it requires the person's own utmost effort to toil upwards out of the Cave. Few thinkers in philosophy or fiction have given a more striking, and moving, picture of philosophical thinking as a releasing of the self from undifferentiated conformity to a developing and enriching struggle for the attainment of truth.

With this picture, and necessary as the other term of the contrast, goes Plato's darkest and most pessimistic picture of the state of those *not* enlightened by philosophy. They are helpless and passive, manipulated by others. Worse, they are used to their state and *like* it, resisting efforts to free them from it. Their satisfaction is a kind of false consciousness about their state; they cannot even recognize and respond to the truth about their terrible condition. This picture notably puts *all* the ordinary person's beliefs on the same level; it does not fit the picture we have had so far, namely that most of the beliefs people have are all right as long as they are about unproblematic matters of experience, and that knowledge is only lacking about difficult and disputed matters like justice. In the imagery of the Cave Plato presses so far his antipathy to the passive and acquiescent state of the unreflective that the unenlightened state is presented as being totally substandard. We shall see that this blanket condemnation leads to a problem of interpretation, but even without this it is clear that to liken all our ordinary beliefs to the seeing of shadows creates a sharp cut-off between the state of the enlightened and that of the unenlightened. They do not inhabit the same cognitive world. The Cave has always provided the main support for those who interpret Plato as holding that the philosopher has knowledge which has nothing to do with experience, and as consigning everyone else to a mental state no better than that of illusion, one quite cut off from knowledge and pathetic by comparison with the real thing.

At 517a Socrates tells Glaucon that the image must be applied as a whole to what has gone before. Clearly the cave and fire correspond to the visible world, and the world outside the cave to the realm of thought. But how detailed is the correspondence? This is a subject of great dispute. Traditionally the Cave has been taken to fill out the scheme of the Line; and it is very plausible that something like this is meant—what else could Plato be referring to? If we do this, then the state of the bound prisoners will be that of *eikasia,* and when they are turned around painfully to see the puppets and fire they get to the

stage of 'belief'. The ascent out of the Cave is the ascent from the world
of the senses and what they tell us to the world of thought; seeing
reflections is the stage of 'thinking', *dianoia,* while seeing the real
thing is 'intellect' or *noēsis,* and the sun is the Form of Good.

We would perhaps be tempted to harmonize Line and Cave even
without Plato's encouragement, since there is an obvious continuity of
interest in the relation of image to original. But apart from the fact
that the Cave does not divide neatly into four sections, there are two
problems of harmonization which both point up the problems latent
in the Cave.

Firstly, while the Line stresses the passage from the world of sense
to that of thought, and by making this a case of the image/original
relation stresses its continuity with what happens within those worlds,
the Cave stresses the sharp division between them. The journey out of
the Cave is unlike anything that happens *in* the Cave or out of it; there
are, as in the Sun figure, two worlds, contrasted and not continuous.
This is pointed up by the Cave's insistence on the inexplicable nature
of the conversion to enlightenment; the prisoner's release from bonds
is an unexplained intervention, not an extension of anything done before. The Line, on the other hand, presents each move to more clarity
as a comprehensible example of something done before: a move from
image to original.

Secondly, how can the prisoners be in a state of *eikasia,* as they
must be if correspondence with the Line is to be maintained? *Eikasia*
in the Line was literally looking at shadows and reflections. But the
prisoners represent the ordinary person's beliefs in general. Of course,
Plato wants us to see everyday beliefs as no better than seeing shadows
and reflections. But what are we to do about the state of 'belief'? In the
Line this is the normal state of seeing trees and people. In the Cave it
is painful, requires effort, and induces bewilderment.

There are two obvious ways to remove the problem. One is to inflate
*eikasia* in the Line, claiming that Plato means it there to cover all ordinary beliefs. He introduces the class by means of the easy examples of
literal reflection only to prepare us for the idea that *all* everyday beliefs
are, properly considered, really about mere shadows and reflections.
But this interpretation cannot survive a careful reading of the Line; the
contrast there drawn between *eikasia* and belief is quite straightfor-
ward, gives us a clear literal case of the image/original relation, and
would never have suggested further inflation to anyone not aware of
the problem with the Cave.

The other response is to admit that *eikasia* in both Line and Cave means simply looking at shadows, and to urge that what needs expansion is the notion of *looking at shadows*. The prisoners in the Cave are described as looking at the shadows of puppets, but what this signifies is the taking over, in unreflective fashion, of second-hand opinions and beliefs. If the prisoners are 'like us' when bound and not when turned round, then their state must, surely, include more than literally looking at shadows of objects. But both moves fail to avoid the problem that if, on the natural way of making Line and Cave correspond, the prisoners are in a state of *eikasia,* then *eikasia* has a different range in Line and Cave. In the Line, it covers looking at reflections, something we spend a fraction of our time doing. In the Cave, it covers what we spend nearly all our time doing.

This shift can be partly explained by the fact that the whole tenor of the Cave is to downgrade our ordinary beliefs, to urge us to regard them as being no better than looking at shadows. The Cave is more pessimistic than the Line about even the best of our everyday beliefs. There is also, though, a more precisely specifiable cause of the problem. The whole Cave is an image, an extended metaphor. Within the metaphor, the prisoners are literally looking at shadows cast by physical objects (a state which looks like that of *eikasia* in the Line). But then we find that within the metaphor another layer of metaphor has been added: the puppets are within the whole image literally puppets, but they also stand for moral qualities the prisoners dispute about shadows of justice and the like (517d–e). So within the whole image the shadows are literally shadows and metaphorically are any ordinary opinions about things like justice, taken over unreflectively and based on acquiescence in the way things appear rather than effort to find out how they really are. No wonder it is tempting both to compare and to contrast the prisoners' state with the state of *eikasia* in the Line. Given the logic of the whole image of the Cave, the states do correspond, but Plato has, once again, overloaded his imagery, and, in order to make the low state of the prisoners a plausible picture of the human condition, has got us to think of their state not just as part of the whole image, but on a further level of metaphor; this makes his point graphically but wrecks correspondence with the Line. Once more he has himself illustrated the dangers in the philosophical use of images, dangers which he warns against without seeming strikingly alive to. For if Line and Cave are to be interpreted consistently, then the Cave cannot be a picture of the universal human need for enlightenment, which it is clearly meant to be. Plato has got so carried away by his desire to stress the utterly contemptible nature of the state unenlightened by philosophical thought that the imagery, memorable though it is, has no consistent overall interpretation.

Sun, Line, and Cave are philosophically frustrating; they point us in too many directions at once. Their power has always lain in their appeal to the imagination, and the harsh forceful contrast they draw between the life content with appearance and superficiality, and the richly rewarding life dedicated to finding out the truth. Their appeal is so strong that interpreters are perennially tempted to try to harmonize them in a consistent philosophical interpretation, despite Plato's own warnings on the limits of the kind of thinking that is guided by images and illustrations.

All three images stress vision and sight, and two of them use light as a metaphor for the truth. The Cave is especially rich in visual detail. However, it and the Sun resist visual representation; only the schematic Line can be successfully turned into a visual aid, while attempts to picture Sun and Cave, for all their pictorial suggestiveness, render them merely bizarre. The only successful visual translation of the Cave's terms of metaphor that I am aware of is Bernardo Bertolucci's movie *The Conformist.* (This is based on a novel of the same title by Alberto Moravia, but the use of the Cave imagery to interpret the story is entirely Bertolucci's idea, and indeed is something that can only be done in cinematic terms.) It has often been pointed out that the Cave is a 'dynamic' image whereas the other two are 'static', and no doubt this is why we have had to wait for the availability of movie techniques for Plato's image to be successfully interpreted in other than philosophical terms. It is worth considering the movie briefly, because it brings out in two very interesting ways points which we are likely to forget if we concentrate on the Cave solely for its significance for the 'theory of Forms'.

One point is that, although the Cave represents the general condition of 'people like us', it has features that suggest a particularly bad society. The human condition is not a social vacuum; there are people in the Cave manipulating the prisoners, as well as the prisoners themselves. The prisoners are prisoners within a given political system; they are political conformists. The protagonist of Bertolucci's film, Marcello, is a conformist in Mussolini's Italy. Fascist Italy is portrayed cinematically in terms of images, reflections, and fragmented appearances. Such a society models for us particularly well the kind of society that Plato saw in contemporary Athens: a society interested in surface and *bella figura,* impressed by showy and unsound schemes and grandiose buildings, a society where what matters is not truth but presenting a good 'public image' and manipulating public opinion. (Cf. Gorgias 517a–519b.) A society like this has no interest in encouraging its citizens to develop their own moral views. It has every interest in encouraging conformity to received opinion by dominating 'the media' (as we put it) and getting people to care only about the images presented to them, seeing no need for a positive moral response of their own. Bertolucci's development of Plato's Cave brings out how much an individual is encouraged to make false choices, and to do things he can recognize to be unworthy of him, if he lives in a society that positively rewards false and superficial values and encourages intelligent people to make only a cynical use of their abilities. This is a point which it is easy to miss in the Cave if we are concentrating on the philosopher's struggle for enlightenment; Plato, though, does not forget the importance of society and the formative power it has over the kind of lives people lead. He is so concerned with reforming education to produce good people that we are justified in seeing in the Cave not only a general point about humanity but a picture of false education and the wrong kind of society.

*The Conformist* is also interesting for one important way in which Plato's image is put to a characteristically twentieth-century use which reveals itself as highly un-Platonic. For Marcello does in the end make the painful turn towards the fire, and we are left in no doubt that he will, even at considerable outward cost, no longer live by what he can see to be factitious values. But even a Marxist like Bertolucci makes the beginning of Marcello's intellectual liberation come from his realizing and facing the implications of particular facts about himself. His failure to make genuine moral choices comes from his failure to face truths about himself which he is unwilling to recognize because of their implications. The knowledge represented in the movie by the turning to the fire is *self*-knowledge, and we are given to understand that it is the denial of truths about the self that leads people to live unauthentic lives, lives that are fragmented, unintegrated, and spent pursuing false and superficial values. To us this seems the natural place to begin. We tend to think that wisdom is built on self-knowledge, and that the beginnings of wisdom are found in facing facts about oneself. We find it natural to think that the false consciousness of the prisoners, their failure to recognize the state they are in, is due to ignorance of the ways in which their lives are deformed by the manipulations of others. They are ignorant of themselves. It is important to see that Plato does not think in this way. The prisoners *are* ignorant of their real nature and real needs, but no role at all is played in the intellectual awakening to these needs and natures by particular facts about individuals. The knowledge that the prisoners wake up to is impersonal; individual scrutiny of self plays no role at all. Plato sees no intellectual value in particular facts about particular individuals. The prisoner's mysterious release from bonds is to be achieved by abstract and impersonal studies like mathematics. The ascent out of the Cave offers no personal interest or fulfilment, not even the satisfaction of having shed inauthentic roles. Plato is at pains to stress how much at odds the ascent puts you with other people, and how peculiar they think you (516e–517a, 517b–d). The culmination of the whole journey is comprehension of the Form of Good—and this is precisely not what is good for the seeker, or good for others, or good in relation to anything or anyone, but simply and unqualifiedly good, in a way that is completely impersonal and indifferent between individuals.

One result of this is that it is indeed mysterious why anybody would be impelled to start the journey. In the *Symposium,* Plato stresses the force of personal love in turning us from the unthinkingness of everyday life to the eternal and impersonal Forms, and in the *Phaedrus* (250b–d) says that Beauty is the Form that is first and most easily found attractive. (These themes are pursued in many of the novels of Iris Murdoch.) But the *Republic* is more austere. The philosophers turn towards the impersonal Good because that is where they are led by impersonal disciplines like mathematics. Although Plato does elsewhere say that philosophers will feel desire for the truth (cf. 485b, d, 486a), the message of Sun, Line, and Cave is that it is mathematics that leads to the Forms. But why should future philosophers ever in the first place see the importance of studies of such an abstract kind, not directed to any self-promoting end? Plato has no answer, and in making the prisoner be freed and forced to turn round by someone else, is perhaps admitting that he has no answer, other than the fact that some people just are by nature dissatisfied with materialistic self-seeking and conformity, and are 'impelled', as we put it, by their own intellectual bent to see the value in studies that everyone else regards as a waste of time.

Sun, Line, and Cave all in different ways stress the impersonal nature of the knowledge of the Good that is the basis of the just person's understanding and grounds all explanation of matters of fact. The Line tells us that the disciplines that first lead us to real knowledge are not concerned directly with moral aspects of the world, but are, surprisingly, abstract and mathematical (and this at a point where such a claim has not been at all filled out). The Sun and Cave have stressed the extreme difference between any of our ordinary thinking about personal concerns and the thinking that can amount to knowledge. We are left in no doubt about the difficulty of being a philosopher and turning through abstract studies to the Form of Good, the good which is absolute and in no way relative to anybody's or anything's interests or needs. We would not have expected these developments just from the actual discussions of Forms, but they are unmistakably there.

But these developments ought to worry us. For if we recall the main argument, Socrates showed that justice was the harmonious state of a person's soul, as part of an argument to show that justice was worth having *for the person.* Justice in the soul is like health in the body. It is the state controlled by knowledge of what is best for all the factors concerned. Reason in the soul knows what is best for *all* the soul's parts, including personal aspirations and particular desires. Now we find, however, that this knowledge requires an abandonment of one's personal concerns. The Good that is the supreme object of knowledge has nothing to do with one's *own* good; it is the purely impersonal Form of Good. But how can the knowledge that produces harmony in my soul, caring for all my concerns, require me to turn away from the world I share with others and concentrate on what is simply just and good, not just or good *for me?* How can the knowledge developed by mathematics, the kind of understanding it engenders, make my soul harmonious? And if not, why should it be something that I would obviously want to have? But the whole argument of the *Republic* was meant to show that justice, and the knowledge it involves, was something that I should want to have. Something seems to have gone very wrong.

This problem can be restated in terms of a distinction between two conceptions of what the philosopher is like. For the developments of Sun, Line, and Cave have made the philosopher's knowledge appear to be no longer practical, but rather theoretical, and we can distinguish two conceptions of the philosopher that correspond to this: the *practical* one, and what (following Irwin) I shall call the *contemplative* one.

Plato has claimed that to be truly just one needs to be a philosopher—that is, not simply be right by accident or luck in one's upbringing, but have full and properly based articulate understanding. But all the same, the philosopher's knowledge should, if the argument is to work, be of a practical kind. That is, even if knowledge requires grasp of Forms, it must be applicable to experience in such a way as to guide the person to make good particular choices; it must enlighten the process of moral development that he or she actually goes through, and be of use in particular cases. (Plato himself makes the point at 484c–d, 520c.) The just person's knowledge, however much it may require theoretical grounding and the ability to give reasons of a highly abstract kind, must be practical in the sense that having it makes a difference in experience and particular decisions. Practical knowledge is what makes the just person *just,* when he or she might not have been. This is the point of comparing the ideally just rulers to skilled pilots or doctors, who make the right decisions in practice because they know what they are doing; they do not just have a happy knack, but understand their subject. Plato has claimed that this kind of knowledge is worth having because it is a condition of having psychic harmony, that is, a fulfilled and integrated personality rather than a confused and frustrated one. If this is what the just person's knowledge is, then while it may require grasping Forms it cannot be limited to them but must be displayed in experience; one's understanding of Forms and the Good is shown in the making of rational and grounded decisions instead of unreflective and prejudiced ones.

On this way of looking at the philosopher's knowledge, we do not need to squeeze out of the discussions of Forms more than the obvious results of them: namely, that in some important matters we need thought, and not just the ordinary course of experience, to attain understanding, and that the wise person's claim to make others' decisions better than they do lies in superior understanding of disputed and difficult matters, something that requires study not necessary in unproblematic matters of fact.

We have seen, however, that Sun, Line, and Cave suggest a different picture of the philosopher—the contemplative picture, where what characterizes him or her is the desire to escape entirely from the world of practical affairs. Philosophical knowledge is associated with impersonal disciplines like mathematics rather than with the desire to sort out actual tangled moral problems. The knowledge that involves understanding of the Forms is represented as so infinitely worthwhile in itself that everything else—everything typical of the human condition—is mere trash by comparison. It is completely unclear how such knowledge could ever have application to matters concerning the two lower parts of the soul, which are concerned with particular and personal things; and these parts are downplayed in these passages in favour of a stress on reason and mathematical thinking as being the capacity in virtue of which a philosopher rises above his or her fellows.

The idea that study of Forms is an end in itself and is to be contrasted with the lowly status of practical concerns goes naturally with the view that knowledge not only begins but ends with Forms, that there is properly speaking no knowledge of particulars, only an inferior state of belief; if Forms are the only objects of knowledge, then particular people, things, and actions are not capable of being known, just because they are particulars. The Sun begins with a wholesale contrast between objects of thought and objects of perception (507b); the Line suggests that different cognitive states are correlated with different objects; and the philosopher emerges from the Cave into another world, leaving the original environment behind. If knowledge is only of Forms, then it does require a wholesale downgrading of our originally accepted beliefs. The people who advance to understanding will not check their discoveries against our intuitions, or beliefs about matters of fact; they will resolutely turn away from consideration of any particular matters of fact—from the 'darkness' into the 'light' of Forms.

These are very different ways of looking at the rule of reason and what it requires in the soul. Why does Plato not see that they are very different? How can the just rulers be compared to doctors and pilots when the beginning of wisdom is to turn away from mortal trash? Plato seems to have drifted away from what the argument needs, the philosopher as practically wise, the good person who is the norm for moral judgments because judging rationally and from understanding. We now find the philosopher raptly contemplating Forms and only Forms, dismissing the world we experience as being on the level of a shadow or a dream.

The practical conception of the philosopher, though it does not entail that there be Forms only for a restricted range of terms, fits much more happily with that idea; and the contemplative conception likewise, though it does not entail that there are Forms for every term, fits more happily with that view. For if knowledge requires grasp of Forms, and also requires a wholesale rejection or downgrading of our beliefs about everything, there seems absolutely no point in limiting Forms to a restricted range of terms. It is therefore all the more frustrating that Plato's position on this issue is not unambiguously clear in the *Republic*. The actual passages of argument that involve Forms depend on a restricted range of Forms, but Plato is not explicit or clear about this, and the considerations that produce this range seem to be of diverse kinds. Further, Plato sometimes talks of Forms as though what characterized them was changelessness, and in Sun, Line, and Cave talks as though there were something inherently defective about the whole world of experienced particulars just as such. And in Book 10 (admittedly an odd production as a whole) he brings in Forms in a way guaranteed to cause conflict with the accounts in Books 5 and 7. This means, unfortunately, that we cannot rely on what is claimed about Forms to settle the question, whether Plato is confused about shifting from the practical to the theoretical conception of the philosopher. For Plato gives us no independent way of getting clear precisely what his claims about Forms are; and the apparent move of generalizing from a restricted range of Forms is just part of the shift from the practical to the theoretical conception of the philosopher, not something that can independently explain it.

One thing that is clear is that nothing *compels* Plato to the contemplative conception of the philosopher. Certainly it is not merely the recognition of Forms. Plato could have stressed as much as he liked the value of studying the Forms and the perspective from which all worldly concerns seem infinitely little, and still have held the practical conception. The philosopher would then be a person in whom this knowledge grounds and directs his or her practical judgments and makes them good ones, that display understanding and promote justice in the world. This would make plausible, if anything could, the just person's claim to rule those who are not just. Plato does not need to stress those features of the philosopher's knowledge, which surface in Books 6 and 7—the stress on mathematics, the Cave's insistence on wholesale rejection of everyday beliefs and downgrading of everyday concerns. These seem to spring from the contemplative conception of the philosopher, not just from recognition of Forms and the need to grasp them.

Further, the two views are destined for conflict. For the contemplative view makes the philosopher's detached study of Forms infinitely more valuable than anything he or she could achieve in the practical sphere. There is no comparison: everything but the studies that lead one out of the Cave are mere rubbish. So on the political level we are moved to ask what it is about this knowledge that fits philosophers to *rule* themselves and others. And on the individual level we have to ask whether this incomparable supremacy of the aims of reason allows reason to function as the best arbiter of the interests of *all* the soul's parts. How can it allow any weight at all to the claims of the other parts, when these are compared with the claims of reason? The objects of every faculty but reason have already been judged to be, in comparison with its objects, worthless trash. But if reason's claims are so incomparably superior, how can its rule produce harmony and unity in the whole soul, as was so much stressed? The practical conception of the philosopher is a comprehensible development of the main argument; the contemplative conception undermines it. Why should exclusive study of Forms lead to psychic harmony?

Plato may simply be confused here in letting the contemplative conception develop without warning from the practical one. He may just be so predisposed to think that study of Forms is all-valuable that he does not notice the problems that this causes for his argument. However, before ascribing simple muddle to him, we should look for a better explanation. The problem, after all, should be as obvious to Plato as to us; and it is Plato who both spends pages of Book 6 discussing the need for philosophers to have a knowledge which is practical and directive, and then from the very beginning of the Sun figure makes the Good that they seek into a separate Form. The problem comes because Plato is being over-ambitious and treats two very different things as parts of a single project. (We have seen something analogous already in his desire to show that soul and state are both just in exactly the same way.) Plato does not want to allow that practical and theoretical reasoning (the notions of reason uppermost in the practical and contemplative conceptions of the philosopher) ever *could* conflict. He thinks of reason as a *single* faculty that can be displayed either in practical contexts or in theoretical contemplation and reasoning; and so no matter how much he stresses the disinterested and detached nature of contemplation of the Forms, he wants this to be an exercise of the *same* reason as is shown in good practical judgement. He would reject any distinction of practical and theoretical reasoning, and hence of the 'practical' and 'contemplative' conceptions of the philosopher; he would say that there was only one conception, that of the person in whom reason is supreme *both* in contemplating the Forms *and* in making good practical decisions.

But we have seen that this will not do; this idea is inherently unstable, because the claims of contemplation as they are presented deny the value to practical and individual concerns that is required for good practical judgement. Plato is led by his desire to see reason as a unity to give unsatisfactory answers as to how it operates. Aristotle, in his *Nicomachean Ethics* (especially the sixth book), reacts sharply against Plato in a way we find sympathetic; he clearly distinguishes practical reasoning from theoretical, and insists that a person outstanding in one may be undistinguished in the other. Young men, he says, can be excellent mathematicians but morally immature, for sound moral judgement comes with experience. (This is undoubtedly a hit at the *Republic*'s mathematically-based programme for pure moral understanding.) Theoretical reasoning concerns universals, whereas action and practical choice are inevitably concerned with particulars; so the two are quite distinct in form and operation. (However, in spite of his clarity on this point Aristotle himself sometimes succumbs to the temptation to assimilate the form of practical reasoning to that of theoretical, and he also fails to reconcile the claims of both forms of reasoning in a single life. Plato's ambitious idea is not a *gratuitous* one; it is one that has appealed to many.)

It is in terms of the distinction between the practical and contemplative conceptions of the philosopher, and his assimilation of them, that we can best understand a famous problem that besets Plato in the *Republic*. The Guardians' progress is the journey out of the Cave; so if they are to rule others they must leave the studies that they excel in and find pleasant and rewarding, and go back down into the Cave. Plato makes it clear that they will not want to do this (519c–521b) and that it will be a matter of 'persuasion and compulsion'. (He does not specify how much compulsion, or how it will work.) Now given the practical conception of the philosopher, there is no obvious reason why he or she should be unwilling to rule: previous training will have developed those capacities and that knowledge which (even if unobviously) best fit a person to decide better than others. The Guardians' reluctance comes from the contemplative conception of the philosopher (significantly it arises within the Cave imagery). Someone engrossed in the study of impersonal Forms, someone who has rejected as trash the claims of the world we experience, can hardly be keen to conduct interviews and sit on boring committees. Once the Guardians are thought of as finding their natural fulfilment in detached intellectual study, there is an obvious problem, why they should return to the Cave. Plato offers several reasons for why they will none the less go. Some are bad or obviously inadequate: thus, they owe it to the city for their privileged upbringing (520a–c); rulers who don't want to rule are better than those who do (520d). The real ground is stated at 519e–520a, and is repeated at 520e in the claim that we are making a 'just order to just people'. The Guardians know what is just because they have the knowledge that is based on the Form of Good. Their return is demanded by the justice that prescribes disinterestedly what is best for all (519e–520a). They do not go down because it is better for them; they would be happier and better off doing philosophy. Nor do they sacrifice themselves altruistically for the others; the others do benefit by their rule, but so do they, for under any other rule they would suffer, deprived of their appropriate role of organizing society for the best. They go down because they realize that that is best—simply *best*, not best *for* any particular group of people. They know what is really good, not good relative to the interests or situation of anyone. And it demands their return; so they go. Their motivation is thus very abstract. They are not seeking their own happiness. Nor are they seeking that of others. They are simply doing what is impersonally best; they make an impersonal response to an impersonal demand. They are not swayed by considerations of their own happiness or their own interests; they consider these merely as part of the workings of the whole, and give them their due place and value along with everybody else's. They take a wholly impersonal attitude to their own happiness, along with everybody else's; and this is because their judgements are made in the light of the impersonal Good, the separated Form which is what is simply *good*, not good relative to anything. They can act in the light of what justice requires because they can detach themselves from their own personal standpoint; for they have experienced the enlightenment which the Cave portrayed as a turning away from one's own personal concerns towards the light of abstract studies and the separated Forms.

But this throws us right back on the problem already raised: why should *I* do what justice requires? The *Republic* began from the inadequacy of act-centered theories, which presented justice as a set of arbitrary and external demands. The discussion of the state, and of the soul's parts and virtues, allowed Plato to show that justice is not this, but is a state of the person that is clearly in their interests, because it is the condition for psychic health and unity. But the central books seem to have undermined this claim, by showing that the knowledge required to be just is knowledge of what is *impersonally* just. Now this does not give us an answer to something that worried us before: why should just people not act against the interests of others? Now we have seen that they will not do this. But in the process we have ruled out their acting in their own interests either. For it has turned out that they do not act in, or against, *anybody*'s interests, but in accordance with the impersonal prescriptions of what is absolutely just and good. However, Plato made Socrates accept the strongest form of Glaucon's challenge: show me that it is in my interests really to be, rather than only to seem, just. If this was accepted as legitimate, why is it not legitimate to ask, why *should* a Guardian go down to the Cave, when it is so clearly not in his or her interests? Why should a Guardian be, rather than seem, just? Why not, for example, try to get out of the descent by faking some incapacity for practical affairs?

Many people try to rescue Plato from this problem by pointing out that the Guardians themselves do not perceive the requirements of justice as conflicting with their interests. For, although they are (given the contemplative conception of the philosopher) happiest doing their abstract studies, they have attained a complete understanding of themselves and their role in the light of the impersonal Good, and so they can think of their own happiness impersonally and accept without resentment its sacrifice to the requirements of impersonal goodness. They accept a personal loss; but they have been trained to think impersonally about themselves as well as the rest of the world. For if knowledge, and the attainment of understanding in the light of the Good, require one to reject the importance of particular claims and individual interests, why should one's attitude to oneself be any exception? The Guardians can abstract from the personal viewpoint, from which one cares about one's own happiness and interests in a specially intimate way, and come to see themselves externally, as being merely parts of the whole, citizens with a part to play (and a specially vital part at that). And because they can take this viewpoint, and indeed do so in so far as they are thinking as wise and enlightened beings, they judge, and act, from a point of view from which sacrifice of mere personal happiness is not really a sacrifice that matters, or causes grief or resentment. We have seen that their treatment of the others in the state was done from a point of view that abstracted from the importance of individual concerns and values and thought of people entirely rationally, purely in the light of their objective social contribution (pp. 92–94). Now we see that they are quite consistent; they extend this attitude to themselves. And so we can see that they do not see the sacrifice of going down into the Cave as a real sacrifice, really against their interests; the loss it entails is one that they regard in a detached and impersonal way. There is no reason for a Guardian to care more about the loss of his or her personal happiness than to care about such a loss on the part of another person; it is not something that is judged to have any real value by comparison with the claims of what is rationally and impersonally required.

But this only raises the more urgently the question, why in that case *I* should want to be a Guardian? This matters, because the Guardians are not just a fanciful idea; they are what just people in a perfectly just society are supposed to be like. But now we see that justice demands that I retreat to a point of view from which I can judge my own happiness and interests in exactly the same impersonal way as everybody else's. I must come to cease to care about my own happiness in a specially intimate way. But why ever should it be in *my* interests to want to do that? Plato did not undertake to show that you have a reason to be, rather than seem, just if you are intellectually gifted and capable of taking an entirely rational and impersonal attitude to your own interests. This would have been totally irrelevant to Thrasymachus' challenge. What he undertook to show was that anyone has a reason to be, rather than seem, just. But it is far from clear that anyone has a reason to be just if that implies taking the viewpoint on one's own interests that the Guardians do. Justice was to have been shown to be in *my* interests. But now it requires that I abstract completely from my interests. But this seems no less external a demand on *me* than the rules of justice as put forward by Polemarchus. We seem to be right back at the beginning.

The Guardians' return to the Cave has always been recognized as a major problem in the *Republic*. For the results are very ugly whether the Guardians suffer real loss by doing it or not. If they suffer real loss, because their own prospects of happiness are sacrificed, then justice is not in their interests—and yet they are the paradigms of justice in a just society, and Plato set out to show that justice was in the agent's interests. But if they do not suffer real loss, because they view their own happiness as rationally and impersonally as they do everybody else's, then justice seems to demand an ideal, impersonal viewpoint which is not in the interests of any actual people to adopt. We thought that Plato's account had the virtue of taking seriously the claims of justice on us as we are; now justice demands that we positively stop being human. The more the Guardians' justice requires that they conform their own viewpoints to that of impersonal reason and impersonal goodness, the more any actual person is driven to ask why, if this is what justice requires, there is any reason for *him,* or *her,* to be just. Plato cannot have it both ways. Justice cannot be shown to be good for

me *and also* good in a way that has no reference to anybody or anything particular at all.

Why *should* I be just? By demanding that the just person be a philosopher and by then turning the philosopher into a contemplator only
of eternal Forms who abstracts from everything individual and personal, Plato has forced us to ask this question all over again.

In fact, the main argument, resumed in Books 8 and 9, does remain
alive to the question that was posed at the beginning and answered
in Book 4. The central books are not forgotten, and sometimes the
philosopher appears in the contemplative role, but the main thrust of
the following books follows through the attempt to show that justice
is worth my while, is something that it benefits the individual agent to
have. The glorious impersonality of the just person's viewpoint disap-
pears from the main argument. The central books, for all their striking
effect, have sent the moral argument in a new, and disturbing, direction.

We have seen that the most obvious source of Plato's difficulties is
his shift from the practical to the theoretical conception of the philosopher. This is *not* due simply to the introduction of Forms, which is
quite compatible with the practical view. It stems partly from Plato's
own predilection for contemplation and theoretical study as the activity
that has highest worth, and his tendency to contrast everything else
with this as paltry and perishable. But it stems also from his refusal to
allow that in developing the contemplative picture of the rule of reason
in the soul he is doing anything *new*. He will not allow that the functions of reason might ever be divided; he does not think that intellectual absorption will make claims on a person that cannot be reconciled
with the claims of practical judgement. Hence the reason that made
just decisions for me and for others becomes identified with the reason
that studies what is absolutely just, just unqualifiedly and not just for
me or for anyone. Plato does not see that such a notion of reason is
bound to split, and to threaten the coherence of his argument for the
worthwhileness of justice. This is not, however, a simple mistake.
There is a grandeur in the way that Plato makes the wise ruler be an
intellectual genius *as well,* refusing to allow that the detached study of
eternal truths is not an extension of the same thing as the just person's
powers of practical judgement, but is something entirely different.

# 10

## *The Sovereignty of Good* (excerpt)

### *Iris Murdoch*

Beauty and the τέχναι [crafts] are, to use Plato's image, the text written in large letters. The concept Good itself is the much harder to discern but essentially similar text written in small letters. In intellectual disciplines and in the enjoyment of art and nature we discover value in our ability to forget self, to be realistic, to perceive justly. We use our imagination not to escape the world but to join it, and this exhilarates us because of the distance between our ordinary dulled consciousness and an apprehension of the real. The value concepts are here patently tied on to the world, they are stretched as it were between the truth-seeking mind and the world, they are not moving about on their own as adjuncts of the personal will. The authority of morals is the authority of truth, that is of reality. We can see the length, the extension, of these concepts as patient attention transforms accuracy without interval into just discernment. Here too we can see it as natural to the particular kind of creatures that we are that love should be inseparable from justice, and clear vision from respect for the real.

That virtue operates in exactly the same kind of way in the central area of mortality is less easy to perceive. Human beings are far more complicated and enigmatic and ambiguous than languages or mathematical concepts, and selfishness operates in a much more devious and frenzied manner in our relations with them. Ignorance, muddle, fear, wishful thinking, lack of tests often make us feel that moral choice is something arbitrary, a matter for personal will rather than for attentive study. Our attachments tend to be selfish and strong, and the transformation of our loves from selfishness to unselfishness is sometimes hard even to conceive of. Yet is the situation really so different? Should a regarded child be kept at home or sent to an institution? Should an elderly relation who is a trouble-maker be cared for or asked to go away? Should an unhappy marriage be continued for the sake of the children? Should I leave my family in order to do political work? Should I neglect them in order to practise my art? The love which brings the right answer is an exercise of justice and realism and really *looking*. The difficulty is to keep the attention fixed upon the real situation and to prevent it from returning surreptitiously to the self with consolations of self-pity, resentment, fantasy and despair. The refusal to attend may even induce a fictitious sense of freedom: I may as well toss a coin. Of course virtue is good habit and dutiful action. But the background condition of such habit and such action, in human beings, is a just mode of vision and a good quality of consciousness. It is a *task* to come to see the world as it is. A philosophy which leaves duty without a context and exalts the idea of freedom and power as a separate top level value ignores this task and obscures the relation between virtue and reality. We act rightly 'when the time comes' not out of strength of will but out of the quality of our usual attachments and with the kind of energy and discernment which we have available. And to this the whole activity of our consciousness is relevant.

The central explanatory image which joins together the different aspects of the picture which I have been trying to exhibit is the concept of Good. It is a concept which is not easy to understand partly because it has so many false doubles, jumped-up intermediaries invented by human selfishness to make the difficult task of virtue look easier and more attractive: History, God, Lucifer, Ideas of power, freedom, purpose, reward, even judgment are irrelevant. Mystics of all kinds have usually known this and have attempted by extremities of language to portray the nakedness and aloneness of Good, its absolute for-nothing-ness. One might say that true morality is a sort of unesoteric mysticism, having its source in an austere and unconsoled love of the Good. When Plato wants to explain Good he uses the image of the sun. The moral pilgrim emerges from the cave and begins to see the real world in the light of the sun, and last of all is able to look at the sun itself. I want now to comment on various aspects of this extremely rich metaphor.

The sun is seen at the end of a long quest which involves a reorientation (the prisoners have to turn around) and an ascent. It is real, it is out there, but very distant. It gives light and energy and enables us to know truth. In its light we see the things of the world in their true relationships. Looking at it itself is supremely difficult and is unlike looking at things in its light. It is a different kind of thing from what it illuminates. Note the metaphor of 'thing' here. Good is a concept about which, and not only in philosophical language, we naturally use a Platonic terminology, when we speak about seeking the Good, or loving the Good. We may also speak seriously of ordinary things, people, works of art, as being good, although we are also well aware of their imperfections. Good lives as it were on both sides of the barrier and we can combine the aspiration to complete goodness with a realistic sense of achievement within our limitations. For all our frailty the command 'be perfect' has sense for us. The concept Good resists collapse into the selfish empirical consciousness. It is not a mere value tag of the choosing will, and functional and casual uses of 'good' (a good knife, a good fellow) are not, as some philosophers have wished to argue, clues to the structure of the concept. The proper and serious use of the term refers us to a perfection which is perhaps never exemplified in the world we know ('There is no good in us') and which carries with it the ideas of hierarchy and transcendence. How do we know that the very great are not the perfect? We see differences, we sense directions, and we know that the Good is still somewhere beyond. The self, the place where we live, is a place of illusion. Goodness is connected with the attempt to see the unself, to see and to respond to the real world in the light of a virtuous consciousness. This is the non-metaphysical meaning of the idea of transcendence to which philosophers have so constantly resorted in their explanations of goodness. 'Good is a transcendent reality' means that virtue is the attempt to pierce the veil of selfish consciousness and join the world as it really is. It is an empirical fact about human nature that this attempt cannot be entirely successful.

Of course we are dealing with a metaphor, but with a very important metaphor and one which is not just a property of philosophy and not just a model. As I said at the beginning, we are creatures who use irreplaceable metaphors in many of our most important activities. And the decent man has probably always, if uncertainly and inexplicably, been able to distinguish between the real Good and its false double. In most ideological contexts virtue can be loved for its own sake. The fundamental metaphors as it were carry this love through and beyond what is false. Metaphors can be a mode of understanding, and so of acting upon, our condition. Philosophers merely do explicitly and systematically and often with art what the ordinary person does by instinct. Plato, who understood this situation better than most of the metaphysical philosophers, referred to many of his theories as 'myths', and tells us that the *Republic* is to be thought of as an allegory of the soul. 'Perhaps it is a pattern laid up in heaven where he who wishes can see it and become its citizen. But it doesn't matter whether it exists or ever will exist; it is the only city in whose politics [the good man] can take part' (*Republic* 592).

I want now to continue to explain the concept of the Good and its peculiar relation to other concepts by speaking first of the unifying power of this idea, and secondly of its indefinability. I said earlier that as far as I could see there was no metaphysical unity in human life: all was subject to mortality and chance. And yet we continue to dream of unity. Art is our most ardent dream. In fact morality does actually display to us a sort of unity, though of a peculiar kind and quite unlike the closed theoretical unity of the ideologies. Plato pictures the journeying soul as ascending through four stages of enlightenment, progressively discovering at each stage that what it was treating as realities were only shadows or images of something more real still. At the end of its quest it reaches a non-hypothetical first principle which is the form or idea of the Good, which enables it then to descend and retrace its path, but moving only through the forms or true conception of that which it previously understood only in part (*Republic* 510–11). This passage in the *Republic* has aroused a great deal of discussion but it seems to me that its general application to morality is fairly clear. The mind which has ascended to the vision of the Good can subsequently see the concepts through which it has ascended (art, work, nature, people, ideas, institutions, situations, etc., etc.) in their true nature and in their proper relationships to each other. The good man knows whether and when art or politics is more important than family. The good man sees the way in which the virtues are related to each other. Plato never in fact anywhere expounds a systematic and unitary view of the world of the forms, though he implies that there is a hierarchy of forms. (Truth and Knowledge, for instance, come fairly closely underneath Good, *Republic* 509A). What he does suggest is that we work with the idea of such a hierarchy in so far as we introduce order into our conceptions of the world through our apprehension of Good.

This seems to me to be true. Plato's image implies that complete unity is not seen until one has reached the summit, but moral advance carries with it intuitions of unity which are increasingly less misleading. As we deepen our notions of the virtues we introduce relationship and hierarchy. Courage, which seemed at first to be something on its own, a sort of specialized daring of the spirit, is now seen to be a particular operation of wisdom and love. We come to distinguish a self-assertive ferocity from the kind of courage which would enable a man coolly to choose the labour camp rather than the easy compromise with the tyrant. It would be impossible to have only one virtue unless it were a very trivial one such as thrift. Such transformations as these are cases of seeing the order of the world in the light of the Good and revisiting the true, or more true, conceptions of that which we formerly misconceived. Freedom, we find out, is not an inconsequential chucking of one's weight about, it is the disciplined overcoming of self. Humility is not a peculiar habit of self-effacement, rather like having an inaudible voice, it is selfless respect for reality and one of the most difficult and central of all virtues.

Because of his ambiguous attitude to the sensible world, of which I have already spoken, and because of his confidence in the revolutionary power of mathematics, Plato sometimes seems to imply that the road towards the Good leads away from the world of particularity and detail. However, he speaks of a descending as well as an ascending dialectic and he speaks of a return to the cave. In any case, in so far as goodness is for use in politics and in the market place it must combine its increasing intuitions of unity with an increasing grasp of complexity and detail. False conceptions are often generalized, stereotyped and unconnected. True conceptions combine just modes of judgment and ability to connect with an increased perception of detail. The case of the mother who has to consider each one of her family carefully as she decides whether or not to throw auntie out. This double revelation of both random detail and intuited unity is what we receive in every sphere of life if we seek for what is best. We can see this, once more, quite clearly in art and intellectual work. The great artists reveal the detail of the world. At the same time their greatness is not something peculiar and personal like a proper name. They are great in ways which are to some extent similar, and increased understanding of an art reveals its unity through its excellence. All serious criticism assumes this, though it might be wary of expressing it in a theoretical manner. Art reveals reality and because there is a way in which things are there is a fellowship of artists. Similarly with scholars. Honesty seems much the same virtue in a chemist as in a historian and the evolution of the two could be similar. And there is another similarity between the honesty required to tear up one's theory and the honesty required to perceive the real state of one's marriage, though doubtless the latter is much

more difficult. Plato, who is sometimes accused of over-valuing intellectual disciplines, is quite explicit in giving these, when considered on
their own, a high but second place. A serious scholar has great merits.
But a serious scholar who is also a good man knows not only his subject but the proper place of his subject in the whole of his life. The
understanding which leads the scientist to the right decision about giving up a certain study, or leads the artist to the right decision about his
family, is superior to the understanding of art and science as such. (Is
this not what καίτοι νοητῶν ὄντων μετὰ ἀρχῆς [they can be understood, when combined with a first principle] means? *Republic* 511D.)
We are admittedly specialized creatures where morality is concerned
and merit in one area does not seem to guarantee merit in another.
The good artist is not necessarily wise at home, and the concentration
camp guard can be a kindly father. At least this can seem to be so,
though I would feel that the artist had at least got a starting-point and
that on closer inspection the concentration camp guard might prove
to have his limitations as a family man. The scene remains disparate
and complex beyond the hopes of any system, yet at the same time the
concept Good stretches through the whole of it and gives it the only
kind of shadowy unachieved unity which it can possess. The area of
morals, and ergo of moral philosophy, can now be seen, not as a hole-
and-corner matter of debts and promises, but as covering the whole of
our mode of living and the quality of our relations with the world.

Good has often been said to be indefinable for reasons connected
with freedom. Good is an empty space into which human choice may
move. I want now to suggest that the indefinability of the good should
be conceived of rather differently. On the kind of view which I have
been offering it seems that we do really know a certain amount about
Good and about the way in which it is connected with our condition.
The ordinary person does not, unless corrupted by philosophy, believe
that he creates values by his choices. He thinks that some things really
are better than others and that he is capable of getting it wrong. We
are not usually in doubt about the direction in which Good lies. Equally
we recognize the real existence of evil: cynicism, cruelty, indifference
to suffering. However, the concept of Good still remains obscure and
mysterious. We see the world in the light of the Good, but what is the
Good itself? The source of vision is not in the ordinary sense seen.
Plato says of it 'It is that which every soul pursues and for the sake of
which it does all that it does, with some intuition of its nature, and yet
also baffled' (*Republic* 505). And he also says that Good is the source

of knowledge and truth and yet is something which surpasses them in splendour (*Republic* 508–9).

There is a sort of logical, in the modern sense of the word, answer to the question but I think it is not the whole answer. Asking what Good is is not like asking what Truth is or what Courage is, since in explaining the latter the idea of Good must enter in, it is that in the light of which the explanation must proceed. 'True courage is . . .' . And if we try to define Good as *X* we have to add that we mean of course a good *X*. If we say that Good is Reason we have to talk about good judgment. If we say that Good is Love we have to explain that there are different kinds of love. Even the concept of Truth has its ambiguities and it is really only of Good that we can say 'it is the trial of itself and needs no other touch'. And with this I agree. It is also argued that all things which are capable of showing degrees of excellence show it in their own way. The idea of perfection can only be exemplified in particular cases in terms of the kind of perfection which is appropriate. So one could not say in general what perfection is, in the way in which one could talk about generosity or good painting. In any case, opinions differ and the truth of judgments of value cannot be demonstrated. This line of argument is sometimes used to support a view of Good as empty and almost trivial, a mere word, 'the most general adjective of commendation', a flag used by the questing will, a term which could with greater clarity be replaced by 'I'm for this.' This argument and its conclusion seem to me to be wrong for reasons which I have already given: excellence has a kind of unity and there are facts about our condition from which lines converge in a definite direction; and also for other reasons which I will now suggest.

A genuine mysteriousness attaches to the idea of goodness and the Good. This is a mystery with several aspects. The indefinability of Good is connected with the unsystematic and inexhaustible variety of the world and the pointlessness of virtue. In this respect there is a special link between the concept of Good and the ideas of Death and Chance. (One might say that Chance is really a subdivision of Death. It is certainly our most effective *memento mori*.) A genuine sense of mortality enables us to see virtue as the only thing of worth; and it is impossible to limit and foresee the ways in which it will be required of us. That we cannot dominate the world may be put in a more positive way. Good is mysterious because of human frailty, because of the immense distance which is involved. If there were angels they might be able to define good but we would not understand the definition. We are largely mechanical creatures, the slaves of relentlessly strong selfish forces the nature of which we scarcely comprehend. At best, as decent persons, we are usually very specialized. We behave well in areas where this can be done fairly easily and let other areas of possible virtue remain undeveloped. There are perhaps in the case of every human being insuperable psychological barriers to goodness. The self is a divided thing and the whole of it cannot be redeemed any more than it can be known. And if we look outside the self what we see are scattered intimations of Good. There are few places where virtue plainly shines: great art, humble people who serve others. And can we, without improving ourselves, really see these things clearly? It is in the context of such limitations that we should picture our freedom. Freedom is, I think, a mixed concept. The true half of it is simply a name of an aspect of virtue concerned especially with the clarification of vision and the domination of selfish impulse. The false and more popular half is a name for the self-assertive movements of deluded selfish will which because of our ignorance we take to be something autonomous.

We cannot then sum up human excellence for these reasons: the world is aimless, chancy, and huge, and we are blinded by self. There is a third consideration which is a relation of the other two. It is *difficult* to look at the sun: it is not like looking at other things. We somehow retain the idea, and art both expresses and symbolizes it, that the lines really do converge. There is a magnetic centre. But it is easier to look at the converging edges than to look at the centre itself. We do not and probably cannot know, conceptualize, what it is like in the centre. It may be said that since we cannot see anything there why try to look? And is there not a danger of damaging our ability to focus on the sides? I think there is a sense in trying to look, though the occupation is perilous for reasons connected with masochism and other obscure devices of the psyche. The impulse to worship is deep and ambiguous and old. There are false suns, easier to gaze upon and far more comforting than the true one.

Plato has given us the image of this deluded worship in his great allegory. The prisoners in the cave at first face the back wall. Behind them a fire is burning in the light of which they see upon the wall the shadows of puppets which are carried between them and the fire and they take these shadows to be the whole of reality. When they turn round they can see the fire, which they have to pass in order to get out of the cave. The fire, I take it, represents the self, the old unregenerate psyche, that great source of energy and warmth. The prisoners in the second stage of enlightenment have gained the kind of self-awareness which is nowadays a matter of so much interest to us. They can see in themselves the sources of what was formerly blind selfish instinct. They see the flames which threw the shadows which they used to think were real, and they can see the puppets, imitations of things in the real world, whose shadows they used to recognize. They do not yet dream that there is anything else to see. What is more likely than that they should settle down beside the fire, which though its form is flickering and unclear is quite easy to look at and cosy to sit by?

I think Kant was afraid of this when he went to such lengths to draw our attention away from the empirical psyche. This powerful thing is indeed an object of fascination, and those who study its power to cast shadows are studying something which is real. A recognition of its power may be a step towards escape from the cave; but it may equally be taken as an end-point. The fire may be mistaken for the sun, and self-scrutiny taken for goodness. (Of course not everyone who escapes from the cave need have spent much time by the fire. Perhaps the virtuous peasant has got out of the cave without even noticing the fire.) Any religion or ideology can be degraded by the substitution of self, usually in some disguise, for the true object of veneration. However, in spite of what Kant was so much afraid of I think there is a place both inside and outside religion for a sort of contemplation of the Good, not just by dedicated experts but by ordinary people: an attention which is not just the planning of particular good actions but an attempt to look right away from self towards a distant transcendent perfection, a source of uncontaminated energy, a source of *new* and quite undreamt-of virtue. This attempt, which is a turning of attention away from the particular, may be the thing that helps most when difficulties seem insoluble, and especially when feelings of guilt keep attracting the gaze back towards the self. This is the true mysticism which is morality, a kind of undogmatic prayer which is real and important, though perhaps also difficult and easily corrupted.

I have been speaking of the indefinability of the Good; but is there really nothing else that we can say about it? Even if we cannot find it another name, even if it must be thought of as above and alone, are there not other concepts, or another concept, with which it has some quite special relation? Philosophers have often tried to discern such a relationship: Freedom, Reason, Happiness, Courage, History have recently been tried in the role. I do not find any of these candidates convincing. They seem to represent in each case the philosopher's admiration for some specialized aspect of human conduct which is much less than the whole of excellence and sometimes dubious in itself. I have already mentioned a concept with a certain claim and I will return to that in conclusion. I want now to speak of what is perhaps the most obvious as well as the most ancient and traditional claimant, though one which is rarely mentioned by our contemporary philosophers, and that is Love. Of course Good is sovereign over Love, as it is sovereign over other concepts, because Love can name something bad. But is there not nevertheless something about the conception of a refined love which is practically identical with goodness? Will not 'Act lovingly' translate 'Act perfectly', whereas 'Act rationally' will not? It is tempting to say so.

However I think that Good and Love should not be identified, and not only because human love is usually self-assertive. The concepts, even when the idea of love is purified, still play different roles. We are dealing here with very difficult metaphors. Good is the magnetic centre towards which love naturally moves. False love moves to false good. False love embraces false death. When true good is loved, even impurely or by accident, the quality of the love is automatically refined, and when the soul is turned towards Good the highest part of the soul is enlivened. Love is the tension between the imperfect soul and the magnetic perfection which is conceived of as lying beyond it. (In the *Symposium* Plato pictures Love as being poor and needy.) And when we try perfectly to love what is imperfect our love goes to its object *via* the Good to be thus purified and made unselfish and just. The mother loving the retarded child or loving the tiresome elderly relation. Love is the general name of the quality of attachment and it is capable of infinite degradation and is the source of our greatest errors; but when it is even partially refined it is the energy and passion of the soul in its search for Good, the force that joins us to Good and joins us to the world through Good. Its existence is the unmistakable sign that we are spiritual creatures, attracted by excellence and made for the Good. It is a reflection of the warmth and light of the sun.

Perhaps the finding of other names for Good or the establishing of special relationships cannot be more than a sort of personal game. However I want in conclusion to make just one more move. Goodness is connected with the acceptance of real death and real chance and real transience and only against the background of this acceptance, which is psychologically so difficult, can we understand the full extent of what virtue is like. The acceptance of death is an acceptance of our own nothingness which is an automatic spur to our concern with what is not ourselves. The good man is humble; he is very unlike the big neo-Kantian Lucifer. He is much more like Kierkegaard's tax collector. Humility is a rare virtue and an unfashionable one and one which is often hard to discern. Only rarely does one meet somebody in whom it positively shines, in whom one apprehends with amazement the absence of the anxious avaricious tentacles of the self. In fact any other name for Good must be a partial name; but names of virtues suggest directions of thought, and this direction seems to me a better one than that suggested by more popular concepts such as freedom and courage. The humble man, because he sees himself as nothing, can see other things as they are. He sees the pointlessness of virtue and its unique value and the endless extent of its demand. Simone Weil tells us that the exposure of the soul to God condemns the selfish part of it not to suffering but to death. The humble man perceives the distance between suffering and death. And although he is not by definition the good man perhaps he is the kind of man who is most likely of all to become good.

# 11

## A Metaphysical Paradox

*Gregory Vlastos*

The paradox of which I wish to speak is the one Plato presents in its most arresting form in Book Ten of the *Republic*: the Form of a bed is the "real" bed;[1] the physical bed, the one made by the carpenter, is not "perfectly real,"[2] is "a shadowy sort of thing by comparison with reality."[3]

Western philosophy offers no better example, to my knowledge, of a pure metaphysical paradox. In any case it is the one I have lived with the longest. I was still an undergraduate when it first got under my skin—that is to say, my metaphilosophical skin, for I cannot pretend that I was tempted then or at any time thereafter to doubt that the bedmaker's bed was as real as anything could possibly be. What astounded, indeed worried, me was that someone else—not a crackpot, but a great philosopher—should have not only felt that temptation but yielded to it and in such a way as to claim for his conclusion demonstrative truth. I wondered how this could have happened. As the years passed that question was replaced by another: Just what did happen? For, as I came to see, if that second one could be properly answered, the first would answer itself. This is what I hope to show you in this address.

On the textual data I shall be very brief. That passage in Book Ten harks back to a discussion in Book Five (475E ff.) where Plato expounds, doubtless for the first time in his published works, what has since come to be called the notion of *grades* or *degrees* of reality. These rubrics, of course, are not in his text, and I shall use them as mere names for what we do find there: the deliberate use in the comparative form of *to be* or *to be real* and their derivatives, asserting or

181

implying that being or reality pertains in higher degree to the Ideas or Forms than to their sensible "namesakes." This may be done directly, as in the *Republic*, where Plato uses with great gusto expressions like "more real" and "less real."[4] But the same thing can—and is—done by the use of that striking expression, "the really real," for which there is no known precedent in earlier Greek prose. In so scrupulous a stylist we could have guessed that the apparent redundancy—which in one place (*Phaedrus* 247C) becomes even a triplication, "the really real reality"—is not inflated rhetoric, but is meant to put on "real" an added intensive force, matching that of the explicit comparatives in the *Republic*. And we do not need to guess. For already in that dialogue "really real"[5] is used as a variant for "perfectly real" in contrast to the "dimmer" reality of sensible things. Plato can also convey the same thing by just saying "real" or "being" with a special emphasis, as though italicizing. This too is clear in the *Republic*, for example, where it is said that the physical bed is not "the real" one (597A4–5). Applying these data to the dialogues we can plot the course of the grades of reality doctrine in Plato's works, finding that it extends as far out as the *Timaeus*,[6] and also the *Philebus*,[7] a dialogue which all scholars acknowledge as one of Plato's latest compositions. So the doctrine staked out in the *Republic* remained one of his permanent convictions, weathering the storm of perplexity and self-criticism recorded in the *Parmenides*.

What, then, does it mean? One may say that something is, or is not, real to express either of two quite different things. Consider:

1. Unicorns are not real.
2. These flowers are not real.

In *1* the real is the existent in contrast to the fictitious, the imaginary. This can scarcely be its sense in *2*. In saying of *these* flowers—the ones I am pointing to—that they are not real, I presuppose their existence. This proves that neither would I have asserted their existence if I had said that they are real. All I would then have said is that they *are* flowers, adding "real" or "really" to distinguish them not from figments of the imagination or of hallucinated perception but only from other objects which are also "real" enough in the first, existential, sense of the word but which are not *real flowers,* because they do not have those crucial properties things must have if they are to bear out, on investigation, the assertion that they *are* flowers, though they do have some of the *bona fide* properties of such objects—same size, shape, color—and are therefore liable to be mistaken for them.

This nonexistential sense of *real* has always been in common use and is recognized as such in the Oxford English Dictionary, immediately after the existential: "that which is actually and truly such as its name implies; possessing the essential qualities denoted by its name; hence *genuine.*" But modern philosophers have ignored it all too often. Kant's classical pronouncement on the hundred real thalers makes no allusion to a hundred counterfeit ones. G. E. Moore, so eager to learn philosophy from language, missed this sense of *real* in his celebrated essay, "The Conception of Reality" (1917).[8] And this has been fairly typical of the recent trend. With a few distinguished exceptions,[9] English-speaking philosophers of the twentieth century allowed the nonexistential sense of "real" to remain a sleeping dog in their discussions. It was after the Second World War, in Austin's Oxford lectures, that this sleeping dog woke up to let out some very frisky philosophical barks. In Lecture VII of *Sense and Sensibilia*[10] this other sense of "real" came at least into its own. But what has all this to do with Plato?

If we were to come to him obsessed with the existential sense of "real" it would be a small miracle if we managed to avoid falling into the assumption that when he says that some things are "more real" than others he must mean that they *exist* more than others. This assumption has in fact been made by the overwhelming majority of modern interpreters, philologists and philosophers alike,[11] and continues to turn up in the latest studies, even those by analytically oriented philosophers, as in the philosophical commentary on the *Republic* by R. C. Cross and A. D. Woozley,[12] who start off their exposition of Plato's grades of reality doctrine by saying point-blank: "in what follows the expressions 'exists,' 'is real,' occur as synonyms" (p. 145). Now if this were true almost everything I want to say in elucidation of Plato's paradox would be off the track. I must, therefore, take time off to show why it cannot be true. I asserted as much in the paper I contributed to R. Bambrough's symposium, *New Essays on Plato and Aristotle* (London and New York, 1965). Here I must argue. I do so with due respect for scholars, some of them in this very audience, who think otherwise. If one disagrees with esteemed colleagues on a fundamental point, the least one can do is to give reasons.

The only one adduced by Cross and Woozley for saying that "exists" and "is real" are synonymous for Plato is that "[he] does not make this distinction" *(loc. cit.)*. They mean, of course, that there is no statement or discussion or analysis of the distinction in the *Republic*. They could go farther and say that there is no such thing in any of Plato's writings, and they would still be right: I agree with G. E. L. Owen[13] against John Ackrill[14] and others that the method of analysis by paraphrase in the *Sophist* which isolated perfectly the "is" of identity from its other uses was not pushed far enough to sort out in the same way the "is" of existence from that of predication. But what does that prove? Noam Chomsky has forcefully reminded us of that linguistic knowledge which consists in being able to use rules of language even in the absence of any awareness of them, to say nothing of any ability to state them.[15] This kind of knowledge of the difference between the "is" in *Troy is famous* and *Troy is* (lame English, but good Greek) even a Greek child would have had. The only question then is whether Plato did or did not observe the difference—in the sense of "observe" in which one observes a rule by following it—even if he never stated or discussed it. This question admits of a conclusive answer.

Scattered throughout his prose, quite often in untechnical, even un-philosophical contexts, we come across expressions like these: "the really good and noble man"; "the real sophist"; "a really divine place"; "he had really stopped talking."[16] If we were to suppose that Plato was using "real" as a synonym of "existing", what would we do with "really"? "Existingly"? The fact that this is odd, indeed impossible, En-glish would not be of itself a good reason for holding that Plato could not have used its Greek equivalent. Would anyone seriously suggest that Plato by uncanny foresight coupled with exquisite consideration for posterity had decided to use only such Greek as could be literally translated into impeccable English? The objection to "existingly" for Plato's "really" in the examples is that, even if we did have the word, "existingly" would simply not fit these contexts. That "really good and noble man" Plato is talking about would be really good and noble even if he did not exist. If you think this too subtle for Plato, consider his statement in the *Politicus* (293E) which contrasts "the only correct constitution" with others which "are not genuine, nor really real." Here it is certain that "really real" cannot mean "existingly existing," since it cannot even mean "existing": the constitutions which are said *not* to be really real are precisely the existing ones—those which, to Plato's disgust, clutter up the political map of Greece. In such a sen-tence as this Plato evidences knowing the nonsynonymy of "existing" and "real"—evidences it as conclusively as would one who remarked, "she did not wear her cape when she sailed around the cape," of knowing the difference between the tailor's cape and the geographer's.

Now anyone who has such knowledge of the difference in "real" as between *unicorns are not real* and *these flowers are not real* would know in the same Chomskyan way that while the second "real" often admits of degrees the first one never does. If you are inquiring whether goatstags are or are not real, your language—Greek or English, it would be all the same in this respect—would not hand you a third possibility, that they might half-exist. To get any such alternative you would have to invent it; and the invention would be uphill work; it would go against linguistic gravity, as it were. Not so in the case of the nonexistential use of "real." It is easy to miss this because in the case of this example, and in that of many others I could add to it (diamonds, teeth, ducks, etc.), the possibilities are also restricted to either "real" or "not real." But here it is nature, not language, that imposes the restriction. It is because the world is what it is that goatstags, diamonds, *et cetera,* are subject to that brutally exhaustive disjunction. There are other things whose nature is more accommodating. If twenty-four carat gold is indisputably "real" gold, and copper is as indisputably not, we can easily interpolate specimens by forming alloys. If the example seems farfetched, think of the ones I cited from Plato a moment ago. Take that "really good and noble man." Between him and the cunning villain who simulates his sterling qualities there are all sorts of cases of ambiguous or speckled virtue where, knowing the facts, we would still find it hard to decide whether a man is or is not good and noble, and might wind up saying, "he is and he isn't." And this is generally true wherever the qualifying predicate—the $F$ in "a real $F$" or "really $F$"—is instantiable more or less adequately, as happens so conspicuously in those $Fs$ which are of special interest to Plato: value-predicates, *good, beautiful, just, pious,* and so forth. In all these cases language, instead of repelling the intermediate between the real and the not real, has a built-in provision for it, and a typical symptom of it is our ability to say, for example, "he is not really educated," without implying that he is *not* educated.

If we now look at Plato's behavior—his linguistic behavior—in that passage in the *Republic* (end of Book Five) where he unveils the grades of reality doctrine, we will see that it bears all the earmarks of an extension of the sense of "real" I have just been discussing. The thesis that sensibles "are and are not"—which, on first hearing, sounds ominously as though it meant "exist and do not exist"—turns out, the moment Plato starts arguing for it,[17] to be an ellipsis for "are and are not $F$," the first three values of *F* in his argument being *beautiful, just, pious,* that is to say, predicates of that very kind in which our experience so often gives us cause to fall in with the *"F and not F"* verdict on the status of actual cases. To get the same result from the existential "real" which, as his language-sense informs him, rules out as monstrosity a *tertium quid* between existence and nonexistence, he would have had to fight his native language all the way, and some sign of the combat would have shown up in the text. Moreover, in that case the thesis would have been unwelcome to him. Plato does not believe that while the Form does exist, its sensible instances do and do not. In the *Timaeus* (52A) he declares "that there are first, the unchanging Form . . . ; second, its namesake and like, sensible, generated, ever changing, . . . ; third, Space. . . ." In full view of the greater reality of the Form, and the lesser reality of the other two members of the trio, Plato says that all three *exist,* and says it again without qualification a few lines later (52D2–4). Where the "is" is clearly existential, it is applied distributively to each, and conjunctively to all, grades of reality. So when the sensible instance is said to be less real than its Form, this is not said to ambiguate its existence, but on the contrary to disambiguate the sort of existence it has. By the same token the Form is said to be "really real" not to assert, but to categorize, its existence—to tell us what kind of existence *it* has.

So this is why I must reject the view that when Plato says "more real" he means "more existent." What then is there left for him to mean? More than I could hope to explore exhaustively in this address. Here I shall be content to bring out what is, at any rate, a part of what he means[18]—the part that can be plotted by tracking down the answer to the following question: What could his Forms or Ideas have in common with real gold, real coffee, real courage, real beauty, in contrast to debased gold, adulterated coffee, feeble or feigned courage, coarse, brittle, or superficial beauty? Two things, I suggest: In the first place, in all of these examples, the real *F* would be the *cognitively reliable F.* Thus, if you want to investigate the nature of gold, coffee, courage, beauty, you must look to the genuine article; the other kind will trick you sooner or later, for along with some *F*-properties, it has also, perhaps cunningly concealed, some not-*F* properties, and if you were to take the latter for the former your mistake would be disastrous. In the second place, the real *F* would be the *reliably valuable* one, the kind of thing that brings fully and durably the satisfaction an *F*-thing can be counted on to yield, instead of a spurious or, at best, an inferior satisfaction, falling far short of the one you are after, or would be, if you had known the real *F*. Plato, I submit, has both of these things in mind when he speaks of his Form as "really real."

The first answers strictly to their epistemological function. On this I can be very brief, for I have expounded it at length and argued for it in the paper to which I referred above, and there would be no point in repeating myself here.[19] Here then is the gist of it: The key to it is Plato's conviction that the Forms are the objects of knowledge *par excellence*. They are incomparably the most rewarding to the mind of all the things to which it can turn in its search for truth, for their natures are logically perspicuous, or can be made so with adequate training in dialectic, and all their properties follow from their natures in conjunction with the natures of other similarly luminous and stable objects. Their physical instances are, by contrast, intellectually opaque and shifty. They do not display their intelligible structure on their sensible surface. And when we try to dig it out of them by inference and extrapolation we cannot be sure that the cluster of properties any one of them happens to have here and now it will still have later on or that other things, to all appearance similar, will have the same set of properties now or later. A thing which is *F* at one time, or in one way, or in one relation, or from one point of view, will be all too often not-*F* at another time, in another way, *et cetera*. So, generalizing with that reckless audacity characteristic of Greek philosophy at its best as at its worst, Plato infers that this is true of all sensible *F*s. All of them will always be so infected, hence none of them could ever be a *real F*, and if we take any of them to be such, we will be sure to be deceived. The Form, conversely, will never deceive, for it is by hypothesis invariantly and wholly the special *F* it is its nature to be. It is, therefore, the real *F*, the genuine one, which can be trusted absolutely in our pursuit of knowledge.

But the Forms have another function to which I barely alluded in the published paper. This I must now try to make clear. We get an inkling of it when we see the philosopher introduced in the *Republic* (474C ff.) not just as a Formknower, but as a Formlover, in dramatic contrast to sightlovers, soundlovers, and the like. And so he remains throughout the rest of the *Republic*. At first one is not sure how much to make of this. Could it not be that he is expected to love the Forms simply as objects of knowledge? Certainly, some ardent inquirers do grow fond of their peculiar subject-matter—some biologists of their rats and hamsters, some physicists of their particles, subparticles, and antiparticles.

But merely to make these similes explicit is to see at once how flat they fall by comparison with the depth of feeling Plato has for the Ideas. Where is the difference? Is it just that the kind of knowledge he expects them to yield is in so many cases knowledge of value? This is indeed true, but still not enough. Aesthetic theory, for example, so far as it succeeds in being knowledge, would be for Plato knowledge of the Form of beauty. If we could come to know this Idea, as Plato thinks we can, we would be assured of a remarkable science of aesthetics—deductively articulated, demonstrative in its certainty, unrestrictedly general in its scope. One would expect Plato to be elated at the prospect of such an accomplishment and to crow over it whenever he had the chance to speak of the philosopher as a student of the Idea of Beauty. Why doesn't he then in the *Republic,* the *Symposium,* or the *Phaedrus*? It is because this aspect of the Idea, important as it is, is overshadowed in these dialogues by another. Beauty is here above all the lure for love, the Idea of Beauty being itself the most alluring thing there is, the one most worth loving. A beautiful body, a beautiful mind, a beautiful work of artistic creation, political contrivance, or scientific insight—each of these will satisfy completely. They are cursed by their particularity. In the very act of giving one kind of beauty, they deny another. And so this Platonic lover, whose appetite for beauty is not only voracious but omnivorous, finds always a residue of frustration in their presence. There is an overtone of restlessness in his enjoyment of them which makes him keep moving from one to another. Only when he reaches that "wonderful sort of Beauty" that waits for him at the peak of his ascent in the *Symposium* (210E) is his restlessness stilled. Here at last he has found "real" Beauty.

The experience of which and from which Plato speaks here and in kindred passages which depict the vision of the elite Forms—Beauty, Goodness, Justice, Temperance, Holiness, Knowledge—has had little attention in English-speaking philosophical commentaries in recent years. With rare exceptions, their authors seem as embarrassed by these passages as was my mother by certain indelicate lines in the Old Testament stories she read us, skipping when she reached those lines, or rushing through them in a thin, dry voice. For serious efforts to see what can be made of this part of Plato's work we would have to go back to older books like Santayana's *Platonism and the Spiritual Life,* Cornford's early work, *From Religion to Philosophy,* or still earlier, Walter Pater's *Plato and Platonism.* But in these works sound insights are marred by license of interpretation, or inaccurate scholarship, or sentimentality, or all three. The job has to be done all over again and from the bottom up, as it surely must if we are to understand Plato. Needless to say, I am not volunteering to do it now. The best I can do here is to refer you to certain of Plato's own statements which would be fundamental data for such an inquiry regardless of what conclusions were drawn from it. What I shall make of their significance will have to speak for itself, since I shall be unable to argue for it.

For the felicity of this experience Plato makes one of the most astounding claims that any philosopher has ever made for anything. He does this in Book Nine of the *Republic* (582A ff.) when winding up his great argument that the good man at fortune's worst will still be happier than the bad one at fortune's best. He implies that as a source of happiness this experience will excel all others, will indeed outdo all others put together. A man who had but this and what would come to him directly from it, even if he had nothing else besides, would still be happier than another who, lacking this, had everything else his heart could wish for. What sort of experience could it be that so floods Plato's soul with bliss? An aesthetic experience it would have to be, for one thing, if it sates his thirst for Beauty. It must be also intellectual, since it marks a climactic point in the pursuit of knowledge. At the same time it is a profoundly moral or, more exactly, moralizing experience. It is the sort of experience that makes men moral. In one passage in the *Republic* the philosopher is pictured as gazing daily at the Forms, which are "orderly and ever constant, neither wronging, not being wronged by, one another, but abide in harmony and the rule of reason" and, as he does so, finds that his character takes on the impress of theirs. "Or do you think," asks Socrates, "it would be possible not to imitate that with which one consorts in love?" "Impossible," says Glaucon, and Socrates concludes that "the philosopher, consorting with the divine and harmonious, will himself become as harmonious and divine as any man may" (500C2–D1). You notice that Plato passes here within a single sentence and without any transitional marker from the moral to the religious dimension. And this he does time and time again. The religion to which he alludes in such contexts is not that blend of high-order patriotic entertainment and white magic which makes up so much of the public cult of the city-state, but that radically different kind of piety, intense, fervent, and other-worldly, fostered by the mystic rites, Bacchic or Eleusinian, the only kind that touched Plato personally and moved him deeply. He sees vision of Form as an analogue of this kind of piety. In one of his most elevated passages he speaks of vision of Form as "celebration of perfect mysteries" (*Phaedrus* 249C). He does this even in low-temperature discourse, as in the *Phaedo* (69CD), where he remarks that the true *Bakchos*—the mystic initiate at the moment at which he feels god-possessed, one with his god—is he "who has philosophized rightly." In this sublimated rite Plato puts Form in place of God. Not only does he call the Forms "divine," but distinctly implies that they are more divine than the gods. If the latter seems preposterous, we need only recall those attributes of divinity—eternity, perfection not flawed by passion or risked in action—of which the gods of cult and myth were more caricatures than exemplars. It is, therefore, understandable that one who exalted these attributes above all others should have found in the Forms of his philosophy, and only there, entities fully worthy of his adoration and felt his vision of them as a sacred communion. Thus in one and the same experience Plato finds happiness, beauty, knowledge, moral sustenance and regeneration, and a mytical sense of kinship with eternal perfection. The Forms then are for him not only guideposts to their best instances in common experience, but are themselves the focal points of a most uncommon experience which he discovered for himself and found incomparably more satisfying than any other. The Forms are "more real" than their instances in that sense as well.

With this account before us, let us take stock of its results. It has taken the grades of reality theory as an implied analogy or, more precisely, as a bundle of implied analogies, telling us that if we think of things which are "real" because they are genuine, true, pure, in contrast with those which are not, we will have a clue to the relation of the Platonic Form to its mundane instances. Now there are many ways in which things can have, or fail to have, this kind of "reality." I offered you a range of examples: real gold, real courage, and the like. These could be easily extended to include, for instance, the real Socrates in contrast to a young admirer who parrots his dialectic and even apes his grimaces, or to the real crown, work of a master silversmith, copied by lesser craftsmen, who cannot create, and only imitate. That Plato himself should not have fastened the analogy to any one example or set of examples is significant. He doubtless needs the freedom of maneuver this ellipsis permits him. Mindful of this proviso, we may nevertheless seize on a single example to bring out the most important of the considerations I have put before you—two major ways in which we may still think of the "real" once we have laid aside the existential sense of this term which, I have argued, is irrelevant to Plato's grades of reality theory, since in this theory to be real in any given degree is to *exist with just that degree of reality.* Suppose Plato had said: The Form, *F,* is to sensible *F*s as is real gold to gold alloyed with baser metals. My major contention has been that this ostensibly single analogy is in fact two quite different ones, either of which pure gold would exemplify, depending on whether we think of gold as something to *know* or something to *covet:*

First analogy: Just as one who sought to investigate the nature of gold should remember that the essential properties of this metal are those of pure gold, *so* if we want to know the nature of anything, we must concentrate our study on its Form.

Second analogy: Just as one who bought gold at the bullion price, anxious to increase his assets, should insist on gold of standard purity, *so* if what we are after is the most valuable experience that life can offer, we must seek vision of Form.

These two analogies are the vehicles of two entirely distinct, though not unrelated, doctrines, generating two different paradoxes:

The first analogy is the vehicle of a purely epistemological doctrine— one we could have had even if Plato had not been an all-around meta-physician, but only an epistemologist, and his single philosophical discovery had been limited to the availability of *a priori* knowledge. If in the flush of that one discovery he had but gone on to do what we know he did in his middle dialogues—restrict knowledge to the *a priori*—he would have generated epistemological paradoxes galore, all of which he could have stated *via* the grades of reality doctrine. In modern philosophy, more plausible and at times quite fashionable theories of knowledge have armed their exponents with paradoxes which Plato could have repeated verbatim: I do not *know* this is my hand, or that I even have a hand; I do not *know* this is a table, that is a bed. The paradox becomes perhaps more vivid, but is no more startling in its implications, if locked into Platonic grades of reality language: The real bed, object of knowledge, is not the carpenter's product, object of mere opinion. It is the Form, *Bed.*

The other analogy is the vehicle of a still more hazardous philosophical venture, the construction of a metaphysical system, one of those very rare ones in secular Western philosophy which are grounded in mystical experience. I use this last term advisedly, for I refuse to think of mysticism as something confined to sporadic states of ecstatic awareness. The methodological propriety of that assumption is dubious for mystical consciousness at focal intensity admits of many varieties, ranging, for example, from that qualityless, undifferentiated, unity achieved in Oriental and Western mysticism by emptying consciousness of every possible content, to Proust's total recall of a past sensation, where consciousness of vivid particularity, so far from being reduced to zero, seems heightened to the $n$th degree. In this respect Platonic vision of Form differs as much from Plotinian union with a One which transcends form or even being, as from Proustian resurrection of a fragment of one's perceptual past in the immediate present. Its closest affinities are with Spinoza's *amor intellectualis Dei,* where also beatitude is achieved in a miraculous junction of love, knowledge, moral resolve, and spiritual exaltation. But even this parallel is far from perfect. Plato's mystical experience at dead center, carefully examined, will reveal at least as many differences from Spinoza's as similarities with it. To find what Plato shares more fully with him, though no more with him than with other mystics, we should look for it in the foreground and aftermath of ecstatic consciousness. The foreground is a disillusionment with those things whose "lesser reality" every mystic would acknowledge with Plato, convinced that he can never find in them ultimate security and fulfilment. If he places such trust in things which can be seen and touched, the mystic feels, he becomes their slave, exposing himself to the torment of unsatisfied desire and of those vicissitudes or "fluctuations of the mind," as Spinoza called them, states of suspense and anxiety bordering at times on terror. He also becomes their dupe. For when he does succeed in reaching the very ones that most enthralled him, he finds the fascination they produced in absence answers to nothing in their presence; the reality he had counted on has eluded him, and what he has finally possessed is shadow, smoke, vanity, and vexation of spirit. Now whatever it be that happens inside the mystical state, we are left in no doubt as to what comes out of it. A man who has felt bound, incarcerated, buffeted, fooled, exiled, in the world of sense—the metaphors are Plato's, but many other mystics have used the same or equivalent ones—finds a liberation and peace which he expresses typically, as Walter Stace has reminded us,[20] in terms of the contrast of time with eternity. Here time without eternity represents the state of bondage; eternity, the blessedness of release; time under the aspect of eternity, regeneration. In vision of Form Plato discovers—one might almost say, invents—his own personal bridge from the first to the third *via* the second. How natural then for him to say that the eternal things, the Forms, are the "really real" ones. In seeing them a creature of time touches eternity, and the contact makes it possible for him to master time, to live in it as though not of it. If he had been a poet—or, more exactly, if he had been only a poet—he would have made of this a lyrical or epic theme. Being a metaphysician he uses it rather as the clue for a redescription of reality, tracing out a pattern, absolutely new in Greek thought, where eternity is incorporeal Form, and the corporeal world has meaning and value so far as it copies, or can be made to copy, Form, and where time itself is redeemed as the image of eternity.[21] This re-structuring of what there is on the scaffolding of what is more and less real is one of Plato's great achievements, perhaps his greatest.

To be great an achievement need not be flawless. I have no wish to disguise the flaws in Plato's. All of them can be traced to defective analysis: *ontological* analysis, which would have explained the difference between the sense of "real" that fits the comparatives of his theory from the existential one which does not; *semantic* analysis, which would have noted that in the required sense—that of "real" in "a real *F*"—"real" is syncategorematic and, therefore, relativized to the predicate which completes its sense; *logical* analysis, which would have spotted an error that has had much, perhaps too much, attention in recent controversy under the none too happy rubric of "self-predication"; *methodological* analysis, which would have sorted out clearly within the grades of reality theory its epistemological from its metaphysical content and—what is still more important—propounded the latter as a personal vision for which demonstrative certainty cannot be claimed.

If Plato had understood his own theory better in these and other ways, he might have saved his readers some unprofitable misinterpretations and spared himself some quite gratuitous errors. For instance, he could have shown us that his Forms are not meant to be "more real" in every possible way. Thus, would he not have been the first to agree that, if what we want is a good night's sleep, the ordinary, bedroom variety, bed is considerably more real? Again, the ends of his epistemology are not advanced by the assumption that in general the Form for *F* is itself *F*. The Form, *Circle*, would not be a more reliable object of knowledge if it were circular, nor the Form, *Beauty*, if it were beautiful. Only when Forms assume their other role, as objects of value, and of the kind of value Plato claimed for them, would the self-characterization of Forms like Beauty have any point whatever. The Form, *Beauty*, would indeed have to be exceedingly beautiful to hold its place at the terminus of the lover's quest, and the Forms, *Justice* and *Temperance*, would have to be just and temperate if they are to have moral attributes that rub off on their contemplators. But not even here would the fault be irreparable. Plato could have reclaimed a metaphorical sense for these literally senseless predications.

The gravest flaw in the theory, one which could not be mended without altering radically Plato's conception of metaphysics and of morality and politics as well, issues from his imperfect understanding of that very experience which meant more to him than any other—vision of Form. For if he had understood it as deeply as he felt it, how could he have thought of it as certifying cognitive and even political infallibility? What troubled me about Plato's metaphysical paradox when I first came across it was his confidence that he could prove it. Now that, understanding his paradox better, I admire it all the more, I think that I was right to be troubled. The mystic is the last person in the world who can afford to be an authoritarian.

### Notes

1. τὸ ὄν, 597A4; "that which bed *is*" (ὃ ἔστι κλίνη) 597A2.

2. τελέως ὄν, 597A2.

3. Cornford's translation of ἀμυδρόν τι, . . . πρὸς ἀλήθειαν, 597A10. Shorey has "dim adumbration" for ἀμυδρόν τι.

4. 515D, 585B–E.

5. κλίνης . . . ὄντως οὔσης, of the Form, Bed, 597D2.

6. 27E–28A; 52C5–6.

7. 58A2; 59D4.

8. His polemic against Bradley in this essay *(Philosophical Studies* [London 1922]) is premised on the assumption that his adversary could not consistently assert the existence of something while denying its reality, unless he gave some esoteric sense ("some highly unusual and special sense," p. 208) to "real." That there might be a perfectly common and natural sense in which one could say of some existent that *it* is not real does not seem to have occurred to Moore in this essay.

9. Chiefly among neo-Hegelians, as in Bradley who presupposes and often asserts the existence of the items—finite individuals, time, space, etc.—whose unreality he seeks to prove, and in Royce, whose discussion of "popular ways of expressing reality" identifies clearly the use of *real* to mean *genuine, true, what you can depend on* (*The World and the Individual,* First Series New York, 1899, 54). Among the critics of the idealists the most valuable contribution to the nonexistential sense of *real* is made by C. I. Lewis who insists that it is "systematically ambiguous" (*Mind and the World-Order,* New York, 1929, 11), so that a real *F* may be an unreal *G*.

10. Reconstructed from the Manuscript Notes by G. J. Warnock (Oxford, 1962).

11. An honorable exception was pointed out to me by Professor Howard DeLong after the delivery of this address: R. G. Collingwood in *The Idea of Nature* (Oxford, 1945), pp. 55 ff.—a penetrating, if brief, interpretation of the Platonic theory, which seems to have been completely overlooked in the subsequent literature: no account is taken of it in N. R. Murphy (1951), W. D. Ross (1951), or in any other scholarly treatment of the topic thereafter to my knowledge.

12. *Plato's Republic* (London, 1964).

13. His view, adumbrated in his essay in the Bambrough symposium (1965, 71, note 1), is now expounded and defended in his contribution to *Plato, I : Metaphysics and Epistemology, A Collection of Critical Essays,* edited by G. Vlastos (New York, 1970).

14. "Plato and Copula: *Sophist* 251–59," *Journal of Hellenic Studies* 77 (1957), 271–87.

15. *Aspects of the Theory of Syntax* (Cambridge, Mass., 1965), 8 *et passim*.

16. *Republic* 396B; *Sophist,* 268D; *Phaedrus* 238C; *Prt.* 328D.

17. 479A5 ff.; note especially 479B9–10.

18. A wholly distinct, though related, part of the meaning, expressed by Plato's phrase "being in itself" in contrast to "being in another" (cf. *Symposium,* 211A8–B1; *Republic,* 516B4–5; *Phaedrus,* 247E1; *Timaeus,* 52C–D1), will fall outside the present investigation.

19. See "Degrees of Reality in Plato," in Gregory Vlastos, *Platonic Studies,* 2nd printing, Princeton, 1981, pp. 56 ff.

20. *Time and Eternity* (Princeton, 1952). I must also record my debt to the extremely suggestive discussion of "reality" in chapter 7 of this book.

21. *Timaeus,* 37D ff.

# 12

# The Defense of Justice in Plato's *Republic*

*Richard Kraut*

In this essay I will try to identify and explain the fundamental argument of Plato's *Republic* for the astonishing thesis that justice is so great a good that anyone who fully possesses it is better off, even in the midst of severe misfortune, than a consummately unjust person who enjoys the social rewards usually received by the just.[1] Plato's attempt to defend this remarkable claim is of course the unifying thread of the dialogue, but his argument ranges so widely over diverse topics that it is difficult to see how it all fits together, and anyone who attempts to state his argument must take a stand on interpretive issues about which there is considerable scholarly controversy.[2] The dialogue's difficulty is increased by Plato's failure to give any explicit justification for the complex moral equation he boldly announces: Justice discounted by pain and dishonor is more advantageous than injustice supplemented by the rewards of justice. Even if he manages to show that justice is the greatest single good, we are still left wondering whether its value is high enough to make this equation come out right. My main thesis is that the theory of Forms plays a crucial role in Plato's argument for that equation, but that the precise way in which that theory contributes to his defense of justice is difficult to recognize. It is hard to overcome a certain blindness we have to one of Plato's principal theses—a blindness we can find in one of Aristotle's criticisms of Plato's conception of the good. My goal is not to show that Plato's theory is defensible against all objections, once we correct for the mistake Aristotle makes. But I do think that there is something powerful in Plato's argument, and by criticizing Aristotle I hope to bring this feature to light.

# I

I said that I will focus on Plato's "fundamental" argument that justice is in one's interest, but it might be wondered why any one argument should be singled out in this way and given special attention. For on the surface, the *Republic* seems to present four independent attempts to support the conclusion that justice pays apart from its consequences.[3] First, at the end of Book IV, we learn that justice is a certain harmonious arrangement of the parts of the soul. It is therefore related to the soul as health is related to the body, and since life is not worth living if one's health is ruined, it is all the more important to maintain the justice of one's soul (444c–445c). Second, in Book IX, Plato compares the five types of people he has been portraying in the middle books—the philosophical ruler, the timocrat, the oligarch, the democrat, and the tyrant—and declares that the happiest of them is the philosopher, since he exercises kingly rule over himself (580a–c). Third, Book IX immediately proceeds to argue that the philosophical life has more pleasure than any other, since the philosopher is in the best position to compare the various pleasures available to different types of people and prefers philosophical pleasures to all others (580c–583a). And fourth, the pleasures of the philosophical life are shown to be more real and therefore greater than the pleasures of any other sort of life (583b–588a).

Does Plato single out any one of these arguments as more fundamental than the others? It might be thought that his fourth argument—the second of the two that concern pleasure—is the one he thought most important, for he introduces it with the remark that "this will be the greatest and supreme fall [of injustice]" (*megiston te kai kuriōtatōn tōn ptōmatōn,* 583b6–7). This could be taken to mean that pleasure is the most important good in terms of which to make the decision between justice and injustice, and that the argument to come is the one that most fully reveals why justice is to be chosen over its opposite. But I think that such a reading would give this argument far more significance than it deserves, and that Plato's words can and should be given a different interpretation. As I read the *Republic,* its fundamental argument in defence of justice is the one that comes to a close in Book IX *before* anything is said about how the just and unjust lives compare in terms of pleasure. This is the argument that Plato develops at greatest length, and if it is correct it makes a decisive case in favor of the just life. It shows precisely what it is about justice that makes it so worthwhile. By contrast, the two arguments that connect justice and pleasure are merely meant to assure us that we do not have to sacrifice the latter good in order to get the former. They add to the attractiveness of the just life, but they are not by themselves sufficient to show that justice is to be chosen over injustice, as is the lengthier argument that precedes them.

Why should we read the *Republic* in this way, despite Plato's statement that "the greatest and supreme fall" of injustice comes with his final argument? The answer lies in the way he poses, in Book II, the fundamental question to which the rest of the dialogue is an answer. The thesis he there undertakes to prove is phrased in various ways: It is better (*ameinon*) to be just than unjust (357b1); justice must be welcomed for itself if one is to be blessed (*makarios*, 358a3); the common opinion that injustice is more profitable (*lusitelein*) must be refuted (360c8); we must decide whether the just man is happier (*eudaimonesteros*) than the unjust (361d3);[4] justice by itself benefits (*oninanai*) someone who possesses it whereas injustice harms (*blaptein*) him (367d3–4); we must determine the advantages (*ôpheliai*) of justice and injustice (368c6). Plato does not give any one of these phrases a special role to play in his argument, but moves back and forth freely among them. And he surely must be assuming that once the consummately just life has been shown to be more advantageous, even in the midst of misfortune, than the consumately unjust life, then he has given decisive reason for choosing the former over the latter.

Notice, however, that Plato never promises, in Book II, to show that justice provides greater pleasures than does injustice, and never even hints that he would have to defend this thesis in order to show that we should choose the just life. This suggests that the question whether the just or the unjust life has more pleasure will still be an open one, even after the greater advantages of the just life have been demonstrated. And of course, this suggestion is confirmed in Book IX: Having shown that the just person is happiest, Plato thinks it requires further argument to show that the just person also has the greatest pleasure. So, in order to accomplish the task Plato assigns himself in the *Republic* it is both necessary and sufficient that he show why justice is so much more advantageous than injustice. But he never says or implies that if he can show that justice brings greater pleasures, then that by itself will be a sufficient or a necessary defense of justice. By supporting justice in terms of pleasure, Plato is showing that there is even more reason to lead the just life than we may have supposed. But the fundamental case for justice has been made before the discussion of pleasure has begun.[5]

What then should we make of his statement that the "greatest and supreme fall" for injustice occurs in the battle over pleasure? A simple and plausible explanation of this phrase is provided by the fact that at the end of his last argument Plato claims that the philosopher's pleasure is 729 times greater than the tyrant's (587e). Whether Plato is serious about this precise figure or not—and I am inclined to think he is not—it provides an explanation of why he says that this last argument gives injustice its greatest defeat.[6] In no other argument had he tried to portray the gap between justice and injustice as so great in magnitude. Once we realize that Plato's remark admits of this interpretation, we can rest content with our earlier conclusion that pleasure has a modest role to play in the overall scheme of the *Republic*.

## II

I will therefore set aside the two hedonic arguments Plato gives in Book IX and concentrate entirely on the single complex defense of justice that precedes them. But it might be thought that this material contains two separate arguments, for by the end of Book IV Plato already seems to have come to the conclusion that since justice is a harmony of the soul comparable to physical health, it is far superior to injustice.[7] We might therefore suppose that after Book IV Plato launches on a second and independent defense of justice, one that concludes in Book IX with the pronouncement that the life of the philosophical ruler is happiest. But Plato himself makes it clear that these two segments—Books II–IV on the one hand, Books V–IX on the other—cannot be isolated from each other in this way. For at the beginning of Book VIII we are told that the victorious pronouncement of Book IV—that the best person and city had been found—was premature (543c7–544b3). This means that the argument of Book IV is not complete after all, but is in some way strengthened by additional material presented somewhere between Books V and IX. For by admitting that Book IV did not yet discover who the best person is, Plato indicates that he had not at that point presented a full enough picture of the just life.[8] It would therefore be a mistake to examine the argument of Books II–IV in isolation from later material as though they were meant to provide a complete defense of justice.

Nonetheless, Plato clearly thinks that he has given at least a partial defense of justice by the end of Book IV; the fact that he goes on to strengthen the argument by giving a fuller picture of the just life does not mean that by the end of Book IV we have no reason at all to think that justice is superior to injustice. To understand the single argument that runs from Book II through Book IX, we must see why Plato arrives at a preliminary conclusion in Book IV and how the additional material that comes in later books strengthens that argument.[9]

To make progress on this interpretive question, let us begin with an observation with which all scholars would agree: One of the fundamental ideas that Plato puts forward in his defense of justice is that we should look for a *general* theory of goodness. His proposal is that when we say of a human body, or a human soul, or a political community, that they are in good condition, there is some common feature that we are referring to, and it is because they share this common feature that they are properly called good.[10] He expects his audience to agree with him that the goodness of a body—health—consists in a certain natural priority among various physical components; and he appeals to this point to support his claim that one's soul is in good condition if it too exhibits a certain order among its components (444c–e).[11] But the analogy between health and psychic well-being is by itself only of limited value, because it does not tell us anything about what sort of order we should try to achieve in the soul. What Plato needs, if he is to give a stronger argument from analogy, is a structure that has the same kind of components and can exhibit the same kind of balance as the soul. He thinks he can accomplish this by examining the question of what the best possible city is, for he believes he can show that the tripartite structure of the best political community corresponds to the structure of the human soul.[12] If he can convince us that these correspondences do exist, and if he can get us to agree that the city he describes is ideal, then he has some basis for reaching the conclusion that the ideal type of person is someone whose soul exhibits the same kind of order that is possessed by an ideal political community.[13]

But in Book IV Plato has not yet given us all of his arguments for taking the political community he is describing as ideal. For one of his main reasons for favoring the kind of city described in the *Republic* is that it alone is governed by individuals who have the wisdom needed to rule well; and that kind of political expertise is only presented in Books VI–VII. This is one reason for saying that the argument from analogy presented at the end of Book IV is incomplete. Furthermore, Plato has not yet said in Books II–IV everything he wants to say about the kind of order that should be established in the soul. He tells us that reason should rule and look after the well-being of the rest of the soul, that spirit should be its ally, and that the appetites should be kept in check (441e–442a). But what is it for reason to rule the soul? In what way can spirit help it? What would it be for appetite to grow too large? Of course, Plato has already given some content to these notions, for he has been describing the proper education of these elements of the soul since the end of Book II, and this gives us some sense of how they should be related to each other. But that education has not yet been fully described; the most important objects of study have still to be presented. When we find out more about what reason must occupy itself with, we will have a fuller idea of what it is for it to rule.[14]


## III


We must now turn to Books V through VII to see how Plato's depiction of the philosophical life contributes to the argument that justice pays. We want to know what it is about this life that makes it so much more worthwhile than any other; and we must understand how this new material is connected to the argument from analogy that comes to a preliminary conclusion at the end of Book IV.

An answer to these questions must in some way or other appeal to Plato's belief in Forms—those eternal, changeless, imperceptible, and bodiless objects the understanding of which is the goal of the philosopher's education.[15] For the philosopher is defined as someone whose passion for learning grows into a love of such abstract objects as Beauty, Goodness, Justice, and so on (474c–476c). And as soon as Plato introduces this conception of who the philosopher is, he lets us know that it is precisely because of the philosopher's connection with these abstract objects that the philosophical life is superior to any other. Those who fail to recognize the existence of Forms have a dreamlike kind of life, because they fail to realize that the corporeal objects they perceive are only likenesses of other objects (476c–d).[16] In a dream, we confusedly take the images of objects to be those very objects. Plato's claim is that nonphilosophers make a similar mistake, because they think that the beautiful things they see are what beauty really is; more generally, they equate the many observable objects that are called by some general term, "*A*" with what *A* really is.[17] The philosophers are those who recognize that *A* is a completely different sort of object, and so they rid themselves of a systematic error that in some way disfigures the unphilosophical life. This is of course the picture Plato draws in the parable of the cave (514a–519d): Most of us are imprisoned in a dark underworld because we gaze only on the shadows manipulated by others; to free ourselves from this situation requires a change in our conception of what sorts of objects there are.

Plato's metaphysics is of course controversial, but our present problem is to understand how it contributes to the defense of justice. Suppose we accept for the sake of argument that at least these central tenets of his metaphysics are correct: There are such abstract objects as the Form of Justice, and to call acts or individuals or citizens just is to say that they bear a certain relationship to this Form. Calling an act just is comparable to calling an image in a painting a tree: The image is not what a tree is, and it is correct to speak of it as a tree only if this means that it bears a certain relation to living trees; similarly, just acts, persons, and cities are not what justice is, and it is correct to call them just only if this means that they participate in the Form of Justice.

If we accept this theory, we avoid the errors of non-Platonists; we recognize that a wider variety of objects exists than most people realize, and that our words constantly refer to these objects. Even so, we should still ask: Why would having this Platonic conception of the world make our lives so much better than the lives of non-Platonists? One possible answer Plato might give is that since knowledge of reality is a great intrinsic good, a life in which we know the truth about what exists is far superior to one in which we remain ignorant of the fundamental realities of the universe. But this strikes me as a disappointing answer, and I will soon argue that Plato has a better one. It is disappointing because it makes an assumption that would be challenged by anyone who has doubts about the merits of the philosophical life. To those who are not already philosophically inclined, it is not at all obvious that knowledge of reality is by itself a great intrinsic good. They can legitimately ask why it is worthwhile for us to add to our understanding of reality, if our failure to do so would not impede our pursuit of worthwhile goods. Plato cannot simply reply that knowledge is intrinsically worthwhile, apart from any contribution it may make to the pursuit of other goals. That would beg the question in favor of the philosophical life.

It might be thought that for Plato knowledge of the Forms is valuable precisely because it is a means to some further goal. For example, he might claim that unless we study the Form of Justice, we are likely at some point to make errors in our judgment of which acts, persons, or institutions are just; and when we make errors of this sort, we will also make bad decisions about how to act. But if this is Plato's argument, then he again begs the question. For we can ask why it is so important to discover how to act justly in all situations. Of course, if acting justly is good for the agent, and knowledge of the Forms is an indispensable means to this end, then one must acquire that knowledge. But this argument merely assumes the thesis that Plato sets out to prove: that acting justly is a good for the agent.

Perhaps he assumes that knowing the Forms is worthwhile not merely as a means to action but because in coming to understand the Forms we develop our capacity to reason.[18] Human beings are not just appetitive and emotional creatures; we also have an innate interest in learning, and if this aspect of our nature is not developed our lives become narrow and impoverished. One problem with this answer is that people differ widely in the degree of intellectual curiosity they possess, and the kinds of objects that satisfy their curiosity also differ widely. Those who have little or no bent for abstract studies can satisfy their curiosity in simple ways, and again Plato would be begging the question if he simply assumed that having an easily satisfied appetite in matters of reasoning disqualifies one from leading a good life. Furthermore, as Plato is aware, it is possible to spend a great deal of one's time on intellectual matters without ever arriving at the realization that the Forms exist. Those who study the universe and seek to explain all phenomena without appealing to Forms surely develop the reasoning side of their nature; it is not sheer emotion and appetite that leads them to their theories. Even so, they are not leading the philosophical life, according to Plato's narrow conception of philosophy, and so they don't have the best kind of life. If he thinks that intellectuals who deny the existence of Forms fail to develop their capacities and therefore fall short of happiness, he owes his reader some argument for this thesis.

## IV

I believe that Plato's answer to this question is staring us in the face, but that we fail to recognize it because initially it strikes us as doubtful or even unintelligible. My suggestion is that for Plato the Forms are a good—in fact they are the greatest good there is.[19] In order to live well we must break away from the confining assumption that the ordinary objects of pursuit—the pleasures, powers, honors, and material goods that we ordinarily compete for—are the only sorts of goods there are.[20] We must transform our lives by recognizing a radically different kind of good—the Forms—and we must try to incorporate these objects into our lives by understanding, loving, and imitating them, for they are incomparably superior to any other kind of good we can have. This is why Plato thinks that the philosopher is so much better off for having escaped the confines of the dreamlike existence of the ordinary person: The objects with which the philosopher is acquainted are far more worthy objects of love than the typical objects of human passion. So Plato is not claiming that it is intrinsically good to have a complete inventory of what exists or that developing and satisfying our intellectual curiosity is inherently worthwhile, regardless of the sorts of objects to which our curiosity leads us. Rather, he takes the discovery of the Forms to be momentous because they are the preeminent good we must possess in order to be happy, and he takes reason to be the most worthwhile capacity of our soul because it is only through reason that we can possess the Forms. If there were nothing worthwhile outside of ourselves for reason to discover, then a life devoted to reasoning would lose its claim to superiority over other kinds of life.[21]

The interpretation I am proposing has some resemblance to the way Aristotle treats Plato's moral philosophy. According to Aristotle, we can discover what kind of life we should lead only by determining which good or goods we should ultimately pursue. He considers competing conceptions of this highest good and takes the Platonist's answer to be that it is not some humdrum object of pursuit like pleasure or virtue but is rather the Form of the Good. Aristotle of course rejects this answer, but it is significant that he takes the Platonist to be saying that a certain Form is the highest good and should therefore play the role non-Platonists assign to pleasure, honor, or virtue. So interpreted, the Platonist is not simply saying that the Form of the Good is an indispensable means for determining which among other objects are good; it itself is the chief good.[22] My interpretation is similar in that I take Plato to treat the Forms in general as a preeminent good; the special role of the Form of the Good will be discussed later.

At this point it might be asked whether the theory I am attributing to Plato is intelligible. For perhaps a Form is simply not the sort of thing that a person can have or possess. Of course, a Form can be studied and known, but studying something does not by itself confer ownership. The moon, for example, might be a beautiful object worthy of our study, but no one in his right mind would say that the moon is a good he possesses by virtue of studying it. Similarly, the claim that the Form of the Good is not the sort of thing that can be possessed is one of Aristotle's many objections to the Platonist conception of the good (*N.E.* 1096b35). Aristotle takes Plato to be saying that the ultimate end is the Form of the Good, and objects that it is disqualified from playing this role because it is not an object of the right type. It might be thought that this objection is so powerful that out of charity we should look for a different interpretation from the one I am proposing.[23]

But I think Aristotle's objection is weak. Of course it is true that if we take the possession of a thing to be a matter of having property rights to it, then studying the Form of the Good does not confer such rights, and it is hard to understand what it would be to possess a Form. But we can speak of having things even though we have no property rights in them; for example, one can have friends without possessing them. And we can easily understand someone who says that in order to live a good life one must have friends. What it is to *have* a friend is quite a different matter from what it is to possess a physical object; it involves an emotional bond and activities characteristic of friendship. What it is to have a certain good varies according to the kind of good it is; different types of goods do not enter our lives in the same way. And so the mere fact that a Form cannot be possessed (that is, owned) gives us no reason to reject Plato's idea that if one bears a certain relationship to Forms—a relationship that involves both emotional attachment and intellectual understanding—then one's life becomes more worthwhile precisely because one is connected in this way with such valuable objects.

In fact, there are similarities between the way in which persons can enter our lives and improve them and the way in which Plato thinks we should be related to the Forms. We can easily understand someone who says that one of the great privileges of his life is to have known a certain eminent and inspiring person. Even if one is not a close friend of such a person, one may have great love and admiration for him, and one may take pleasure in studying his life. That is the sort of relationship Plato thinks we should have with the Forms—not on the grounds that loving and studying are good activities, whatever their objects, but on the grounds that the Forms are the preeminent good and therefore our lives are vastly improved when we come to know, love, and imitate them.

Suppose it is conceded that if the Forms are a good, then they are the sorts of things that can improve our lives when we are properly related to them. Nonetheless, it might still be asked whether we can make sense of the idea that they are good. If someone says that water is a good thing, we might be puzzled about what he has in mind, and we might even be skeptical about whether water is the sort of thing that can be good in itself (as opposed to a mere means).[24] Similarly, we might have doubts about Plato's Forms: How can such objects, which are so different in kind from such mundane goods as health and pleasure, be counted as good? And if he cannot convince us that they are good, then of course he has no hope of persuading us that they are vastly better than such ordinary goods as pleasure, health, wealth, power, and so on.

For Plato's answer to our question, What is it to say of something that it is a good thing? we might turn for help to his discussion of the Form of the Good. But although he insists on the preeminence of this Form, he does not say precisely what he takes goodness to be; he simply says that it is not pleasure or knowledge (505b–506e). There is a marked contrast here between the fullness of his account of what justice is and the thinness of his discussion of goodness. We learn what it is to call a person, act, or city just, and we see the feature that they all have in common, but Plato points to no common feature of all good things. So he does not take up the project of showing that Forms are preeminent by stating what property goodness consists in and arguing that they exhibit that property more fully than anything else.

Perhaps we can discover why Plato thinks of Forms as goods if we focus on their distinguishing characteristics and ask which of them Plato might put forward as points of superiority over other objects. For example, he thinks that Forms are more real than corporeal objects, and presumably he counts this as evidence of their superiority in value.[25] But this point will not take us as far as we need to go, because he thinks that objects that are equally real can nonetheless differ greatly in value. Consider two bodies, one of them healthy, the other diseased: One is in better condition than the other, but Plato never suggests that one of them must therefore be more real than the other. Though Forms are more real than other types of objects, we cannot treat differing degrees of reality as what in general constitute differences in value.

But our example of the healthy and diseased bodies suggests another line of reasoning: Plato equates health, the good condition of the body, with a certain harmony among its elements; and he argues that justice, the good condition of the soul, is also a certain kind of harmony among its parts; and so the thought suggests itself that he takes the goodness of anything of a certain kind to be the harmony or proportion that is appropriate for things of that kind. According to this suggestion, the goodness of Forms consists in the fact that they possess a kind of harmony, balance, or proportion; and their superiority to all other things consists in the fact that the kind of order they possess gives them a higher degree of harmony than any other type of object.[26]

Clearly Plato does think that the Forms exhibit the highest kind of orderly arrangement. He says that the philosopher looks away from the conflict-ridden affairs of human beings to things that are unchanging and ordered (*tetagmena*, 500c2); by studying the divine order (*kosmos*, c4) her soul becomes as orderly and divine as it is possible for a human soul to be (c9–d1). Even the beautiful patterns exhibited in the night sky fall short of the harmonies present in true shapes and numbers, since the corporeality of the stars makes deviation inevitable, whereas the incorporeality of the Forms ensures that the orderly patterns they exhibit will never deteriorate (529c7–530b4). But he does not say precisely what the orderliness of the Forms consists in; bodies, souls, and political communities exhibit order (and therefore goodness) when their parts or components are related to each other in suitable ways, but we are not told whether the Forms have parts or whether they achieve their order in some other way. Perhaps this explains Plato's refusal to say what the Form of the Good is (506d–e); though goodness simply is some kind of harmony, he had not yet reached a firm grasp of what this harmony is in the case of Forms, and so he could not put forward a general characterization of harmony that would apply equally to the various kinds of harmony exhibited by living bodies, souls, stars, and Forms. But in any case, we can now see how Plato would try to address doubts about whether Forms are the sorts of objects that can intelligibly be called good. He would reply by appealing to his discussion of politics, the soul, and health: In all of these cases, the goodness of a thing consists in a kind of order; and so if the Forms can be shown to have the kind of order that is appropriate for things of that kind, they too will be good. And if they necessarily have a higher degree of order than anything else, then they are the best goods there can be.[27]

## V

It may now be asked how any of this provides Plato with a defense of the virtue of justice. Even if we see why he thinks that the philosophical life is best, we still can ask why this should be regarded as a defense of *justice*. Why is the philosopher the paradigm of the just person? Part of Plato's reply, as I understand it, is as follows:[28] When the ideal state properly educates individuals to become philosophers, their emotions and appetites are transformed in a way that serves the philosophical life, and these affective states no longer provide a strong impetus toward antisocial behavior, as they do when they are left undisciplined (499e–500e). Someone who has been fully prepared to love the orderly pattern of the Forms will be free of the urge to seek worldly advantages over other human beings or to engage in the sort of illicit sexual activity to which people are led by unchecked appetites. Furthermore, such a person is in the best possible position to make wise political decisions; having understood the Forms, she can see more clearly than others what needs to be done in particular circumstances (500d–501a). One of the things we look for, when we seek a paradigm of the just person, is someone who has these intellectual and affective skills.[29]

It is tempting to protest at this point that Plato is being extremely naive. After all, we all know people who have impressive intellectual abilities but who are hardly models of justice. And of course there is nothing to prevent such individuals from recognizing the existence of abstract objects, and even loving the contemplation of the orderly pattern among such objects. Consider a Platonist mathematician who occasionally gets drunk and indulges in other behavior that conflicts with Plato's description of the just individual. Aren't such individuals living refutations of Plato?

I believe not, for I don't take him to be making the implausibly strong claim that the love of abstract objects by itself guarantees just behavior or the emotional discipline that characterizes the just person. Rather, his weaker and more plausible claim is that one will be in the best position to lead a life dominated by the love of Forms if one trains the nonrational components of one's soul to serve one's love of philosophy. It is this weaker claim that lies behind his portrayal of the philosopher as the paradigm of human justice. By putting oneself into the best position to lead the philosophical life, one develops the intellectual and emotional skills that we look for in a completely just person. The mere existence of unjust lovers of abstract objects does not by itself refute Plato, for the issue is not whether they exist but whether the psychological condition that underlies their injustice makes them less able to profit from their recognition of abstract objects. It might be argued, against Plato, that sensuality, greed, and large appetites for food and drink make one all the more able to understand and love the orderly realm of the Forms, but it is far from obvious that this is so. He is not being unreasonable in assuming that these emotional states are on the contrary obstacles to the philosophical life.

We should recall, however, that Plato promises to do more than merely show that justice is a great good. He has to show that it is a greater good than injustice, so much so that even if the normal consequences of justice and injustice are reversed it will nonetheless be better to be just than unjust. The paradigm of justice must be punished because he is thought to be unjust; and the paradigm of injustice is to receive the honors and rewards because he appears to be just. How can Plato show that even in this situation it is better to be just?

The answer lies partly in the way he describes the situation of the completely unjust person, that is, the tyrant. Such a person is allowed to live out his fantasies of power and eroticism without restraint, and Plato's case against such a life is that this lack of restraint will inevitably exact a devastating psychological toll. When erotic desires are allowed to grow to full strength, they become impossible to satisfy; rather than leading to a life of peace and fulfillment, they leave one with a chronic feeling of frustration (579d–e). Similarly, tyrannical power inevitably gives rise to continual fear of reprisals and an absence of trust in one's associates (576a, 579a–c). The failure to impose any order on one's appetites makes one the victim of frequent and disorganized internal demands (573d). So, in order to achieve great power and intense sexual pleasure, the tyrant must lead a chaotic life filled with anguish, fear, and frustration. No one who reads this account of the tyrannical life could seriously hold it up as a model of how human beings should live. When the immoralist praises the life ruled by unrestrained desires for power and pleasure, he simply fails to think through the consequences of giving these desires free rein. He responds to something in human nature, for Plato agrees that no one is completely free of the impulses that the immoralist champions (571b–572b). The presence of these illicit urges seems to lend some credibility to the immoralist's doubts about whether justice is a virtue, for the praise of immorality answers to something within us. Plato's response to the immoralist is that when we seriously consider the psychological consequences of magnifying the power of our illicit urges, the life of maximal injustice loses its appeal. This is something he thinks we will be able to see without having the benefit of the theory of Forms; he invokes the Forms because they are the objects around which the best kind of human life must be built, but he makes no appeal to these objects when he tries to convince us that the tyrannical life is miserable.

Again, it is possible to protest that Plato's argument is naive. It seems to rest on the empirical assumption that anyone who possesses tyrannical power will also have sexual obsessions, and this makes it easier for him to make such a life look unattractive. But in fact such an empirical assumption is unwarranted: It is certainly possible to tyrannize a community and hold all other passions in check.[30] Here too, however, I think Plato is less vulnerable to criticism than we might have thought. His portrait of the tyrant is not meant to be an exceptionless empirical generalization about what such individuals are like. Rather, he is developing the portrait of the unjust life that is presented in Book II when Glaucon and Adeimantus try to make such a life look attractive. According to their portrait, the unjust man can seduce any woman who appeals to him; he can kill anyone he wants (360a–c). Plato's idea is that if these features of injustice capture its subrational appeal, then it is fair to describe the paradigm of injustice as someone whose sexual appetites and murderous tendencies are extreme. If that is how he is proceeding, then it is irrelevant that in fact tyrants need not be dominated by sexual appetite.

Plato's portrait of the tyrant makes it clear that his argument for justice does not rest solely on the metaphysics of the middle books and the political theory of the early books but also relies on various assumptions about human psychology. Certain desires, if unchecked, lead to the sorts of consequences—frustration, fear, pain—that everyone tries to avoid and that no one regards as compatible with a fully happy human life. What Plato is assuming is that the life of the completely just person is not marred by these same features. Fear, frustration, and chaos are not the price philosophers must inevitably pay for having a love of the Forms and for giving this passion a dominant role in their lives. On the contrary, those who are in the best position for studying the Forms will have modest and therefore easily satisfied appetites, and will be free of the competitive desire for power that typically sets people at odds and destroys their tranquillity. So the philosophical life will include the felt harmony of soul that everyone can recognize and value, as well as the more complex kind of harmony that one can understand only through a philosophical investigation of the parts of the soul and of the metaphysical objects that enter one's life when reason rules.

We can now see why Plato is confident that he can prove that justice pays even when he allows the just person and the unjust person to reverse their roles in Book II. Even if the just person is mistakenly dishonored and punished, she will still be at peace with herself; she will be free of the chaos and frustration that make the life of the tyrant so repellent. In place of the great physical pain imagined for the just person, the tyrant must endure great psychological pain. Neither is in an enviable condition, but there is a major difference that Plato thinks counts decisively in favor of the just person: her understanding and emotions gain her entrance into a world of completely harmonious objects, and so she possesses the greatest good there is. We have finally answered the question with which we began: The consummately unjust person has troubles that counterbalance the pain and dishonor imagined for the just person, and if these were the only factors involved in their comparison, it might be difficult to decide whose situation is worse; but once the possession of the Forms is added to the just person's side of the equation, the advantage lies with her, overwhelmingly so because of the great worth of that nonsensible realm.[31]

## VI

One important feature of Plato's theory has not yet been discussed, and it is best brought to light by considering a well-known internal difficulty in his argument. He says that the philosophers of the ideal city must not be allowed to study Forms without interruption, but must instead return to the darkness of the cave and help administer the political community (519d–521b, 540a–b). Why won't the philosophers be tempted to resist this requirement, however just it may be, since it seems to conflict with their self-interest?[32] After all, life in the open air illuminated by the Form of the Good must be better than life in the subterranean atmosphere in which one must rule the state. Won't the philosophers be strongly tempted to think of ways in which they can escape such service? If so, they cannot be held up as paragons of justice. Furthermore, this example seems to show that justice does not always pay: If one could unjustly escape service to the community and continue contemplating the Forms, one would do what is best for oneself, but one would not act justly.

Plato is completely confident that the individuals he has trained for the philosophical life will accept this requirement. After all, he says, they are just, and the requirement is just (520e1). But why doesn't he see any problem for his theory here? Why doesn't it leap to his eye that ruling is contrary to the philosopher's interests, so that this feature of his ideal state presents a clear counterexample to his thesis that justice pays? One possible answer to this question is simply that Plato is willing to make exceptions to this generalization.[33] But it is unlikely that he would restrict himself to the weak claim that justice is *usually* in one's interests. It is more fruitful, I think, to look at the problem in the reverse manner: Plato thinks that ruling the state is a just requirement, and since he believes that justice is always in one's interest, he must think that somehow it does pay to rule the city. The question is how he could believe this.

He tells us at one point that when philosophers look to the harmonious arrangement of the Forms, they develop a desire to imitate that harmony in some way or other (500c). And then he adds that if it becomes necessary for the philosophers to imitate the Forms by molding human character in their likeness, they will be in an excellent position to do this job well. So it is clear that when the philosophers rule, they do not stop looking to or imitating the Forms. Rather, their imitative activity is no longer merely contemplative; instead, they start acting in a way that produces a harmony in the city that is a likeness of the harmony of the Forms. Furthermore, were they to refuse to rule, they would be allowing the disorder in the city to increase. Were any single philosopher to shirk her responsibilities, and let others do more than their fair share, then she would be undermining a fair system of dividing responsibilities. The order that would be appropriate to their situation would be undermined. And so failure to rule, whether in an individual philosopher or in a group of them, would create a certain disharmony in the world: Relationships that are appropriate among people would be violated. And in creating this disharmony, the philosopher would in one respect cease to imitate the Forms. She would gaze at the order that is appropriate among Forms but would thereby upset an order that is appropriate among human beings.

What this suggests is that Plato has the resources for showing that justice is in one's interests even when it requires forgoing some purely philosophical activity. What he must hold is that one's highest good is not always served by purely contemplating the Forms;[34] rather, one's highest good is to establish and maintain a certain imitative relation-

ship with the Forms, a relationship that is strained or ruptured when
one fails to do one's fair share in a just community. The person who is
willing to do her part in a just social order, and whose willingness arises
out of a full understanding of what justice is, will see the community of
which she is a part as an ordered whole, a worldly counterpart to the
otherworldly realm of abstract objects she loves. When she acts justly
and does her fair share, she sees herself as participating in a social
pattern that approximates the harmony of the Forms, and she therefore takes her good to be served by acting justly. In making this connection between social harmony and the harmony of abstract objects, Plato
offers an account of the positive appeal that justice in human relationships should have for us. We are—or should be—attracted to justice in
human relationships; when we act justly, we should do so not merely
because of the absence of such motives as greed, sensuality, and the
desire to dominate others. Rather, we should see something attractive
about communities and relationships in which each person does his or
her appropriate part, and we should be loathe to violate these relationships because of our love of justice. If I have understood Plato correctly, he recognizes that justice as a relationship among human beings
can have this positive appeal.[35]

## VII

I said at the beginning of this chapter that there is something powerful
in Plato's argument that justice pays. What I have in mind is his thesis
that the goodness of human life depends heavily on our having a close
connection with something eminently worthwhile that lies outside of
ourselves. To live well one must be in the right psychological condition,
and that condition consists in a receptivity to the valuable objects that
exist independently of oneself. If one is oblivious to these objects and
devotes oneself above all to the acquisition of power, or the accumula-
tion of wealth, or the satisfaction of erotic appetites, then one will not
only become a danger to others but one will fail to achieve one's own
good. Psychological forces that lead to injustice when they become
powerful are forces that should in any case be moderated for one's
own good, for when they are too strong they interfere with our ability
to possess the most valuable objects.

Even if we reject Plato's belief in Forms or his thesis that goodness consists in harmony, we should recognize that there are many different ways of trying to sustain his attempt to connect the goodness of human life with some goodness external to one's soul. Christianity provides an obvious example, for it holds that the external good is God and that no human life is worth leading unless God is somehow present in it. Another example can be found in Romantic conceptions of nature, according to which a person who is cut off from the beauty of the natural order has been excluded from his home and must lead an alienated existence. We can even see some similarity between Plato's theory and the idea that great works of art so enrich human lives that the inability to respond to their beauty is a serious impoverishment.

In this last case, the valuable objects are created by human beings, but nonetheless it could be held that one's good consists in learning how to understand and love these objects. Someone can reasonably say that her life has been made better because she has come to love one of the cultural products of her society—a great novel, for example. This does not have to mean that the novel has taught her lessons that have instrumental value or that it has brought forth psychological capacities that would otherwise have lain dormant. It is intelligible to say that a relationship to a certain object—something beautiful in nature, or some work of art, or a divinity—by itself makes one's life better. And that seems to represent the way many people view their lives, for it is difficult to sustain the belief that one's life is worthwhile if one sees and feels no connection between oneself and some greater object.

Plato would of course reject these alternatives to his theory: He claims that the natural world for all its beauty is no model of perfection and that the works of poets are of lesser value still. Perhaps then we should distinguish a weak from a strong form of Platonism: Weak Platonism holds that the human good consists in having the proper relationship to some valuable object external to oneself, whether that object be a work of art, one's family or political community, the natural world, or a divinity. Strong Platonism goes further and holds that the valuable object in question must be some eternal and unchanging realm. What is distinctive of Plato's own view, of course, is that the objects in question are the Forms. But even if his particular version of Platonism is rejected, it should be recognized that some form of this doctrine, strong or weak, is deeply appealing to many. Plato might be pleased and not at all surprised that watered-down forms of Platonism have had such a long history.

## Notes

1. See *Rep.* 360e–362c for the contrast between the just and unjust lives. (All future page references will be to this dialogue, unless otherwise noted.) It should be emphasized that Plato is not trying to show that it is advantageous to *act justly* regardless of one's psychological condition. His claim is that it is advantageous to be a *just person.*

2. I have learned most from these studies: Julia Annas, *An Introduction to Plato's Republic* (Oxford, 1981); Terence Irwin, *Plato's Moral Theory* (Oxford, 1977); C. D. C. Reeve, *Philosopher-Kings: The Argument of Plato's Republic* (Princeton, 1988); Nicholas P. White, *A Companion to Plato's Republic* (Indianapolis, 1979). Among older treatments still worth consulting are R. C. Cross and A. D. Woozley, *Plato's Republic: A Philosophical Commentary* (London, 1964); Horace W. B. Joseph, *Essays in Ancient and Modern Philosophy* (Freeport, N.Y., 1971); N. R. Murphy, *The Interpretation of Plato's Republic* (Oxford, 1951); Richard Nettleship, *Lectures on the Republic of Plato*, 2d ed. (London, 1962).

3. Here I am setting aside the arguments of Book I of the dialogue and concentrating entirely on the issue as it is reintroduced at the beginning of Book II. Plato must have believed that the arguments of Book I were in some way deficient; otherwise there would be no need to reopen the question in Book II. Perhaps their deficiency lies principally in their schematic nature: They need to be buttressed by political theory, metaphysics, and psychology. An alternative reading is that in Book II Plato thinks that the earlier arguments are entirely of the wrong sort. For this interpretation, see Irwin, *Plato's Moral Theory*, 177–84; Reeve, *Philosopher-Kings*, 3–24. I also set aside the further considerations Plato mentions in Book X at 612b*ff*: These are the worldly and otherworldly rewards the just can expect to receive. It is precisely these rewards that Plato agrees to overlook when he promises in Book II to show that justice is in our interest, apart from its consequences. It should be emphasized that Plato thinks these rewards make the just life even more desirable. He agrees that the just person who suffers the torments described at 361e–362a suffers a loss of well-being and is no paradigm of happiness. When he refers to wealth and other "so-called goods" at 495a7, his refusal to call them goods outright should be taken to mean that these ordinary objects of pursuit are not in all circumstances good; he cannot hold the stronger thesis that they are never good, for then the social rewards of justice would be a matter of indifference. There has been considerable discussion of what Plato means by saying that justice is good *in itself.* See Annas, *Introduction*, chap. 3; Cross and Woozley, *Plato's Republic*, 66–9; M. B. Foster, "A Mistake of Plato's in the *Republic*," *Mind* 46 (1917): 386–93; Irwin, *Plato's Moral Theory*, 184–91, 325–6; C. A. Kirwan, "Glaucon's Challenge," *Phronesis* 10 (1965): 162–73; J. D. Mabbott, "Is Plato's *Republic* Utilitarian?" *Mind* 46 (1937): 468–74; David Sachs, "A Fallacy in Plato's *Republic*," this volume; *Philosopher-Kings*, 24–33; Nicholas P. White, "The Classification of Goods in Plato's *Republic*," *Journal of the History of Philosophy* 22 (1984): 393–421.

4. Readers of the *Republic* should bear in mind that Plato does not use

*eudaimonia* (often translated "happiness") and its cognates to refer to the feeling of pleasure. For Plato, to seek one's own happiness is simply to seek one's own advantage, and so to discover what happiness is one must determine where a human being's true interests lie.

5. At 589c1–4 Plato distinguishes between praising justice for its advantages and praising it for its pleasures (cf. 581e7–582a2, 588a7–10). This implies that the two arguments from pleasure in Book IX are not addressed to the issue of whether justice or injustice is more advantageous. For an alternative reading, see J. C. B. Gosling and C. C. W. Taylor, *The Greeks on Pleasure* (Oxford, 1982), 98–101; their interpretation is endorsed by Reeve, *Philosopher-Kings*, 307 n. 33. For further discussion of this alternative, see my review of Reeve's *Philosopher-Kings* in *Political Theory* 18 (1990): 492–6.

6. For discussion of Plato's calculation, see Reeve, *Philosopher-Kings*, 150–1. He argues that the correct figure should be 125.

7. Or following Annas, *Introduction*, 168–9, we might think that Plato is arguing for two different conclusions: The earlier material is designed to show that justice is good in itself, apart from happiness; whereas the later material does try to link justice and happiness. But we should reject her statement that "the notion of happiness has not occurred" in Book IV. When Plato asks at 444e7–445a4 whether justice is more profitable (*lusitelei*) than injustice, he is in effect asking whether the just person is happier. As Book II shows, the thesis Plato is trying to prove can be formulated in several terms that are treated equivalently. Annas's interpretation was proposed earlier by Mabbott, "Is Plato's *Republic* Utilitarian?," 62.

8. Other passages show that Plato does not take himself to have fully revealed in Book IV what justice is: See 472b7 and 484a7–8.

9. For the contrary view—that Plato does not attempt to give *any* argument in Books II–IV for the thesis that justice is advantageous—see Nicholas P. White, "The Ruler's Choice," *Archiv für Geschichte der Philosophie* 68 (1986): 34–41. But I think 444e7–445b7 rules this out: The interlocutors here agree that justice is advantageous and that injustice is not; and surely they think that they have some reason for this conclusion. I take 445b5–7 to mean that the conclusion has not been supported as fully as possible, and that the fuller argument is now to come. Despite this difference, White and I agree that Books II–IX should be read as a single continuous argument in defense of justice.

10. This is of course a consequence of Plato's general principle that whenever we call a group of things by the same name there is something they all have in common. See, for example, *Meno* 72b–c and *Rep.* 596a. Plato's assumption that goodness is a single thing is attacked by Aristotle in the *Nicomachean Ethics* I.6.

11. More fully, the argument is this: (1) Health is the preeminent good of the body, in the sense that life is not worth living when one's body is completely lacking health. (2) What makes health so worthwhile is that it involves a natural balance of elements—certain elements appropriately dominate certain others. (3) Justice involves an analogous balance in the soul. (4) Since justice has the same good-making characteristic as health, it must be equally true that life is not worth living if one is greatly deficient in justice. The crucial premise

is (3), and to support it Plato appeals to the analogy between city and soul. But even if Plato had completely left aside the idea that health involves a balance, the main argument from analogy of Books II–IV would still remain: What is best for the polis is an internal balance, and so we should expect the same to hold true of the individual. The appeal to health is an attempt to strengthen the argument by adding one more case in which advantage can be equated with proper balance.

12. For discussion of Plato's argument for the tripartition of the soul, see John M. Cooper, "Plato's Theory of Human Motivation," *History of Philosophy Quarterly* (1984): 3–21; Irwin, *Plato's Moral Theory*, 191–5; Terry Penner, "Thought and Desire in Plato," in *Plato*, vol. 2, ed. Gregory Vlastos (Garden City, N.Y., 1971), 96–118; Reeve, *Philosopher-Kings*, 118–40.

13. Plato's strategy would fail if it were impossible to say anything about what a good city is without first knowing what a good person is or what human happiness is. Books II–IV try to convince us that we can discover a good deal about how a political community should be organized, even before we address the question of human virtue and happiness. For the view that the argument of II–IV begs the question against Thrasymachus by simply assuming at 427e–428a and 433a–435a that justice is a virtue, see Michael C. Stokes, "Adeimantus in the *Republic*," in *Law, Justice and Method in Plato and Aristotle*, ed. Spiro Panagiotou (Edmonton, 1985). Stokes thinks that Plato is not really addressing his argument to a radical critic of justice like Thrasymachus; rather, he is speaking to Glaucon and Adeimantus, who are already half-convinced when the argument begins. A similar view is defended by Reeve, *Philosopher-Kings*, 33–42; contrast Martha C. Nussbaum, *The Fragility of Goodness* (Cambridge, 1986), 155–6. I believe that Plato is trying to persuade Thrasymachus (see 498d) and that he does not take his argument to beg the question against him, but the issue requires more discussion than I can give it here.

14. The limitations of Plato's argument as it develops from Book II to Book IV are emphasized by John M. Cooper, "The Psychology of Justice in Plato," this volume, pp. 18–20; Irwin, *Plato's Moral Theory*, 216–17; and White, "Ruler's Choice," 39.

15. Among the most important passages characterizing the Forms are *Phd.* 65d–66a, 74b–c, 78c–80b; *Phdr.* 247c; *Rep.* 477a–480e; *Smp.* 210e–211e; *Ti.* 27d–28a, 38a, 52a–b; *Phil.* 59c. For a thorough examination of Plato's reasons for postulating the existence of Forms, see Terry Penner, *The Ascent from Nominalism* (Dordrecht, 1987).

16. For a lucid interpretation of this aspect of Plato's theory, see Richard Patterson, *Image and Reality in Plato's Metaphysics* (Indianapolis, 1985).

17. See Penner, *Ascent from Nominalism*, 57–140.

18. See Irwin, *Plato's Moral Theory*, 236, for the claim that Plato's defense of justice depends on the idea that we must develop all of our capacities.

19. The principal textual support for this reading derives from the many passages in which Plato describes the Forms as the proper objects of love: 476b, 480a, 484b, 490a–b, 500c, 501d. They could not be such unless they are good (*Smp.* 204d–206a). I am not claiming that according to Plato each Form counts as a separate good; rather, it is the ordered whole constituted by the

Forms that is a good, although some of the individual Forms (Goodness, Beauty, etc.) may by themselves be goods. Of course, if my interpretation is to be an improvement over the ones just considered, then Plato cannot simply *assume* that the Forms are a great good. His argument for this claim will be discussed later. It might be asked how the Forms can be the greatest good, since that distinction is reserved for justice (366e9). But there is no real conflict here. When Plato says that justice is the greatest good, he does not mean that the universe has no better object to show than a just human being; the Forms are superior to this. He means rather that possessing justice is better for us than possessing any other type of good; and this is compatible with the claim that the Forms are the supreme objects. For on my reading, being fully just and fully possessing the Forms are the same psychological state, and so there is no issue about which state it is better to be in.

20. It is widely recognized that according to Plato happiness consists in possessing good things—a point he takes to need no argument. See *Smp.* 204e–205a. What is distinctive of my interpretation is the suggestion that Plato defends the philosophical life (and therefore the life of consummate justice) by adding to the conventional list of goods.

21. The pattern of argument in the *Philebus* is similar: Reason is declared to be a more important component of the good human life than pleasure because it is more akin than pleasure to the good. Here, as in the *Republic*, something outside of human life is taken to be ideal, and those elements of human life that most fully approach this ideal are to receive priority.

22. This is why his discussion in *N.E.* I.6 of the Platonic conception of the Good is not out of place. Aristotle also considers the possibility that for the Platonist the Good is not itself a desirable object but is instead a tool for gaining the knowledge we need to make practical decisions. See 1096b35–1097a6. But this is an alternative to the main conception of the Good that he considers in I.6

23. Thus G. X. Santas, "Aristotle's Criticism of Plato's Form of the Good: Ethics without Metaphysics?" *Philosophical Papers* 18 (1989): 154. He takes Aristotle to be obviously right that a Platonic Form is not the sort of thing that can be possessed, and defends Plato by denying that his theory makes any such claim. Instead, he takes Plato merely to be saying that the Form of the Good must be known, the better to possess other goods. A related view seems to be presupposed by Nussbaum, who takes Plato to believe that "the bearers of value are activities." See *Fragility of Goodness*, 148. On this view, the Forms themselves cannot be "bearers of value," since they are not activities. Rather, they have value because they are the objects of pure, stable, truth-discovering activity. See pp. 145–8.

24. See Paul Ziff, *Semantic Analysis* (Ithaca, N.Y., 1960), 210, 216. His view is that when we call something "good" we are saying that it "answers to certain interests" (p. 117). Unless we are provided with further information, it is not clear how water can meet this condition. Of course, on my reading, Plato is not merely saying that the Forms answer to certain interests. They are good quite apart from our interests, and because of their great goodness it is in our interest to possess them.

25. The analogy of the cave (514a–517c) and the critique of artistic imitation in Book X (see esp. 596a–597d) bring out this aspect of the theory most fully. See too 477a, 478d, 479d. For discussion, see Gregory Vlastos, "Degrees of Reality in Plato," in *Platonic Studies*, 2d ed. (Princeton, 1981), 58–75. Vlastos holds that the Forms are fully real in two senses: they have the highest degree of cognitive reliability, and they have a kind of value that "transcends the usual specifications of value" (p. 64). Of course, Plato cannot simply lay it down without argument that Forms have this transcendent value, nor can he infer that they have it merely because of their greater cognitive reliability.

26. So read, the arguments of Books II–IV and of V–IX are mutually supporting: The later material adds content and support to the thesis that justice is a psychological harmony, and that thesis in turn supports the identification of being in good condition with being harmoniously arranged.

27. Some support for this interpretation comes from the *Philebus*, since Plato there appeals to measure and proportion to explain the nature of goodness (*Phil.* 64d–e). Throughout the cosmos, and not merely in human affairs, wherever limit is imposed on the disorder inherent in the unlimited, a harmonious unification is achieved, and this harmony is what makes things good. See *Phil.* 23c–26d. I take Plato to be saying that a thing of one type is better than something of the *same* type if it has a greater degree of the harmony appropriate for things of that type; and a thing of one type is better than something of a *different* type if things of the first type can achieve a higher degree of harmony than things of the second. Harmony is for Plato a form of unification, and so on my view he connects goodness and unity. Note his emphasis on unity as the greatest civic good: 462a–b; cf. 422e–423c. On the role of unity in Plato's argument, see White, *Companion*, 31, 38–40. For further discussion of the Form of the Good, see Cooper, this volume, pp. 20–23; Irwin, *Plato's Moral Theory*, 224–6; G. X. Santas, "The Form of the Good in Plato's *Republic*," in *Essays in Ancient Greek Philosophy*, ed. John P. Anton and Anthony Preus (Albany, 1983), 2:232–63; and Reeve, *Philosopher-Kings*, 81–95.

28. In section VI, I will discuss another part of Plato's answer: Some acts of justice imitate the Forms.

29. For further discussion of the ways in which Plato's novel understanding of justice is related to the ordinary Greek conception, see Gregory Vlastos, "Justice and Happiness in the *Republic*," in *Platonic Studies*, 2d ed. (Princeton, 1981), 111–39. This is a response to Sachs, "A Fallacy in Plato's *Republic*," which argues that these two conceptions are unconnected. Some other responses to Sachs are Annas, *Introduction*, chap. 6; Raphael Demos, "A Fallacy in Plato's *Republic?*" *Philosophical Review* 73 (1984): 395–8; Irwin, *Plato's Moral Theory*, 208–12; Richard Kraut, "Reason and Justice in Plato's *Republic*," in *Exegesis and Argument*, ed. E. N. Lee, Alexander P. D. Mourelatos, and R. M. Rorty (Assen, 1973), 207–24; and Reeve, *Philosopher-Kings*, chap. 5.

30. For this criticism of Plato, see Annas, *Introduction*, 304.

31. Here my reading differs from that of Nicholas P. White, "Happiness and External Contingencies in Plato's *Republic*," in *Moral Philosophy*, ed. William C. Starr and Richard C. Taylor (Milwaukee, 1989), 1–21. He denies that Plato

tries to defend the thesis (one that White labels "absurd") that "every just person is at every moment better off than every unjust person," regardless of differences in their good or bad fortune (p. 16). Rather, he takes Plato to hold the weaker view that justice "is the best strategy" over the long run, and he thinks Plato's defense of this thesis is not completed until Book X. On this reading, when the just person is on the rack, he is at that point worse off than an unjust person basking in undeserved glory. This commits Plato to the view that if the just person *dies* on the rack, and so has no long run, then despite the fact that he chose the best strategy, his life is worse than the lives of some who are unjust.

32. The philosophers' motivation for ruling has received much discussion but no consensus has emerged. For some of the conflicting views, see Annas, this volume, pp. 161–8; Cooper, this volume, pp. 23–8; Irwin, *Plato's Moral Theory*, 242–3, 337–8; Richard Kraut, "Egoism, Love and Political Office in Plato," *Philosophical Review* 82 (1973): 330–44; Reeve, *Philosopher-Kings*, 95, 197–204; White, *Companion*, 44–8, 189–96; White, "Ruler's Choice."

33. For the view that Plato makes an exception in this one case, see White, "Ruler's Choice."

34. I do not believe that Plato ever claims or commits himself to the thesis that the best human life is the one that has the greatest amount of purely contemplative activity. What he does clearly hold is that such activity is better than political activity (520e–521a); but this does not entail that pure contemplation that creates injustice is more advantageous than political activity that is justly required.

35. For a fuller presentation of the interpretation I have given in this section, see my "Return to the Cave: *Republic* 519–521," in *Proceedings of the Boston Area Colloquium in Ancient Philosophy*, vol. 7, ed. John J. Cleary (Lanham, 1993).

# 13

## Plato and the Poets

### *James O. Urmson*

Our greatest goods come to us through madness, says Socrates in the *Phaedrus*, provided always that it is one of the kinds of madness that are the gift of the gods. One god-given type of madness is that of the poet (*Phaedrus* 244a). Indeed, the poet could be thought of as possessed, as being but the mouthpiece of the Muse herself. Thus the *Iliad* begins with the words: "Sing, goddess, the destructive anger of Achilles the son of Peleus." This must not be thought of as merely a conventional gesture, though it was conventional, any more than Milton's invocation of the heavenly Muse at the beginning of *Paradise Lost* is mere convention:

> Of man's first disobedience . . .
> Sing, Heavenly Muse, that, on the secret top
> Of Oreb, or of Sinai, didst inspire
> That shepherd who first taught the chosen seed
> In the beginning how the heavens and the earth
> Rose out of Chaos . . .

Philosophers are not accustomed either to asking for or to receiving much in the way of divine guidance; but this should not blind them to the fact that many people do ask for it and sincerely believe that they get it. Likewise the Muses spoke to Hesiod on Mount Helicon and made the peasant farmer a poet—the Muses make some men poets as Zeus makes some men kings (*Theogony* 33ff and 94ff.).

Parallel with and most strictly compatible with the idea that the Muse spoke through the poet's mouth was the notion that she inspired the poet. Nowadays we are inclined to think of poetic inspiration as the gift of artistry, of expressive mastery. But that was not the old idea. Milton's heavenly Muse, as the reader will have noticed, was the source of information for the first few chapters of the book of *Genesis*, and is being asked by Milton for more information on the topic; in this Milton was showing himself the accurate classical scholar that he was. In the *Iliad* Homer's first request to the Muse was that she would tell him what caused Achilles and Agamemnon to quarrel, and throughout the *Iliad* he continues to ask the Muses, the daughters of Memory, for factual information: 'For you are goddesses, and are present, and know all things, but we have only hearsay and know nothing' (*Iliad*, Book II.I. 484–85). Similarly in the first two lines of the *Odyssey* Homer asks the Muse to tell the story of Odysseus and makes clear that the need is for solid facts. As reasonably accurately and totally absurdly translated by Pope he pleads with her:

> Oh, snatch some portion of these acts from fate,
> Celestial Muse! and to our world relate.

Plato would not challenge this tradition. Though philosophically an innovator, he was in practical matters a committed conservative. He was trying desperately to shore up the old ways, the old morality, the old patriotism, or what seemed such to his nostalgic eyes. He never wrote anything that could be construed as being inconsistent with or derogatory from the ancient religion of Greece. In the *Laws* he somewhat archaically advocates worship of the sun and the moon, visible gods in a visible heaven. But it is hard to believe that his writings on these matters accurately reflect his own beliefs; it is rather that he thinks that the only religion of which the common herd is capable should be supported by the elite. To this extent he was of like sentiment with Lord Melbourne, who admitted that he was not a pillar of the established church but claimed to be a buttress thereof, since he supported it from the outside. Plato therefore conformed, but in the *Timaeus* he tells us that the maker and father of this world is hard to find and when found is impossible to tell to the masses (28c). In the *Laws* he permits himself to describe the inspiration of the poets as a *palaios muthos* (719c), an ancient myth or tale, but he never denies it and often affirms it. But, in any case, in allowing inspiration to the poets Plato was not committing himself to the view that they always spoke truth. The Muses told Hesiod that they were capable of telling a pack of lies as well as of truth telling. <u>If Plato regarded the poets as inspired, or spoke as though he did, this was in no way incompatible with regarding them as a danger to society.</u> How and why he so regarded them will be the subject of the rest of this chapter.

By the end of the ninth book of the *Republic* Socrates has finished his task of showing that justice is an intrinsic good for those who practice it. At the beginning of the tenth book Socrates looks back over the discussion and says that one of the best things they had done in building the ideal city was to exclude all mimetic poetry from it. He says that the rightness of this decision is now clearer than it had been initially as a result of the subsequent proof of the tripartite nature of the soul. I want to consider what he was rejecting and, second, why he rejected it. I do not propose to argue that Socrates' position is satisfactory nor that it is unsatisfactory. But I do believe that it will emerge that the discussion in the *Republic* is by no means as irrelevant to modern attitudes to imaginative literature as is commonly suggested.

First, then, what is Socrates rejecting? In his own words, literally translated, it is "Poetry, so much of it as is mimetic." Whatever these words may mean, I take it that they do not mean the same as "such parts of mimetic poetry as are undesirable"; he is talking about all mimetic poetry. What, then does he mean by "mimetic"? Since he refers us back to the earlier discussion in book 3, it is a perfectly natural and reasonable expectation that he now means by "mimetic" what he very clearly explained that it meant in book 3. There he tells us that mimetic poetry is to be distinguished from narrative poetry; mimetic poetry is that in which the reciter plays the part of some character and utters what are supposed to be that character's words; it is *oratio recta*, it is direct dramatic representation, it is vocal acting. Narrative poetry is that in which the poet or reciter describes *propria persona* the events portrayed; insofar as speech of others is reported, it is reported in *oratio obliqua*.

But reasonable as the initial presumption is that this will be what he means by "mimesis" in book 10, it is, it seems clear, a quite different position, employing a different conception of mimesis, which is defended in that book. In book 3 Socrates maintains, as a canon of elementary education, that the young should not be permitted to play the part of bad or ridiculous characters—actually to play the part is damaging to the character in a way that narration is not; we may read about Thersites, but not act Thersites. Such is the gist of the argument on Stephanus pages 392 to 398. So, in contrast with the total elimination of mimetic poetry in book 10, not all even of directly dramatic acting is forbidden in book 3, not all of *mimetike*, as here defined, but only a portion of it.

Moreover, it cannot be this notion of *mimesis* that Socrates is employing in book 10, for two reasons. First, Socrates introduces the discussion in book 10 not by saying, as we might expect, that he has already given a perfectly clear account of *mimesis*, but by saying (595c) that he is not at all clear what mimesis is supposed to be; he then gives the famous account of it in terms of the three beds, which affords absolutely no basis whatever for the distinction of drama and narrative made in book 3. If we were to attempt to apply the distinction of book 3 to painting, I suppose that painting a piece of canvas to look like a bed would be narration, and painting oneself to look like a bed would be mimetic. There is no hint in the *Republic* of such absurdities.

Second, as we shall see, the objections to mimetic poetry in book 10 have as much relevance to narrative poetry as to mimetic poetry as defined in book 3. The book 3 distinction is simply irrelevant to book 10. With an amiable desire to make Socrates consistent, such writers as Cross, Woozley, and Tate have held that when he speaks of mimetic poetry in book 10 he really means only bad poetry that is mimetic in the sense of book 3. But not only do all the objections of book 10 apply to narrative as easily as to drama, most of them apply with at least equal force to the portrayal of the good and the beautiful as to the portrayal of the bad and the ugly. In book 3 we were concerned with censorship, the elimination of the morally undesirable—not the elimination of the equivalent of sensational pulp literature, but of the objectionable parts of Homer and other good literature. In modern terms, it is like a prosecution of *Lady Chatterley's Lover or The Naked Lunch*, not of cheap pornography. But in book 10 the strictures are intended to apply with equal force to the equivalent of *War and Peace* and *Crime and Punishment*. The complete works of Homer, Aeschylus, Sophocles, and Euripides are to be eliminated. We can represent the argument of book 10 as resuming that of book 3 only by doing gross violence to one or the other or both.

I think that Socrates' basic objection to mimetic poetry as a whole is given on page 595b5. Mimetic poetry is destructive of the intelligence of those of its hearers who do not have the protection of knowing what sort of thing it is—that is to say, who are not philosophers. Nonphilosophers do not know that what is offered by the poet is at two removes from reality. The lover of sights is even unaware that the world of becoming is anything other than the truly real; still less does he realize that what is depicted in mimetic poetry is one grade still farther away from reality. Philosophers are safe from the intellectual corruption of mimetic poetry, as they are from the lures of advertisements of breakfast cereals; but other men are not, and for the sake of the city as a whole, mimesis must go. All mimesis, of good men as of bad men, of heroic deeds as of vice, is a dream of a dream. Most men cannot distinguish dream from reality. ⋏

The illustration of the three beds is not designed as an attack on painting; it is a highly stylized illustration to clarify the nature of mimesis. What is said is intended to be directly applicable to mimetic poetry; it includes the following three points:

1. He who understands beds is primarily the user and secondarily the maker of beds. The painter of pictures of beds needs no understanding of beds.

2. The painter of pictures of beds does not attempt to paint beds as they are known to be but the way they look; to do this convincingly is precisely his skill.

3. At a distance a child or a fool may be deceived into taking a picture of a bed for a bed.

How is this highly stylized account of *trompe-l'oeil* painting to be applied to mimetic poetry, Plato's serious prey?

If we were to insist on an overliteral parallelism, the answer would have to be that the poet was trying to reproduce the world of becoming in such a way that not too attentive children and idiots would be deceived into believing that what they were witnessing was some transaction in the world of becoming. They would believe that in the theater they were actually witnessing a quarrel between Creon and Antigone, Oedipus questioning Teiresias, or Medea threatening vengeance. This sort of mistake can indeed be made; there were a number of halfwits in England who sent wreaths to the funeral of a character in a radio serial. But I do not think that Plato was seriously worried about this possibility, any more than by *trompe-l'oeil* painting. I do not even think that he was worried about the falsification of history—after all, in his earlier discussion of falsehood he had suggested that one of its more permissible uses was to fill up gaps in known history (382d).

But Plato does wish seriously to maintain in some sense that the

mimetic poet has no need to understand the world of becoming that
he depicts, that he does not even attempt to depict the world as it is
but only the way that it appears to be—that is his skill—and that people
who are not philosophers can be misled into thinking that he gives
insight into reality rather than the plausible imitation that in fact he
offers. We must try to understand this view in more detail.

In the *Ion* Homer is called the best and divinest poet of all (530b), a
view to which Plato without a doubt sincerely assented. Prominent in
Homer's alleged merits, however, is the fact that he has "described war
for the most part, and the mutual intercourse of men, good and bad,
lay and professional and the ways of the gods in their intercourse with
each other and with men" (531c). The rhapsode Ion is now represented as taking Homer as an authority on the various themes on
which he writes: Ion even claims that as a result of being a specialist
on Homer and having an intimate knowledge of Homer's descriptions
of strategy he himself is now the best general in Greece: "Be sure of it,
Socrates; and that I owe to my study of Homer" (541b). But Socrates
points out again that the *techne* of Homer was that of the poet and
that as a poet he has no understanding of war or chariot-racing or
medicine, though much advice on these topics is given by alleged au-
thorities in his poems.

It should be noted that it is Homer's skill in and understanding of
matters other than poetic technique that are being called into question.
There is also no suggestion that Plato is worried about possible historical inaccuracies in the Homeric narrative. In the passages on censorship in book 3 Plato criticizes some of Homer's descriptions of the
behavior of gods and heroes as blasphemous or inappropriate, not for
mere inaccuracy of fact. But in the *Ion*, and, as we shall see, in book 10
of the *Republic*, it is the lack of skill and understanding of the poet
overall, not his occasional scurrilities, that is criticized. Certainly Homer
and the rest are not being ejected merely on the ground that they are
unreliable historians.

The poets' lack of skill and understanding, insisted on in the *Ion*, is
harped on again in the *Republic*. Socrates (599) asks what Homer was
good at; if he really understood warfare, medicine, chariot-racing, and
the like, why was he not a famous practitioner in these areas as well as
in poetry? But here, more than in the *Ion*, Socrates emphasizes not
merely the poets' lack of the technical skills that they purport to describe; now he argues that the poet as such is not an authority on
excellence and evil. Poets are *mimetai eidōlōn aretēs*—imitators of

images of excellence (600e5). The poet (602b) will produce his imitations not knowing in each case in what way it is good or bad. Not knowing the reality he will, it seems, imitate what appears fine to the ignorant multitude. The poet's skill in writing (601a) gives his product a charm that makes what he says seem plausible. This lack of understanding of the nature of good and evil, accessible only to the philosopher in Plato's view, is surely the main indictment of mimetic poets.

So the first point by Socrates in book 10 of the *Republic* is one made constantly by him. It is made in so early a dialogue as the *Apology*, where Socrates is represented as saying (21d): "The poets say many fine things, but know nothing of that of which they speak." The poet has only the skill of composition, but is treated as a man with skill and understanding of many things, even of good and evil and the soul of man, an understanding he has not but which he seems to have because of the skill he has in producing a spurious appearance of understanding.

But Socrates now (604) has a further point to make, which I do not recollect that he makes elsewhere; presumably it is this point that becomes clear in the light of the tripartite analysis of the soul. It would be dull to represent a man acting in the face of calamity of the sort that occurs in tragedy as a gentleman of good character would behave. A gentleman hides his grief from the public eye, his anger and his joy are restrained, he does not rant and rail. Homer represents Achilles exhibiting frenetic grief at the death of Patroclus in a way in which a man of good character would be ashamed to exhibit it. So not only are the poets ignorant of the nature of moral excellence, they also have a standing temptation to represent people who are supposed to be heroes as behaving in a theatrical and intemperate manner. In the theater we are led to admire what outside of it we would despise. The appeal is to the lowest of the three elements in the soul and we admire characters whose appetites and emotions are in control of their reason.

We have rehearsed what Plato says. At this stage the expositors of Plato begin to speak, if friendly, in an apologetic tone and, if less friendly, with some condescension. Homer, we are told once again, was the bible of the Greeks; they read him as an authority on early history, theology, warfare, and the like, and no doubt this was a mistake. But this, the critics continue, has no relevance to aesthetic or to literary criticism. Plato simply fails to look at things from the aesthetic angle. Maybe Homer was no theologian and a poor strategist—but that is irrelevant to his merits as a poet. Sometimes the critics appear not to be able to assimilate what they read, in their horrified incredulity. Thus Nettleship, in his lectures on the *Republic*, sums up the passage that we have been discussing as follows: "Rightly or wrongly, Plato has here come to the conclusion that nearly all the imitative art of his time has degenerated into indiscriminate catering for common excitement. He treats art as being this and only this, and in consequence the whole passage remains rather an attack on certain developments of art than an adequate theoretical treatment of it." Degenerate imitative art of his time indeed, when all his references are to Homer and the tragedians! Moreover, Plato is not writing a treatise on aesthetics but explaining why poetry of an imitative sort must, in spite of its manifest attractions, be excluded from the ideal state.

I reiterate that I do not want to attack or defend Plato's criticism of imitative poetry. But I do want to say that, justified or unjustified, it is just as relevant to modern literary criticism as to anything in his own day. That is what I now proceed to show.

First let me say again that Plato is attacking mimetic poetry using as examples those poets whom he clearly believes to be the best. He has primarily in mind his beloved Homer and the great tragedians of the fifth century. It is the tragedian who is said (597e6) to be at two removes from reality and the attack is explicitly stated (598d7) to be on tragedy and its leader, Homer. Actual examples are mostly taken from Homer, although (595b9) "a certain love and respect that I have had from childhood makes me hesitate to speak about Homer." Further, it is now the whole of their works that are to be banished.

It is clear who would be the modern equivalent of these great literary figures whom Plato banishes. Certainly the great playwrights, Shakespeare and the rest, must be included. But I have no doubt that the serious novelists may be included also. Plato mentions only poets, but it is not meter that is the target of his criticism. The simple fact is that all fiction in his time and before it was written in verse; there were no prose romances. So let us add Tolstoi, Hardy, Dostoievsky, Henry James, and the rest to our list of the giants of literature whom Plato would expel.

Now, what sort of thing do critics write about these great literary figures and their works? Do they attribute to them the merits that Plato denied them? It would be unwise for me at this stage to offer my own generalizations, so I must ask you to bear with a number of quotations from famous literary critics:

*[margin note: emphasis on political motivation]*

1. "The multitude of things in Homer is wonderful; their splendor, their truth, their force, and variety; he describes the bodies as well as the souls of men." Hazlitt, "On Poetry in General," from *Lectures on the English Poets*

2. "In the first and lowest side of drama . . . I place those pieces in which we are presented with only the visible surface of life. . . . The second place in the scale of dramatic art is due to effective representations of human passions where the deeper shades and springs of action are portrayed. . . . But I conceive that the stage has yet another and loftier aim. Instead of merely describing the enigma of existence, it should also solve it." Friedrich von Schlegel, *Lectures on the History of Literature*

3. "The first and last aim of art is to render intuitively perceptible the process of life itself, to show how the soul of man develops in the atmosphere surrounding him." Hebbel, *Journal* [1838]

4. "It is here [in truth of detail] in very truth that he [the novelist] competes with life; it is here that he competes with his brother the painter in *his* attempt to render the look of things, the look that conveys the meaning, to catch the color, the relief, the expression, the surface, the substance of the human spectacle." Henry James, *The Art of Fiction*

5. "It [the novel] is an attempt to find . . . in the aspect of matter and in the facts of life what of each is fundamental, what is enduring and essential—their one illuminating and convincing quality—the very truth of their existence." Joseph Conrad, preface to *The Nigger of the Narcissus*

6. "A good poem helps to change the shape and significance of the universe, helps to extend everyone's knowledge of himself and the world around him." Dylan Thomas, *On Poetry*

I cease to quote, not from lack of material but lest I exhaust by iteration the reader's patience. I hope to have given, finely expressed by distinguished writers, specimens of the view that Plato is attacking. All these authors, he would hold, mistake the imitation of a shadow for reality. They are prisoners in the cave and what they take for the deep truths of imaginative literature are in fact shadows on the wall. What a revealing picture of remorse and the craving for expiation Dostoievsky

*[handwritten marginalia: the two former are of a different kind than the latter — you can make the claim that philosophy — to some degree — is instrumental in showing the truth... but the philosopher doesn't know... know any more than the poet might... in poetry... medicine...]*

gives us in *Crime and Punishment*, we exclaim. But, Plato asks, why should you think it in any way truthful? It is so utterly convincing, we answer. Indeed, Plato replies, to be convincing is the skill of the writer of fiction, a skill that Dostoievsky has in abundance; but why should we regard the novelist as having any particular insight into the human soul, the criminal mentality, the repentant sinner? To claim such knowledge for Dostoievsky is precisely parallel to the claim that Homer had insight into strategy, medicine, and the virtues and vices of man. It is the philosopher, not the plausible imitator of the world of becoming, who has the insight into good and evil. Such, I think, is the way that Plato would apply his attack to modern literature and the view of it taken by the critics and, no doubt, many lesser readers.

I repeat that it is no part of my design to attack or to defend these views of Plato. The further charge that he would no doubt make, that the great tragic heroes of modern literature, Hamlet, Othello, and the rest, are not heroes but intemperate men whose souls are swayed by appetite, passion, and caprice, I leave also without comment.

What I hope to have established in this chapter is that:

1. Plato is not attacking inferior literature; his attack is on the very best mimetic poets that he knows of, especially Homer, "the best of poets and first of tragedians" (607a).

2. Plato principally attacks them because they give a very convincing show of apparent insight into important matters of which they know nothing. —> *[handwritten: this is not proven, it is an assumption]*

3. So far from Plato's charges being obsolete, they are directed against a view of serious imaginative literature that is still very common in modern times.

*[handwritten: coward]*

Once again, I say that I offer no comment of my own. But I allow myself the luxury of one further quotation from an author who appears to side neither with Plato nor with those whom I take Plato to be criticizing:

So far as we are taken up with the happenings in any novel in the same way in which we are taken up with what happens under our eyes, we are acquiring at least as much falsehood as truth. But when we are developed enough to say: "This is the view of life of a person who was a good observer within his limits, Dickens, or Thackeray, or George Elliot, or Balzac;

but he looked at it in a different way from me . . . so what I am looking at is the world as seen by a particular mind"—then we are in a position to gain something from reading fiction. T. S. Eliot, "Religion and Literature," in *Essays Ancient and Modern*

## Appendix

The Greek verb *mimeisthai* and such derivatives as *mimetikon* and *mimesis* can be translated, as normally employed up to Plato's time, as "imitate," "imitative," and "imitation" with as much accuracy as can be expected from any translation. Plato's extension of this use in book 3 of the *Republic* to denote the direct speech of the actor as opposed to narrative is natural enough, and any inaccuracy it might have as aesthetic theory can be excused in a disquisition on the principles of educational censorship. There is here no suggestion of fraud or misrepresentation but only of playing a part.

The extension in book 10 of the *Republic* is quite different, but equally natural. Here there is the notion of the imitation as a counterfeit, the notion as it occurs in "imitation pearl" or "imitation cream." Plato explains it with regard to a type of painting that was ultrarealistic and seriously aimed at *trompe-l'oeil* effects; there are anecdotes that show that this type of painting was well known in the fourth century B.C., when Plato was writing; Zeuxis is said to have painted grapes at which birds flew, and Apelles a horse at which live horses neighed. This style of painting could deceive children and fools at a distance, Plato tells us, more plausibly and moderately; it is the sort of painting that Plato is here calling mimetic, but it would be absurd to suppose that Plato thought it represented a serious threat to the well-being of society. The aspect of *mimesis* that Plato now goes on to ascribe to fiction no doubt includes its representational character; but the important aspect, as the story of the three beds shows, is its being a counterfeit of reality, a counterfeit of understanding, not of historical truth.

As the term *mimetic* was extended to cover the other arts, its connection with the root meaning of "imitation" was attenuated. To say that instrumental music is mimetic of the passions, as Aristotle does, can mean very little more than that such music can properly be called gay, sad, etc. Plato (*Laws* 669E) was unwilling to call purely instrumental music mimetic.

I do not believe that Plato thought that any other art would lay claims to insight as literature did, and so had no thought of banning any, though he wanted to purge them of undesirable elements. I dare say that such claims are sometimes made for painting nowadays, but they were not in Plato's time. If they had been he would no doubt have banished painting as well as mimetic poetry from the ideal state. The same fate would surely have befallen any art that made the same claims as poetry.

# Suggested Readings

Allen, R. E. *Studies in Plato's Metaphysics*. New York: Humanities Press, 1965.

Annas, Julia. "Plato's *Republic* and Feminism." *Philosophy* 51 (1976): 307–21.

———. *An Introduction to Plato's Republic*. Oxford: Oxford University Press, 1981.

Bar On, Bat-Ami. *Engendering Origins: Critical Feminist Readings in Plato and Aristotle*. Albany: State University of New York Press, 1988.

Bluestone, Natalie Harris. *Women and the Ideal Society: Plato's Republic and Modern Myths of Gender*. Oxford: Berg, 1987.

Burnyeat, Myles. "Platonism and Mathematics: A Prelude to Discussion." In *Mathematics and Metaphysics in Aristotle*, ed. Andreas Graeser. Bern: Paul Haupt, 1987.

Cooper, John. "Plato's Theory of Human Motivation." *History of Philosophy Quarterly* 1 (1984): 3–21.

Cross, R. C., and A. D. Woozley. *Plato's Republic: A Philosophical Commentary*. London: Macmillan, 1964.

Fine, Gail. "Knowledge and Belief in *Republic* V." *Archiv für Geschichte der Philosophie* 60 (1978): 121–39.

———. "Knowledge and Belief in *Republic* V–VII." In *Companions to Ancient Thought 1: Epistemology*, ed. Stephen Everson. Cambridge: Cambridge University Press, 1990, 85–115.

Gosling, J. C. B. *Plato*. London: Routledge & Kegan Paul, 1973.

Gosling, J. C. B., and C. C. W. Taylor. *The Greeks on Pleasure*. Oxford: Oxford University Press, 1982.

Griswold, Charles L., ed. *Platonic Writings, Platonic Readings*. New York: Routledge, 1988.

Grote, George. *Plato and the Other Companions of Socrates*, 4th ed., 4 vols. London: J. Murray, 1888.

Guthrie, W. K. C. *A History of Greek Philosophy*, vol. 4. Cambridge: Cambridge University Press, 1975.

Irwin, Terence. *Plato's Ethics*. New York: Oxford University Press, 1995.

Joseph, H. W. B. *Essays in Ancient and Modern Philosophy.* Oxford: Clarendon Press, 1935.

Klagge, James C., and Nicholas D. Smith. *Methods of Interpreting Plato and His Dialogues.* Oxford: Clarendon Press, 1992.

Klosko, George. *The Development of Plato's Political Theory.* London: Methuen, 1986.

Kraut, Richard. "Return to the Cave." In *Proceedings of the Boston Area Colloquium in Ancient Philosophy,* vol. 7 (1991), ed. John J. Cleary. Lanham, Md.: University Press of America, 1993, 43–61.

———, ed. *Cambridge Companion to Plato.* Cambridge: Cambridge University Press, 1992.

Lesses, Glenn. "The Divided Soul in Plato's *Republic.*" *History of Philosophy Quarterly* 4 (1987): 147–61.

Moline, Jon. "Plato on the Complexity of the Psyche." *Archiv für Geschichte der Philosophie* 60 (1978): 1–26.

Moravcsik, Julius, and Philip Temko, eds. *Plato on Beauty, Wisdom, and the Arts.* Totowa, N.J.: Rowman & Littlefield, 1982.

———. *Plato and Platonism.* Oxford: Blackwell, 1992.

Murdoch, Iris. *The Fire and the Sun: Why Plato Banished the Artists.* Oxford: Oxford University Press, 1977.

Murphy, N. R. *The Interpretation of Plato's Republic.* London: Oxford University Press, 1951.

Nehamas, Alexander. "Plato on the Imperfection of the Sensible World." *American Philosophical Quarterly* 12 (1975): 105–17.

Neu, Jerome. "Plato's Analogy of State and Individual: The *Republic* and the Organic Theory of the State." *Philosophy* 46 (1971): 238–54.

Nussbaum, Martha C. *The Fragility of Goodness.* Cambridge: Cambridge University Press, 1986.

Patterson, Richard. *Image and Reality in Plato's Metaphysics.* Indianapolis: Hackett, 1985.

Penner, Terry. "Thought and Desire in Plato." In *Plato,* vol. II, ed. Gregory Vlastos. Garden City, N.Y.: Doubleday, 1971.

———. *The Ascent from Nominalism.* Dordrecht: D. Reidel, 1987.

———. "Plato and Davidson: Parts of the Soul and Weakness of the Will." *Canadian Journal of Philosophy* supplementary volume 16 (1990): 35–74.

Popper, Karl. *The Open Society and Its Enemies,* vol. 1: The Spell of Plato. London: Routledge & Kegan Paul, 1945.

Price, A. W. *Love and Friendship in Plato and Aristotle.* Oxford: Oxford University Press, 1989.

Reeve, C. D. C. *Philosopher-Kings.* Princeton: Princeton University Press, 1989.

Ross, W. D. *Plato's Theory of Ideas.* London: Oxford University Press, 1951.

Santas, Gerasimos. "The Form of the Good in Plato's *Republic.*" *Philosophical Inquiry* 2 (1980): 374–403.

————. "Two Theories of the Good in Plato's *Republic*." *Archiv für Geschichte der Philosophie* 57 (1985): 2233–45.

Saxonhouse, Arlene W. *Women in the History of Political Thought*. New York: Praeger, 1985.

Vlastos, Gregory. *Plato: A Collection of Critical Essays*, 2 vols. Garden City, N.Y.: Anchor Books, 1970–71.

————. *Platonic Studies*, 2nd printing. Princeton: Princeton University Press, 1981.

————. *Studies in Greek Philosophy*, vol. 2. Princeton: Princeton University Press, 1994.

Wender, Dorothea. "Plato: Misogynist, Paedophile, and Feminist." *Arethusa* 6 (1973): 75–90.

White, Nicholas P. *Plato on Knowledge and Reality*. Indianapolis: Hackett, 1976.

————. *A Companion to Plato's Republic*. Indianapolis: Hackett, 1979.

————. "The Classification of Goods in Plato's *Republic*." *Journal of the History of Philosophy* 22 (1984): 393–421.

————. "The Ruler's Choice." *Archiv für Geschichte der Philosophie* 68 (1986): 22–46.

# Index of Passages

# Authors

**Julia Annas** is Regent's Professor of Philosophy of the University of Arizona. Among her publications are *Aristotle's Metaphysics Books M and N* (translation and commentary), *An Introduction to Plato's Republic, Hellenistic Philosophy of Mind, Modes of Scepticism,* and *The Morality of Happiness.*

**John M. Cooper** is Professor of Philosophy at Princeton University. He is the author of *Reason and Human Good in Aristotle* and of numerous articles on diverse aspects of ancient philosophy. He is also the editor of *Plato: Complete Works* and coeditor and cotranslator of *Seneca: Moral and Political Essays* (with introductions and notes).

**Richard Kraut** is Professor of Philosophy and Classics at Northwestern University. He is the author of *Socrates and The State, Aristotle on the Human Good, Aristotle Politics Books VII and VIII* (translation and commentary), and the editor of the *Cambridge Companion to Plato.*

**Jonathan Lear** is a member of the Committee on Social Thought at the University of Chicago. Among his publications are *Aristotle and Logical Theory, Aristotle: The Desire to Understand,* and *Love and Its Place in Nature.*

**Iris Murdoch** is a renowned novelist and the author of several philosophical works, including *The Sovereignty of Good, Sartre: Romantic Rationalist, The Fire and the Sun* and *Metaphysics as a Guide to Morals.*

247

**C. D. C. Reeve** is Professor of Philosophy at Reed College. Among his publications are *Philosopher-Kings*, *Socrates in the Apology*, and *Practices of Reason*.

**David Sachs** had been, before his death in 1992, Professor of Philosophy at Johns Hopkins University. His research ranged widely over ancient philosophy, moral psychology, Wittgenstein, and Freud.

**Arlene W. Saxonhouse** is Professor of Political Science at the University of Michigan. She is the author of *Women in the History of Political Thought, Fear of Diversity*, and *Athenian Democracy*.

**C. C. W. Taylor** is Fellow of Corpus Christi College, Oxford University. Among his publications are a translation and commentary on Plato's *Protagoras*, and he is the coauthor of *The Greeks on Pleasure*.

**James O. Urmson** was until 1979 Fellow and Tutor at Corpus Christi College, Oxford University, and was Professor of Philosophy at Stanford University from 1975 to 1980. He is the author of many essays and books, including *Philosophical Analysis, Berkeley, The Greek Philosophical Vocabulary*, and *Aristotle's Ethics*; in addition, he has translated some of Simplicius's commentaries into English.

**Gregory Vlastos** had been Professor of Philosophy at the University of California, Berkeley, before his death in 1991. Among his many publications are *Plato's Universe, Platonic Studies, Socrates: Ironist and Moral Philosopher*, and *Studies in Greek Philosophy* (2 volumes).

**Bernard Williams** is Monroe Deutsch Professor of Philosophy at the University of California, Berkeley, and was formerly Provost of King's College, Cambridge University. Among his publications are *Problems of the Self, Descartes, Moral Luck, Ethics and the Limits of Philosophy*, and *Shame and Necessity*.